HOUSING MARKETS AND HOUSING INSTITUTIONS: AN INTERNATIONAL COMPARISON

HOUSING MARKETS AND HOUSING INSTITUTIONS: AN INTERNATIONAL COMPARISON

Edited by

Björn Hårsman
Stockholm Regional Planning Office

John M. Quigley
University of California, Berkeley

Kluwer Academic Publishers
Boston/Dordrecht/London

Distributors for North America:
Kluwer Academic Publishers
101 Philip Drive
Assinippi Park
Norwell, Massachusetts 02061 USA

Distributors for all other countries:
Kluwer Academic Publishers Group
Distribution Centre
Post Office Box 322
3300 AH Dordrecht, THE NETHERLANDS

Library of Congress Cataloging-in-Publication Data

Housing markets and housing institutions : an international comparison
/ edited by Björn Hårsman and John M. Quigley.
     p.   cm.
  Includes index.
  ISBN 0-7923-9084-9
  1. Housing.   2. Housing policy.   3. Urban policy.   I. Hårsman,
Björn.   II. Quigley, John M.
HD7287.5.H66   1990
363.5—dc20   90-5290
                                                                CIP

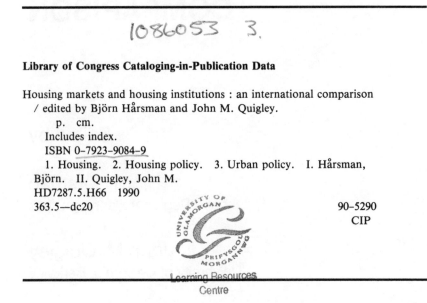

Printed on acid-free paper.

Printed in the United States of America

CONTENTS

1   Housing Markets and Housing Institutions in a Comparative Context
Björn Hårsman and John M. Quigley

2   The Swedish Housing Market: Development and Institutional Setting
Alex Anas, Ulf Jirlow, Björn Hårsman, and Folke Snickars

3   **The Finnish Housing Market: Structure, Institutions, and Policy Issues**
Christer Bengs and Heikki A. Loikkanen

4   **The Functioning of the Housing Market in Amsterdam**
Leo van Wissen, Peter Nijkamp, and Annemarie Rima

PREFACE

International comparisons of economic institutions and government policies are fraught with difficulties. After the selective barriers of language and culture are overcome, differences in programs and outcomes are far more subtle than those that can be revealed by highly aggregated national data. Relatively "soft" comparisons are the norm in international comparative research.

This is particularly true in comparative analyses of housing and the operation of housing markets. Housing markets are local or regional in character, and the effects of government programs on market outcomes depend upon important economic characteristics of the local environment. Moreover, the institutions that influence the production, distribution, and consumption of housing differ enormously across nations.

The distribution of housing and the role of the market in provision depend upon historical and social factors as well. Aggregate national data are unlikely to allow for much depth in comparisons across societies. Yet in the absence of such comparisons, the very visibility of housing may lead to inadequate or erroneous generalizations. Photographs emphasing the aesthetics of "well-planned" housing agglomorations or urban slums are compelling. Documentation that middle-class households must wait in a queue for a decade to be housed is notably less graphic.

This book overcomes some of these difficulties by focusing upon single cities or metropolitan areas within national systems. Each of the chapters in this book presents a description and analysis of a national housing market and an analysis of the development of housing policy and outcomes in a particular metropolitan region. Neither the countries nor the metropolitan areas were selected randomly and thus the analyses and insights cannot be "representative" in a formal sense. However, a major premise of this book is that careful analysis of particular markets and outcomes is likely to be more fruitful than aggregate comparisons of national data provided by housing ministries or census officials. The book is presented, moreover, on the presumption that detailed analysis of the operation of government programs within given markets is more informative than a catalog or taxonomy of national policies.

The countries selected for analysis include Austria, Finland, the Netherlands, Hungary, Sweden, the United Kingdom, and the United States; the metropolitan areas that form the bases of the analyses include Vienna, Helsinki, Amsterdam, Budapest, Stockholm, Glasgow, and San Francisco. Each chapter was written by a group of economists and economic geographers based in a university in that city. Some care was taken to insure that each chapter described the historical development of national housing policy as well as the resources devoted to current programs. Each chapter also includes a detailed analysis of the spatial development of the major city, the operation of the housing market and the pattern of housing occupancy, and the principal institutions that affect the production and distribution of housing. Each group was also asked to provide some explicit evaluation of selected policies. Although each chapter covers all of these aspects, they vary substantially in organization and emphasis.

This collaborative analysis grew out of a series of workshops sponsored by the International Institution for Applied Systems Analysis (IIASA) in Vienna during 1983 and 1984. These workshops were organized by Åke Anderson and Börje Johansson, then of the IIASA staff. Subsequently, a conference was held in Stockholm, sponsored by Bo Wijmark of the Stockholm Regional Planning Office. Logistical support for this collaborative project has been provided by the Institute for International Studies, the Institute for Urban and Regional Development, and the Center for Real Estate and Urban Economics, all of the University of California, Berkeley. Layout and typeset was managed by David Norrgard at Berkeley's Graduate School of Public Policy. Finally, the project could not have been completed without the financial assistance provided by the Swedish Council for Building Research. We are grateful to these individuals and institutions for support and encouragement.

Björn Hårsman
John M. Quigley

CONTRIBUTORS

Alex Anas is Professor of Civil Engineering, Economics, and Industrial Engineering at Northwestern University.

Elizabeth Aufhauser is a Researcher at the Institute for Geography, University of Vienna.

Christer Bengs is Senior Research Scientist at the Technical Research Centre of Finland.

Manfred M. Fischer is Professor of Economic Geography and Chairman of the Department Economic Geography at the Vienna University of Economics and Business Administration.

Andrew Gibb is Director of Development at the University of Glasgow.

Björn Hårsman is Research Director at the Stockholm Regional Planning Office and Professor of Regional Economic Planning at the Royal Institute of Technology, Stockholm.

John A. Hird is Assistant Professor of Political Science at the University of Massachusetts, Amherst.

Ulf Jirlow is Director of Real Estate at the Stockholm Regional Planning Office.

Sàndor Kàdas is Lecturer in Applied Mathematics at the Budapest University of Economics.

Heikki A. Loikkanen is Head of the Research Department at the Statistical Centre of Helsinki and Acting Professor of Economics at the University of Helsinki.

Duncan Maclennan is Professor of Economics and Director of the Centre for Housing Research at the University of Glasgow.

Peter Nijkamp is Professor of Spatial Economics at the Free University of Amsterdam.

John M. Quigley is Professor of Economics and Public Policy at the University of California, Berkeley.

Annemarie Rima is Managing Director of the Tinbergen Institute of the Netherlands Research Institute and the Graduate School for General and Business Economics.

Herta Schönhofer is a Researcher at the Austrian Institute of Regional Planning.

Folke Snickars is Professor of Regional Planning at the Royal Institute of Technology, Stockholm.

Leo van Wissen is Assistant Professor of Spatial Economics at the Free University of Amsterdam and Research Fellow at the Royal Netherlands Academy of Sciences.

Michael L. Wiseman is Professor of Public Affairs, Urban and Regional Planning, and Economics at the University of Wisconsin-Madison.

LIST OF TABLES

LIST OF FIGURES
AND MAPS

HOUSING MARKETS AND HOUSING INSTITUTIONS: AN INTERNATIONAL COMPARISON

1
HOUSING MARKETS AND HOUSING INSTITUTIONS IN A COMPARATIVE CONTEXT
Björn Hårsman
John M. Quigley

INTRODUCTION

(All developed countries have a housing problem in some form, and all nations, regardless of their orientation towards free markets or central planning, have adopted a variety of housing policies.) The production, consumption, financing, distribution, and location of dwellings are controlled, regulated, and subsidized in complex ways. In fact, compared to other economic commodities, housing is perhaps the most tightly regulated of all consumer goods.

This book provides a comparative analysis of the policies adopted in a set of very different countries and analyzes the housing markets in major metropolitan areas in those countries. The policies have been adopted for a variety of economic, political, ideological, and historical reasons. The execution of these policies affects the physical appearance and spatial development of metropolitan areas, the economic well-being of households, and their social environments. This collaborative volume provides a description of the policies adopted in a variety of countries and indicates their specific applications in particular metropolitan contexts. The book also provides a critical analysis of the operation of housing policy and housing markets. Although the analysis is explicitly economic and geographic, a real attempt has been made to analyze policies in their social and historic contexts.

In part, the specialized policies which have developed in different societies to regulate or subsidize housing arise from the peculiar economic characteristics of this commodity. Housing is peculiar, and housing policy is special.

HOUSING IS PECULIAR

Several of the characteristics of housing distinguish it from other economic commodities. First, housing is a complex commodity -- complicated to evaluate, complicated to produce, and therefore, complicated for suppliers and demanders to trade efficiently. A variety of different attributes must be considered to characterize a dwelling or building. A household or landlord must gather and process a great deal of information to make housing market choices that maximize utility or profit.

Second, housing is fixed in space. This means that housing choice is also a choice of neighborhood, a choice of access to workplaces, and a choice of access to a variety of local services such as schools and shopping centers. From the landlord's point of view, it also means that the most important determinants of site rents may be well outside of his or her direct control. Site rents may be substantially influenced by actions of the public sector. Fixity also implies that a residential move is quite typically necessary in order to change the consumption of housing.

Third, housing is expensive to produce. This makes renting a common form of tenure. For owners, this makes mortgage repayment an attractive alternative to outright purchase. This also implies that housing consumption generally constitutes a substantial fraction of household budgets and that new construction of residential housing is a substantial component of net national investment in any year.

Fourth, housing units have extremely long lifetimes. This implies that new construction provides only a small fraction of the total quantity of housing services supplied for consumption in any one period, and that new construction activity is vulnerable to small changes in the demand for housing. This also means that the consequences of local investment activity will affect the physical environment for a long time.

Fifth, housing is a necessity for any individual or for any household desiring to live a normal life in modern industrial society. Although there may be many substitution possibilities within the set of housing services, housing itself has few substitutes. No matter how poor they may be, households "need" to consume housing services.

Other commodities may have one or more of these distinctive features. For example, automobiles are complex commodities that are expensive to purchase. Aircraft are also long lived, farmland is fixed, and food is a necessity. But it is difficult to think of another commodity having all these special attributes. The combination of these attributes defines the special features of the housing market. For example, the complexity and fixity of housing ensure that transactions costs are very high in this market. Consumers must evaluate alternatives personally and must incur substantial monetary and psychic costs to change consumption bundles. The monetary costs include substantial expenditures of time and money in searching for dwellings, as well as the costs of moving and of concluding lease or purchase transactions. The psychic costs may include the loss of attachment to neighbors, schools, and local amenities, attachments which may change with the duration of residence at a particular location.

Fixity and longevity mean that the entire future course of geographical areas is determined when housing investment decisions are made. The consequences of this are likely to be substantial, so substantial that long-range planning by some economic actors may be highly appropriate. The expense and the necessity of housing emphasize the fact that even low-income households must consume some of this expensive commodity; without some form of subsidy, shelter expenditures as a fraction of income will be quite high for poor households.

HOUSING POLICIES ARE SPECIAL

As befits a somewhat peculiar commodity, housing policies as a class are somewhat special. First, since housing is a necessity and since it occupies such a large fraction of household budgets, considerations of housing policy affect all citizens in developed societies. This means that the distribution of housing is an important real issue for producers and consumers, and an important symbolic issue for politicians and government officials.

Second, the direction of housing policy can be changed only rather slowly, especially if subsidies are specific to long-lived dwellings. Even large changes in new commitments to housing subsidy will affect the stock of subsidized dwellings only slowly over a long time horizon. In the parlance of budgeteers, housing subsidies are likely to be "uncontrollables" in the government budget.

Third, housing policy is closely related to many other important objectives of economic and social policy: for example macroeconomic stabilization, social welfare, public health, appropriate land use, economic development, and regional balance. Without coordination, activities and policy initiatives in these other spheres may affect housing outcomes and may thwart housing policy.

Finally, it should be recognized that housing policy is difficult to design and may be difficult to evaluate in many cases. In part, this is because a long time perspective is required and in part because uncertainty is magnified over long time horizons.

The evaluation of housing policies in industrial societies can be made on the basis of the efficiency objectives, equity objectives, and social and political objectives that underly government action.

Efficiency Motives for Housing Policies

One clear reason for the adoption of housing policies is to promote allocative efficiency in the economy. There are many different bases for the argument that government policies in the housing market can promote an efficient use of scarce resources. It appears that government regulation in the market for the building, occupancy, financing, or pricing of housing services may promote efficiency in many rather distinct ways.

First, there are the public good aspects of housing. Many analysts, especially physical planners, believe that certain aspects of dwellings, and indeed some aspects of the entire housing stock, are public goods, consumed by all, without one's consumption infringing on another's. Obviously, individually occupied dwellings are private commodities, rival in consumption, and enjoyed by particular households. Nevertheless, many attributes of individually owned and occupied housing are consumed collectively. The physical appearance of a building, its architecture, and its arrangement in relation to infrastructure and transportation may benefit all. A well-designed building can provide benefits not only to its owner occupant or its tenant but also to those who view it, visit it, or hear about it. Many argue that a well-designed and planned urban landscape arising from the placement of housing in relation to infrastructure is also a public good and a benefit available to all without congestion. Certainly, for these aspects of housing, a free and competitive market with divided ownership will ignore, or at least undersupply, many attributes. From this perspective, some government role is virtually required to foster economic efficiency.

These externalities associated with the housing stock, its design, arrangement, and external quality, have fiscal and pecuniary effects. These externalities can prevent private landlords from investing to maintain quality and to maximize their collective profits. The recognition of these prisoners' dilemma problems for landlords has provided the basis for many kinds of public urban renewal activities. These externalities, however, may be social and fiscal as well as physical. Under a variety of tax arrangements, particularly property taxes, the occupants of large and desirable dwellings may confer fiscal benefits to other residents; conversely, small inexpensive dwellings may increase the financial costs of public services to others. These fiscal externalities provide a clear motive for government regulation and zoning. Prejudice, racial discrimination, and other manifestations of private behavior may lead to outcomes in which negative social externalities are intensified. Public controls over land use and housing can, at least in principle, internalize the positive externalities from dwellings and mitigate their negative consequences. It is clear that free markets with divided ownership do not provide the appropriate incentive for internalizing these market effects.

In addition, there are merit good aspects to housing. Housing is durable and is expensive to alter. It is expected to be used by future as well as current generations. If not, transformation and demolition costs are substantial. Housing is also consumed by many of the current generation who are incapable of evaluating it appropriately: for example, children whose needs, preferences, and demands are not taken into account in market transactions. Housing standards and norms could be considered much like educational standards or medical standards, intended partly to meet the minimums prescribed for captive consumers with few dollar votes: children, the elderly, handicapped, future generations, etc. The merit good argument implies that the needs of these groups will not be appropriately taken into account by an unregulated market, and that society has some collective obligation to take these preferences into account.

A related efficiency argument concerns the effect of expectations on market behavior. It has been widely argued that individuals behave as if they have higher discount rates in private transactions than the so-called "golden rules" of capital accumulation would warrant. With very long-lived investments in housing structures, which may have useful lives of 50 or a 100 years, differences in the appropriate investment strategies for society and for individuals will be magnified. Thus the enforcement of regulations could narrow the difference between the investments undertaken using individual discount rates and the appropriate investments using collective social discount rates. Inefficiencies in resource allocation would otherwise arise-- if, for example, the high discount rates of current consumers led to underinvestment in infrastructure.

As we have noted, housing markets are also characterized by substantial transactions costs both for consumers and producers. Some standardization could reduce these costs for both producers and consumers. A set of common standards may facilitate the negotiations and actions of intermediaries in construction, and uniform rules and codes may result in information economies in consumption as well. This standardization may not only reduce the cost of information about alternative dwellings for potential housing consumers but also reduce the cost of inspection for health and safety and for the enforcement of the police powers of the state.

Moreover, the promulgation of standards and norms for the housing market may encourage economies of scale in production which would not otherwise be feasible. These economies of scale may arise because of the technical character of the production process. Under these conditions, it is not at all clear that the variety of housing produced by an unregulated market is socially efficient.

Intervention in the housing market to stabilize production may also promote dynamic efficiency in house building. In most industrial countries, output per manhour in residential construction lags other sectors, and changes in total factor productivity in housebuilding are notoriously low. If government programs reduce the cyclicality of housing production, they may foster the substitution of capital for labor in production and promote labor-saving innovation in the building trades. Expectations of a more stable output may promote the use of more specialized inputs in the building process and a more appropriate capitalization of the sector.

Finally, government intervention in this market may have beneficial efficiency effects from a macroeconomic perspective. Given the high cost of housing, new construction is quite sensitive to variations in interest rates and in housing demand. Thus, residential construction is quite variable and is subject to cycles with large amplitudes. Explicit policies about the level of housing construction can provide an additional instrument for national and regional development policy.

Equity Objectives in Housing Policy

The equity objectives furthered by housing policy are at least equal to efficiency objectives in importance. In most Western and socialist countries, governmental authorities articulate an explicit policy objective concerning the provision of housing. For example, in the United States every housing bill since 1949 has articulated the goal of a "decent home and suitable living conditions for all citizens." In many cases, such a statement seems to be related to an income distribution objective. This is certainly not the case in all countries; but even in the United States, for example, housing goals are often espoused by those who see housing policy as a second best way of redistributing income (in-kind, as compared to a distribution in cash). In other countries-- for example, Sweden-- housing provision relates to a more sharply and explicitly drawn equity objective. The importance of housing in consumer budgets may make housing policy an attractive tool for achieving equity objectives.

Many economists, of course, would argue that these income distribution objectives are better pursued by explicit transfer policies rather than through the distribution of housing services. Yet in most societies, transfers earmarked for housing consumption are explicitly related to distributional objectives. One reason, noted above, is that some political environments favor redistribution in kind. Under so-called "commodity egalitarianism," redistribution in kind is more palatable than redistribution in cash. In the United States, food stamp programs and medical programs appear to be far more popular than programs that distribute cash to needy households.

A second and less noble reason for intervention in pursuit of equity objectives is the visibility of poor housing. It need not be evident how much or how little people earn in the marketplace or how much or how little people eat, but it is impossible to ignore the existence of low-quality and unsightly housing. The visibility of substandard housing makes the issue salient to politicians, voters, and the owners of property whose value would be improved through housing upgrading.

The merit good aspect of housing, discussed above, may make housing an attractive vehicle for politicians in accomplishing distribution goals. This merit good rationale can also be interpreted paternalistically: politicians or government bureaucrats know more than a badly housed individual about the negative consequences associated with inadequate housing. For example, it is often argued that parents at the lower end of the socioeconomic scale do not realize the importance of good housing or good nutrition for the well-being of their children. Thus unaided, they would use disposable income in ways that were not consistent with this higher knowledge.

Regardless of the motive, however, the existence and importance of equity objectives in developed societies have important consequences for the design and for the evaluation of housing policy measures. Finally, the equity objective may be broader than those objectives associated with particular individuals and may extend to the distribution of income across regions, provinces, or states. An active housing program can greatly advance such objectives.

Social and Political Motives

It is sometimes difficult to distinguish social and political motives for housing policy from the narrower equity and efficiency motives. Nevertheless, the distinction is real and is important. The promotion of order and public safety is perhaps the most basic reason for government. It is also the oldest political motive for housing policy. Governmental policies aimed at improving health and safety have regulated housing since the days of the Romans. For example, in ancient Rome, Caesar Augustus reorganized the water supply system and organized fire brigades to make residential areas safer for the citizenry. To reduce urban flooding, he regulated the water level on the Tiber and forbade private citizens to construct buildings taller than 20 meters.

It was not until the nineteenth century that European countries enacted comprehensive legislation to assure minimum standards of health and safety in residential dwellings. Regulation of the interior conditions of housing-- overcrowding, sewage, and water supply-- was undertaken because such regulation was seen as inhibiting epidemics of cholera, tuberculosis, and other contagious diseases. The first housing legislation in Britain, the Public Health Act, adopted in 1848, was followed by the more comprehensive Salesbury Act. The latter made local governments responsible for proper sanitation and for enforcing a variety of health and safety measures. The Swedish Health Code, enacted in 1874, instructed the local authorities to control housing conditions and to prevent the occupancy of unsafe dwellings. By the end of the 19th century, similar housing regulations were introduced in Amsterdam to improve sanitary conditions. In Vienna, the capital of the Austro-Hungarian

Empire, a comprehensive building code was introduced in 1859. This legislation was designed explicitly to protect safety and health. The minimum standards enacted in Vienna were not considered satisfactory in light of the rapid city growth that followed, so further regulatory measures were enacted. These examples seem to suggest that concern about the most basic functions of government was the driving force justifying housing policy.

It is not clear that these activities are best described merely as efforts to internalize external effects related to housing consumption. Many will argue that these policies were not just intended to correct individual decisions, but that the regulations were also a way of codifying the social character of urban life. The discussion of special housing policies in most industrialized countries during this century gives further credit to this view. Much of this discussion revolves around the rights of citizens to health and safety conditions and the expectation that government will ensure minimum standards in these dimensions. These can be thought of as the minimum requirements of a social contract in the increasingly dense urban areas which arose after the industrial revolution.

The rapid development of housing policies per se after World War I may be attributable merely to rising income and expectations. However, housing policies have also been an important part of a more explicitly political welfare state that has arisen. Sweden is a conspicuous, if somewhat extreme, example of this development. In the general guidelines for housing policy decided upon in 1946, the proposed policy measures were explicitly seen as part of a broader social policy, and hence as complimentary to other policy instruments such as child allowances and pension reform. The revisions of the guidelines undertaken some twenty-five years later strengthened this explicitly political view -- holding that decent housing should be regarded as a "social right" rather than merely as a commodity. At the other extreme, in the United States the Housing Act of 1949 explicitly established the goal of a "decent home and a suitable living environment for all Americans." This slogan has subsequently appeared in the preamble to all American housing acts and policy statements since then, but it does not appear to have infiltrated the dominant political ideology.

Related to this welfare statist view is another: poor housing conditions have high social costs in the form of crime, juvenile delinquency, alcoholism, and other forms of maladjustment. Empirical support for these claims seems quite weak; there is essentially no evidence that bad housing conditions cause these social disorders; nevertheless, the arguments certainly have played an important role in motivating housing policies in many welfare states.

A second political motive for adopting housing policies relates to the division of windfall gains and losses among social and economic classes. The profits made by landlords during periods of rapidly increasing housing demand provide a conspicuous example. In some countries-- for example, the Netherlands-- "excessive" profits have been a major motive for controlling rents in many parts of the housing stock. However, this motivation for intervention is somewhat broader than the rationale for rent control during wartime shortages. Many other activities undertaken routinely as legitimate manifestations of governmental power and collective responsibility provide windfall gains. These unearned profits are in the form of increased site values accruing to particular owners of residential or commercial properties, landlords, and the owners of tracts of land. For example, decisions about the location of infrastructure, the type and routing of roads, public transport, hospitals, and other spatial aspects of urban life may have no explicit distributional motivation. Nevertheless, the outcome of these activities can greatly increase the profits of landlords or landowners in particular areas of the economy. Policies regarding land use, housing, and residential and commercial rents may be derived from political considerations about the "fair" division of these unearned windfalls among different economic actors.

Another set of political motives for housing policy is related to the process itself. There is a very long tradition, especially in Europe, of considering overall urban development as a question of common concern for those living within the area. Thus, integrating housing with other public functions is a matter of common social concern. Of course, this involvement in town planning is partly motivated by efficiency reasons. But it is also strongly rooted in a political and culturally based belief that participation in the resolution of development issues is natural in a democratic society. Moreover, the expectation is that the process itself can foster an improved democracy. Thus participation in the process of planned development or zoning regulation is itself viewed as a politically and socially desirable activity, useful in forming some kind of consensus about the way local areas should develop. This importance of process, for example, provides an explicit rationale for the methods of local decision-making adopted in Holland. Although this political value seems currently less pronounced in North America, "maximum feasible participation" provided a rationale for community action programs and other urban development activities in the 1960s and 1970s.

A fourth important political reason for housing policy is related to the physical characteristics of real estate and its long life. Specific housing investments are lasting monuments to the particular politicians or the political forces initiating them. The promise of housing improvements in the South Bronx is a tangible campaign pledge, and the outcome of housing development can be a lasting monument to the far-sighted politician who facilitated the investment. There are no greater opportunities for monuments and plaques and ribbon cutting ceremonies than investments in physical urban infrastructure.

Control over the spatial development of housing of different kinds also provides local politicians with some mechanism for affecting the socioeconomic mix of area populations and thus of guiding population development in ways that can influence election outcomes. The possibilities for exercising this control are greatest in societies with strong traditions of class and party loyalty. The distribution of households of different economic classes within a metropolitan area can then have important effects upon the makeup of city councils and regional governments; these considerations are themselves of importance to politicians.

In addition, the paternalistic motives for providing housing for those with less knowledge and lower incomes can support a larger governmental structure. Larger governmental structures make the elected and appointed officials who manage such agencies more powerful, as they control larger staffs. Such power can be legitimized by the equity concerns that motivate government policy, and the prestige of officials can be increased by the employment of experts, scientists, engineers, and planners to serve under their guidance and direction.

Finally, an important political reason for housing programs can be seen in the link between regional development policies, labor market policies, and the housing market. Housing investment is a stimulant to a local or regional economy and may be used politically and economically as a tool for redistribution across regions. Similarly, the link between labor market policies and housing availability is close, not only within metropolitan areas (the availability of housing near work sites) but also among regions (the availability of suitable housing in areas with rapidly growing demands for labor). The political and social aspects of these regional development programs are, of course, inextricably linked with the narrowly economic. Nevertheless, it would be a mistake to view these activities as merely economic in scope and lacking a particular political or ideological dimension.

THE RATIONALE OF THIS BOOK

This book presents a series of closely related chapters that analyze the operation of housing markets and market outcomes in very different environments. Each chapter reports on the housing market of a particular metropolitan region, and provides a critical analysis of national and local policies. The studies differ in organizational detail, but each includes some attempt to trace out the link between housing policy and the operation of the market.

Besides the emphasis on policy, the analyses presented in this book provide a wealth of institutional and historical detail about each market-- each analyzes the important spatial dimension of housing markets.

A fundamental rationale for the collection is the belief that understanding and evaluating the operation of housing markets require analysis oriented towards particulars, which are more often local or regional than national in scope. As a corollary, understanding national policy requires a detailed analysis of local market conditions.

Given the importance of long-lived capital, history really matters in the understanding of housing markets and the spatial development of metropolitan areas.

Economic analysis of any individual market also requires some appreciation of the market orientation of a society and of the perceived importance of the collective attributes of housing discussed above. The kinds of policies that can be undertaken and the ways that they can be evaluated depend in a real way on the character of the society itself. Programs may be undertaken routinely in Stockholm that are unthinkable in San Francisco. Individual choice in the San Francisco housing market may be incompatible with the kind of housing allocation mechanism approved by consumers in Amsterdam.

For these reasons, the countries and particular markets analyzed were chosen because a locally based university research group was prepared to collaborate in the effort. Each group was prepared to develop a comprehensive analysis of local conditions and to attempt to link those conditions to national and regional policies and programs. The chapters thus provide a detailed account of urban development at the metropolitan level and provide some depth in analysis at the national level.

The cities and metropolitan areas analyzed are not based upon a grand sampling design and are a decidedly nonrandom sample. As such, they provide a better opportunity for observing market behavior and government programs than in any single country, but it is not clear that comparative inferences are perfectly general.

The next two sections provide some background material for making comparisons. Below we discuss the markets analyzed in terms of economic and political characteristics. We then note some broad policy comparisons.

METROPOLITAN MARKETS IN NATIONAL ECONOMIES

The seven countries represented in this study have high incomes and highly developed economies. Six are member nations of the Organization for European Cooperation and Development (OECD), and they include two of the four richest members of that club. Hungary, the only nonmember, is still quite well off by world standards or by the standard of Comecon member states.

Table 1-1 reports some comparative indicators of living standards among the seven countries in 1970 and 1980. In 1980 private consumption was highest per capita in Sweden, the United States, and the Netherlands, at about $7,200 to $7,600 U.S. Per capita consumption in Austria, Finland, and the United Kingdom was quite similar, at $5,600 to $5,800. The relative pattern of private consumption levels was similar in 1970. Consumption was substantially greater in the United States, followed by Sweden. Consumption in the Netherlands, Finland, and the United Kingdom was just less than half as great as in the United States. In Austria, it was only about a third as large. The relative measures of consumption and wealth in 1980 are borne out by the statistics on autos, television sets, telephones, and physicians per capita in the seven countries. In the United States, there are more than twice as many autos per capita than in Britain; in Sweden, there are almost 30 percent more television sets per capita than in Austria and almost 20 percent more than in neighboring Finland. Except for physicians, consumption indices in Hungary are considerably lower than in the OECD countries.

TABLE 1-1
Some Comparative Indicators of Living Standards,
1970-1980.

	Private consumption per capita (current U.S.$)	Per thousand population			
		Passenger cars	Television sets	Telephones	Doctors
1980					
Austria	$5650	272	296	421	1.60
Finland	5850	257	322	497	1.88
Hungary	--	95	258	118	2.88
Netherlands	7200	288	296	539	1.90
Sweden	7630	345	381	828	2.20
United Kingdom	5581	262	404	507	1.30
United States	7370	526	624	789	2.00
1970					
Austria	1090	162	213	207	1.85
Finland	1350	154	225	257	1.06
Hungary	--	23	171	80	2.27
Netherlands	1360	194	243	280	1.19
Sweden	2220	279	323	557	1.30
United Kingdom	1340	213	298	289	1.18
United States	3010	432	449	604	1.49

Note: -- Not available.
Sources: OECD Economic Surveys, *Basic Statistics: International Comparisons,* 1973-1974, et seq. Hungarian Central Statistical Office, *Statistical Yearbook,* 1970, et seq. Hungarian Central Statistical Office, *Statistical Pocketbook of Hungary,* 1985.

Table 1-2 reports two other measures of well-being for the seven countries-- per capita and per household incomes. The United States, Sweden, and the Netherlands have the highest per capita incomes. The housing markets analyzed also differ in their relative size and importance within the various countries. Five of the metropolitan areas, Vienna, Helsinki, Amsterdam, Budapest, and Stockholm, include the largest cities in their respective countries. But, even here, the relative size of the metropolitan agglomeration varies. In 1980, about 27 percent of the citizens of Austria and Hungary lived in the metropolitan areas containing their capitals. In contrast, only about 9 percent of the Dutch lived in the Amsterdam metropolitan area. In contrast, the cities analyzed in the United States and Britain are much less dominant. The San Francisco metropolitan area is only the thirteenth largest agglomeration in the United States, containing less than 1½ percent of the U.S. population; the Glasgow conurbation is the fourth largest in the United Kingdom, but contains only a little more than 1½ percent of the population.

Table 1-2 indicates the percent of both national and urban population residing in the metropolitan areas analyzed. Metropolitan area population relative to national population, but not absolute size, declined in the decade of the 1970s in three of the metropolitan areas. The Stockholm area population remained at about the same percentage of national population in 1970 and 1980. In Glasgow, Helsinki, and Budapest, however, the concentration of national population increased.

Table 1-3 presents comparative information on the relative size and importance of the public sector in these countries as well as the resources devoted to housing. In 1980, central government expenditures represented almost half of gross national product (GNP) in the United Kingdom and approximately a third of GNP in Sweden and the Netherlands. When all government spending is included, the public sector is even larger, 61 percent of GNP in the Netherlands, 52 percent in Britain, and 62 percent in Sweden. In Austria, central government spending represents 26 percent of GNP, while in the United States and Finland the share is a good bit lower, 21 to 23 percent. Somewhat surprisingly, central government expenditures are a much smaller fraction of GNP in Hungary, at least according to official statistics. In all seven countries, public expenditures as a fraction of GNP have increased during the decade of the 1970s. The increase in all government spending as a percent of GNP is most pronounced in the Netherlands and Sweden. Central government spending as a percentage of GNP increased most in the Netherlands between 1970 and 1980.

Government housing expenditures are not large as a fraction of GNP, but in many countries they represent a significant fraction of government expenditures, as much as 11 percent in Austria. Only in the United States are direct central government expenditures on housing an insignificant share (0.6 per-

TABLE 1-2
Basic Comparative Data on Seven Countries Included in Study,
1970 - 1980.

	Real income[a]		Metro population as percent of:		
	Per capita	Per household	Metropolitan area	National Pop	Urban Pop[b]
1980					
Austria	--	--	Vienna	27.1%	44.0%
Finland	$6,087	$16,356	Helsinki	15.9	26.5
Hungary	--	--	Budapest	26.6	51.1
Netherlands	7,359	15,147	Amsterdam	8.9	17.0
Sweden	7,671	18,251	Stockholm	16.7	20.1
United Kingdom	--	--	Glasgow	1.6	--
United States	9,201	25,763	San Francisco	1.4	1.9
1970					
Austria	--	--	Vienna	28.2	42.5
Finland	4,197	13,705	Helsinki	14.8	29.1
Hungary	--	--	Budapest	26.0	52.2
Netherlands	2,955	6,207	Amsterdam	9.4	18.5
Sweden	6,754	17,896	Stockholm	16.7	20.5
United Kingdom	--	--	Glasgow	1.3	--
United States	3,434	10,999	San Francisco	1.5	2.1

Notes: [a]   Current U.S.$
           [b]   Data are not strictly comparable due to varying definitions of urban
                 population.
           --   Not available.
Source: Survey of participating research groups.

cent) of government spending. In three of the seven countries the share of housing in government expenditures increased during the 1970s.

The seven countries vary substantially in the role of public ownership of the housing stock. Almost a third of the British and Dutch housing stocks are owned by the public sector. More than a quarter of housing units in Austria and Hungary are publically owned, and 23 percent of dwellings in Sweden are owned by the public sector. Only in Finland and in the United States are the shares of publically owned housing very small. For all of these countries except Hungary and the Netherlands, the share of government-owned housing increased in the decade of the 1970s.

Finally, table 1-3 also reports housing consumption as a percent of all private consumption. With one exception, Finland, the share of private consumption allocated to housing increased during the 1970s, and the fractions have converged. Significant differences persist, however. In the Netherlands, housing consumption makes up only 11 percent of private consumption, while in the United Kingdom the fraction is 20 percent.

Table 1-4 presents comparative information on the share of residential construction in real capital formation in these nations. In Holland and Finland, residential construction represented approximately a quarter of fixed capital investment in 1964, and in Sweden, housebuilding represented about one-fifth of new investment in real capital. The fractions in the United Kingdom and the United States were 13 and 18 percent, respectively. During the past decade, there has been a systematic decline in the share of housing investment relative to other real capital investment in Hungary and the Netherlands, but a net increase in its importance in Finland, the United States, and Sweden. For all

TABLE 1-3
Housing and Government Expenditures, 1970-1980.

	Public expend. as % of GNP		Government housing expend. as % of:		Percent of housing	Housing consumption
	All govt.	Central govt.	GNP	Public expend.	owned by Governent	as percent of private consumption
1980						
Austria	--	25.9%	2.9%	11.0%	26.0%	16.8%
Finland	38.2%	21.2	0.7	3.3	5.3	13.0
Hungary	--	11.5	--	--	28.6	--
Netherlands	60.5	32.6	2.7	7.0	31.7	10.7
Sweden	62.3	35.1	2.1	3.4	23.0	18.0
United Kingdom	52.0	46.0	2.2	5.0	32.0	20.0
United States	33.0	22.8	0.2	0.6	1.5	16.0
1970						
Austria	--	24.4	2.2	9.1	23.0	11.6
Finland	31.1	17.7	--	--	3.0	14.7
Hungary	--	10.7	--	--	33.5	--
Netherlands	44.9	24.1	2.5	8.0	37.0	8.4
Sweden	43.9	31.7	0.7	1.6	22.0	17.4
United Kingdom	49.0	--	2.4	6.0	30.0	18.0
United States	31.5	20.6	0.0	0.0	1.4	15.0

Note: -- Not available.
Source: Survey of participating research groups.

TABLE 1-4

Capital Formation in Residential Housing as a
Percent of Fixed Capital Formation, 1964-1981.

	1964	1971	1976	1981
Austria	--	--	--	16.5%
Finland	23.2%	25.1%	27.6%	28.3
Hungary	--	22.6	21.1	12.9
Netherlands	27.8	27.9	21.7	18.5
Sweden	19.5	17.3	26.3	24.0
United Kingdom	12.5	20.7	18.1	20.5
United States	17.6	23.6	25.8	25.8

Note: --   Not available.
Sources: United Nations, *Compendium of Human Settlements Statistics*, 1983, Table
            15; *Compendium of Housing Statistics*, 1975-1977, Table 12, and 1971,
            Table 15.

of these countries the housing sector is quite clearly an important component
of national investment.

Figure 1-1 presents comparative information on the level and cyclical sen-
sitivity of housing investment in the seven nations. It presents the number of
dwellings completed per thousand inhabitants during the period 1960 to 1981.
The two Nordic countries, Finland and Sweden, had the highest averages
during this period, 10.3 and 10.2 dwellings per thousand inhabitants, but they
also had the largest variances (and largest coefficients of variation as well). The
smallest relative variation in housing investment was in the two central European countries, Austria and Hungary, and the smallest average level of housing
construction was in the United Kingdom, which averaged only six dwellings per
thousand inhabitants during the entire period. It is interesting to observe the
common cyclical pattern of residential construction in Sweden, Holland, and
the United States.

Table 1-5 presents a comparison of selected demographic characteristics in
each of the seven countries and in the metropolitan areas analyzed in this book.
Where possible, data are presented for 1970 and 1980. The countries and the
metropolitan areas vary enormously in levels of residential mobility.   In
Budapest, the mobility rate is less than 2 percent; in San Francisco, it is more
than ten times as large. In 1980, average household sizes varied from 2.2 to 2.9
persons. In each country and in each city, average household size declined
during the 1970s. In each of these metropolitan areas, average household size

FIGURE 1-1
Dwellings Constructed per Thousand Inhabitants, 1960-1981.

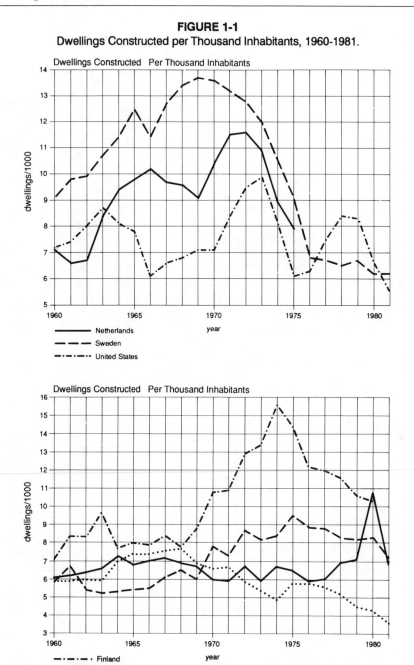

TABLE 1-5

Comparative Demographic Characteristics, 1970 - 1980.

	Annual mobility rate	Persons per household	Single person households	House- holds with child'n	Population less than 24 yrs	Population more than 65 yrs
1980						
Austria	3.8%	2.7	28.3%	48.4%	29.0%	18.4%
Vienna	4.3	2.2	37.0	35.8	29.4	19.4
Finland	11.1	2.7	27.1	51.0	36.1	12.0
Helsinki	15.7	2.4	33.2	42.6	33.2	11.1
Hungary	2.1	2.9	19.4	58.7	35.1	13.3
Budapest	1.8	2.5	--	--	29.8	15.9
Netherlands	10.1	2.8	22.1	49.3	40.5	11.5
Amsterdam	16.3	2.3	31.2	39.8	44.7	10.2
Sweden	13.3	2.3	33.0	29.0	33.0	16.0
Stockholm	14.5	2.2	39.0	26.0	32.0	15.9
United Kingdom	--	2.8	23.0	36.0	--	17.0
Glasgow	--	2.7	26.0	32.0	--	24.0
United States	17.2	2.8	17.1	45.3	41.4	11.3
San Francisco	20.0	2.5	28.5	37.6	35.9	11.2
1970						
Austria	--	2.9	25.6	51.8	37.8	14.3
Vienna	--	2.3	32.7	37.1	29.2	19.1
Finland	--	3.0	23.9	57.6	43.2	9.3
Helsinki	--	2.5	34.0	45.9	39.4	8.9
Hungary	2.7	3.1	17.5	55.0	37.5	11.5
Budapest	2.1	2.7	--	--	32.3	12.6
Netherlands	12.3	3.2	17.1	57.5	44.7	10.2
Amsterdam	15.8	2.7	22.8	46.4	38.9	12.2
Sweden	13.1	2.6	25.0	33.0	28.0	14.0
Stockholm	14.1	2.4	31.0	31.0	35.0	12.0
United Kingdom	--	2.9	18.0	38.0	--	15.0
Glasgow	--	3.1	17.0	39.0	--	19.0
United States	18.7	3.1	22.7	38.4	45.9	9.8
San Francisco	17.0	2.8	29.4	30.1	42.7	9.5

Note: --   Not available.
Source: Survey of participating research groups.

in 1980 was substantially smaller than in the rest of the country. With the exception of Glasgow, this was also true in 1970. In part, this reflects the much greater frequency of one-person households in large metropolitan areas, and the substantially lower incidence of households with children. The relative importance of single-person households is particularly striking in Stockholm and Vienna. The population distribution, given the less frequent incidence of

TABLE 1-6
Comparative Housing Characteristics, 1970 - 1980.

	Owner-occupied	Co-operative	Average rent/income	value/income	Avg. no. of rooms rental	owned	Built since 1900
1980							
Austria	48%	6 %	--	--	2.2	3.6	71%
Vienna	27	7	--	--	2.2	3.1	75
Finland	61	0	14.0	5.4	2.6	3.8	92
Helsinki	55	0	--	4.2	2.6	3.5	94
Hungary	71	0	--	--	--	--	86
Budapest	38	0	--	--	--	--	83
Netherlands	42	30	14.7	12.5	3.6	5.2	92
Amsterdam	18	30	13.8	14.1	3.3	4.3	86
Sweden	42	16	19.0	3.6	2.4	4.3	89
Stockholm	22	19	19.0	4.7	2.3	4.5	93
United Kingdom	59	3	7.3	2.9	3.1	4.5	--
Glasgow	29	4	6.4	3.1	2.5	3.8	--
United States	64	0	--	--	4.0	5.9	98
San Francisco	53	0	--	--	3.6	5.8	99
1970							
Austria	42	--	--	--	--	--	--
Vienna	--	--	--	--	--	--	--
Finland	59	0	--	--	2.5	3.5	--
Helsinki	47	0	--	--	2.4	3.3	--
Hungary	67	0	--	--	--	--	--
Budapest	30	0	--	--	--	--	--
Netherlands	38	29	15.7	13.3	3.5	5.0	--
Amsterdam	13	26	16.8	17.2	3.1	4.3	--
Sweden	39	14	19.0	3.5	2.2	3.6	--
Stockholm	18	16	19.0	5.3	2.1	3.8	--
United Kingdom	49	1	8.6	2.6	--	4.5	--
Glasgow	28	0	7.3	2.8	--	3.9	--
United States	63	0	--	--	4.0	5.6	--
San Francisco	52	0	--	--	--	--	--

Note: --   Not available.
Source: Survey of participating research groups.

children, suggests a larger fraction of young adults. There is no consistent pattern in the fraction of elderly households.

Table 1-6 presents some comparative data on housing. The incidence of homeownership is highest in Hungary, the United States, Finland, and the United Kingdom, and homeownership rates are similar in Austria, Holland, and Sweden. The homeownership rate is consistently lower in the major metropolitan areas than in their respective nations. Cooperative ownership of dwellings is an important form of tenure in the Netherlands and Sweden and is of some significance in Austria. On average, owner-occupied dwellings are larger than rental units, but there are no consistent differences between the sizes of units in these metropolitan areas and elsewhere in the nations.

With the exception of the two countries in central Europe, virtually all dwellings were built in this century.

Table 1-7 presents a comparison of four measures of housing quality in 1970 and in 1980. For most of these measures, there was a substantial quality improvement recorded during the 1970s in the seven countries and metropolitan areas. There are, nevertheless, substantial differences in the average quality of housing across countries. The average number of rooms per household is three times as large in the United States as in Hungary and is more than twice as large as in Austria and Finland. The incidence of overcrowding (defined as dwellings with more than one person per room, kitchen excluded) is four or five times as large in Austria or Finland as in the Netherlands or the United States. Almost three-quarters of the dwellings in Vienna lack central heating, as do almost 60 percent in Glasgow, while virtually all dwellings in Stockholm and San Francisco have this amenity. A significant fraction of the households in Vienna, Amsterdam, and Budapest lacks some or all plumbing facilities.

A TAXONOMY OF HOUSING POLICIES

Not surprisingly, each of the housing markets analyzed in this book deviates from the free market caricature of the economic textbook. All the countries have explicitly stated housing policy goals, and they use subsidies, regulations, or direct controls to pursue their goals.

In addition, government in each country also exerts a substantial indirect influence on the housing market through fiscal and monetary policy, social welfare policy, and in some cases regional development policy.

The extent and focus of the various policy instruments adopted vary quite substantially among countries and over time. As perhaps could be expected, local governments typically play important policy roles. Moreover, in many cases, local authorities in these metropolitan regions seem to have been innovators in the development of housing policy. For one extreme example, as

TABLE 1-7

Comparative Measures of Housing Quality, 1970-1980.

	Rooms per household	Percent overcrowded	Percent lacking central heat	Percent lacking plumbing
1980				
Austria	2.7	29 %	56 %	14 %
Vienna	2.4	24	73	15
Finland	2.7	33	20	16
Helsinki	2.4	28	4	4
Hungary	2.0	--	--	37
Budapest	1.7	--	--	18
Netherlands	3.9	7	34	4
Amsterdam	3.2	9	52	10
Sweden	3.2	10	2	2
Stockholm	2.9	10	1	0
United Kingdom	4.5	--	56	2
Glasgow	3.7	--	58	1
United States	6.0	5	1	1
San Francisco	4.9	5	1	1
1970				
Austria	2.9	33	85	30
Vienna	2.2	40	--	34
Finland	2.3	54	44	39
Helsinki	2.2	48	10	11
Hungary	1.6	--	--	66
Budapest	1.5	--	--	34
Netherlands	4.0	8	68	18
Amsterdam	3.2	--	74	29
Sweden	2.9	25	8	10
Stockholm	2.7	24	5	3
United Kingdom	4.5	--	--	9
Glasgow	3.5	--	--	11
United States	5.6	8	1	1
San Francisco	4.7	6	1	1

Note: --   Not available.
Source: Survey of participating research groups.

described in Chapter 8, the city of Glasgow undertook a program of subsidized construction about a century before any national measures of this kind were undertaken in Britain.

An evident and important implication of these observations is that housing policy must be looked upon as an integral and interdependent part of what could be called the delivery system for housing services. This is schematically illustrated in the figure 1-2.

FIGURE 1-2
Housing Policy and the Delivery of Housing Services.

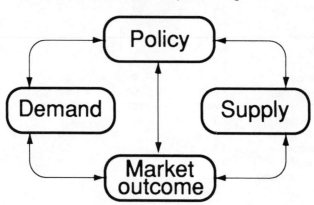

In the figure, the usual interplay between demand and supply is mediated by a policy component. Housing policy, interpreted in a broad sense, affects both housing conditions and market outcomes in three ways: 1.) through demand-oriented subsidies; 2.) through supply-oriented incentives; or 3.) through direct market intervention. Housing allowances, building codes, and rent regulations are examples of these three types of policy instruments.

As indicated in the figure, the causal links also run in the opposite direction. Given a certain ideological orientation, the development of housing market conditions may give rise directly to various policy actions. On the demand and the supply side different pressure groups advocate policies that favor their interests. In some societies such groups may even be given formal roles in setting housing policy. In Sweden, for example, rents are set and revised yearly in formal negotiations between tenants' and landlords' associations.

The presence of these interdependencies underlines the importance of dynamic or historical factors in explaining current housing policy at the national and metropolitan level.

These historical factors also suggest that the observed patchwork of housing policies at any point in time may deviate significantly from the set of policies that would be adopted de novo by the same authorities to advance the same objectives. Indeed in some cases, as is pointed out in subsequent chapters, policies within these metropolitan areas are logically inconsistent with one another.

In figure 1-2, the various policy instruments currently in use can be classified roughly as follows:

Demand-oriented: Housing allowances, tax exemptions;

Supply-oriented: Planning and land use policy, building codes and zoning regulations, construction and interest rate subsidies; and

Direct market intervention: Rent and price controls, rationing and queuing systems, tenant security regulations.

All these policy instruments are used in one or more of the metropolitan regions analyzed in this book. However, as indicated below, the utilization of these policies, subsidies, and controls varies enormously.

In this introduction, we merely note how the various policy instruments relate to the rationalizations discussed earlier: efficiency, equity, and social or political motives. The subsequent chapters provide a more detailed evaluation of outcomes.

On the demand side, cash transfers earmarked for housing consumption or rent rebates are motivated mainly by equity concerns. In some cases-- for example, in Hungary-- a more explicit merit good argument is articulated; the size of the allowance a household obtains depends upon the quality standard of the dwelling occupied. In contrast, tax exemptions and other subsidies to home ownership seem to be motivated by political reasons in each of the seven countries.

In most Western European countries, housing allowances have been introduced only quite recently, much later than other parts of the housing support systems. Sweden is the exception to this general rule; allowances for low-income families with more than two children were introduced in Sweden in the late 1930s. A common feature of the European allowance programs is that the recipients must meet certain qualifications concerning income, wealth, and family size. Subject to specific eligibility rules, the goals of the allowance systems have been expressed in quite general terms. In the Netherlands, however, where housing allowances are confined to renters, the goal of the policy has been made quite specific-- to keep rent expenditures under 10 percent of net income for the lowest income wage earner and under 17 percent for the average industrial worker.

Most housing allowance systems, with the exception of Sweden, are restricted to certain parts of the housing market. For example, in Austria only low-income households in newly constructed or in recently modernized buildings are eligible. In Finland, households in owner-occupied dwellings built before 1974 are excluded from the national program of transfers.

It must be emphasized that public general assistance to households often contains substantial amounts that are used for rent payments by the recipients. For example, although there is no housing allowance system in the United States, public assistance for single-parent families with dependent children is intended to make decent housing more affordable to recipients. In each of the seven countries analyzed in this book, significant subsidies are provided to owner occupants through the national tax codes. Significant differences exist in the operation of these implicit subsidy schemes. Interest payments on home mortgages are typically deductible in computing taxable income (subject to upper limits on qualifying deductions, at least in Finland and Britain) and capital gains on housing escape effective taxation (except in Sweden and Finland). To some extent, these deductions are offset by calculations of imputed income from housing assets (at least in the Netherlands, Finland, and Sweden). Nevertheless, it is quite remarkable that these very different societies-- with ideologies ranging from a conservative appreciation for the free market to a social democratic ethic to a communist peoples' republic-- should find it expedient to provide large subsidies to high-income households through the housing system.

Tables 1-8 and 1-9 provide a rough comparison of these demand-side subsidies in the seven countries. Table 1-8 indicates the relative importance of housing allowances as compared to other items included in direct central government housing subsidies in the seven countries. The value of tax exemptions for owner-occupied housing relative to other subsidies for housing is displayed in table 1-9. Housing allowances are a relatively small demand-side subsidy program-- in absolute terms or when compared with the tax exemption policies adopted in these nations.

On the supply side, strong beliefs about the public good aspects of spatial development and about the importance of externalities in affecting competitive outcomes provide the principal rationale for government planning and land-use policies in Holland and Sweden. Building codes are motivated by their role in reducing information costs, but also in their alleged effects upon the minimum housing quality levels available to lower-income groups.

Supply-side subsidies, usually designed as preferential loans, are motivated by equity concerns and sometimes also by a belief that a free market simply cannot produce enough housing of reasonable quality. As noted below, these political and ideological motives are sometimes made quite explicit. For example, as explained in Chapter 7, the decision of the city of Vienna to construct public housing was motivated by the "inability" of the free market to produce sufficient housing of adequate quality. A common feature of physical planning and land-use policies is that strong powers are vested at the local level. In some countries, as in Finland and Sweden, the term "planning monopoly"

TABLE 1-8

Housing Allowances as a Percent of Direct Central Government
Housing Subsidy, 1970-1980.

Country	1970	1980
Austria	1.2%	12.3%
Finland	9.8	19.7
Hungary	--	--
Netherlands	5.5	35.9
Sweden	100.0	55.0
United Kingdom	--	--
United States	0.0	0.0

Note: --   Not available.
Source: Survey of participating research groups.

TABLE 1-9

Tax Exemptions and Direct Central Government Housing Subsidy as a
Percent of Government Expenditure, 1970-1980.

	Tax exemptions		Government housing subsidies	
	1970	1980	1970	1980
Austria	--	--	3.8%	4.1%
Finland	0.8%	1.8%	5.1	7.9
Hungary	--	--	--	--
Netherlands	6.7	--	1.3	2.5
Sweden	2.9	5.2	3.4	6.0
United Kingdom	--	--	--	--
United States	--	--	--	--

Note: --   Not available.
Source: Survey of participating research groups.

is frequently used. Among other things, the term indicates that planning power rests exclusively with the local government and that an approved plan must always precede building. The highest degree of local independence is to be found in the United States where the federal and regional influence on physical planning is rather insignificant.

At the regional level, the role of the planning bodies is more commonly of an advisory nature. The regional plans, as a rule, are not compulsory or binding but are used as instruments for coordinating local planning activities. The normal regional plan is a land-use plan in accordance with guidelines expressed at the national level. Regional authorities occasionally have the task of ratifying local plans but, except in the Netherlands, this regional power is more apparent than real.

The national influence on physical planning is normally limited to a few strategic matters: for example, conservation areas of great importance or ratification of plans adopted by local or regional authorities.

All of the Western European countries included here use heavily subsidized state or government-sponsored loans to support new construction. The terms of these preferential loans vary with the form of tenure and sometimes by location. As a rule, this supply-side subsidy is combined with controls concerning construction costs and some quality standards. The support is given in the form of below market interest rates or direct capital subsidies. The amortization periods are often long-- up to 50 years-- with the exception of Finland, where the State loans, as well as the first mortgage loans, are repaid in a much shorter time: 18 to 27 years.

In comparison to the European countries included in this analysis, the housing assistance system in the United States is much less extensive. Only a minor fraction of the housing stock is affected by direct supply-side loan programs. These subsidized dwellings (a small fraction of the housing stock) are strictly allocated to households with special needs: for example, low-income households, elderly people, war veterans.

As is discussed more fully in Chapter 6, the system of housing support in Budapest has only nominal resemblances to the systems in the West. The heavy subsidization of municipal construction by long-term loans with very low preferential interest rates means that rents in municipally owned housing do not even cover the costs for maintenance and management.

During the last decade, rehabilitation of the older housing stock has become an important housing policy issue in the European countries included in this book. Most of these countries have adopted special programs for rehabilitation and modernization. The common form for encouraging rehabilitation activities includes preferential public loans combined with restraints on the rent increases which would otherwise be necessitated by increased capital costs. In some cases, these supply-side programs are augmented by special allowances to households that are considered to be especially vulnerable to such increases.

An important feature of the rehabilitation process has been the increasing participation of tenants in decision-making. This participation is explained in the chapters discussing Amsterdam and Vienna among others, but the most radical shift in policy and in responsibility has been in the United Kingdom. In Glasgow, the traditional role of council housing has been transformed by the transfer of ownership to associations formed by the tenants. This has created a circumstance where the responsibility for modernization, maintenance, and management has been transferred from local politicians to local associations composed of the tenants directly affected. As noted in Chapter 8, these policy changes have in fact made the city of Glasgow a leader in the British policy areas of rehabilitating older neighborhoods and in remaking social housing.

Direct intervention in the market through price regulation and rent control is pervasive in the six European housing markets considered in this book. This rent control invariably necessitates rationing and is often linked to strong rights of tenant security.

The rent legislation in Vienna, where rents were actually frozen from 1914 until 1981, represents a most extreme example of rent control; these price controls cover over 90 percent of the rental stock in the metropolitan agglomeration. The other extreme is represented by local regulations in most of the San Francisco Bay Area, where landlords and tenants are free to contract for any rents, subject to rather minimal standards of dwelling quality imposed on landlords for health and safety reasons.

Glasgow, Stockholm, Amsterdam, Helsinki, and the city of San Francisco itself fall between these two extremes. The pattern of price regulation in socialist Budapest is quite intriguing. As noted in Chapter 6, rental units in the Budapest metropolitan area are subject to extensive rent control. Despite this, however, in a large part of the rental market, prices are essentially free; tenants are allowed to buy and sell their rental contracts at unregulated prices.

Table 1-10 indicates the share of the housing stock subject to some degree of explicit price regulation as of 1980. The fraction of the total housing stock subject to rent control ranges from more than 60 percent in Budapest, Glasgow, and Vienna to 30 percent in Helsinki. The corresponding figure for the entire San Francisco Bay Area is certainly considerably lower. Of the seven cities, Budapest is the only metropolitan region making more or less full use of the price mechanism since rental contracts can in fact be freely sold in Hungary. Rent control is complemented by some form of rationing system in six of the seven metropolitan areas (the exception being San Francisco). Priority in these systems is usually determined by a mix of time in the queue and a set of criteria defining a household's need for a dwelling. The most restrictive rationing scheme is used in Amsterdam where a "housing permit" and an "urgency certificate" are needed for almost every residential move in the entire metropolitan area.

Closely linked to rent regulation schemes is the question of security of tenure. Extensive provisions to protect tenants from eviction and "excessive" rent increases were introduced as early as 1922 in Austria. The need for cor-

TABLE 1-10
Extent of Rent Control Regulations in Effect in 1980.

Metropolitan region	Rental units as a percent of total housing stock	Percent of rental units subject to rent control
Amsterdam	52 %	100 %
Budapest	65	100
Glasgow	67	100
Helsinki	30	100
San Francisco	47	--
Stockholm	58	100
Vienna	68	94

Note: --   Not available.
Source: Survey of participating research groups.

responding rules occurred in the other Western European countries as rent regulation systems were initiated, that is, mostly after World War II.

Another legal issue concerning the tenant's right to use his or her rented flat is whether the tenant has the legal right to swap. The most extensive legislation governing swapping seems to be found in Sweden where the right to swap is unlimited in practice. This right, however, does not extend to the right to make or receive side payments. In the other Western European countries, swapping rights are usually limited by rules related to the queue system. For example, when it comes to publicly owned housing in the United Kingdom and Finland, swapping is allowed only when the households can meet certain criteria concerning family size, income, etc.

CONCLUSION

As the reader will come to appreciate, it is hard to rationalize the set of housing market policies analyzed in this book. In comparing the set of institutions and regulations governing the markets in these countries, it is clear that equity concerns are perceived to be far more important than economic efficiency, even broadly defined, in motivating housing policy and in regulating the national and local markets.

These equity concerns are complemented by a more-or-less deep distrust of market mechanisms for housing allocation. This distrust may arise from perceptions about the importance of exernalities in the market. The general reluctance to rely upon market allocation may also be rooted in a political ideology in which the welfare state acts to protect consumers from exploitation by the presumably wealthy landlord class. This is surely the case in several of the housing markets surveyed in this book.

It is also clear from the more detailed analysis presented in this book that history matters a great deal. In the European context, and to a lesser extent in the United States as well, current housing policies and proposals can often be seen as a piece of patchwork. New pieces have been added to deal with specific issues more or less continuously since the forties, or in some cases since the Great War. From this perspective, some of the inconsistencies in policy may be no less glaring, but rather more understandable.

As a consequence of this historical development, the effects of various subsidies and controls are hard to sort out. In several of the countries analyzed in detail in the remainder of this book, policy changes may be more commonly motivated by political or ideological reasons than by a clear analysis of how the system actually works.

The analyses presented in this book attempt to provide a clear documentation of the housing policies in effect in each of the seven countries. They also emphasize the institutional context in which decisions about housing supply and consumer demand are registered. To varying degrees, the chapters also emphasize the historical development of policy and the effects of this development upon the spatial structure of the various metropolitan areas.

Most importantly, however, the analyses attempt to unravel the details of how the housing systems actually work. As such, they provide a detailed evaluation of the effects of government policies on market outcomes and consumer well- being. Each evaluation is in the context of a specific metropolitan housing market. These analyses indicate the benefits and costs of a variety of specific interventions in the market, often with a detailed quantitative analysis.

In most cases, the authors are not unsympathetic to the broad goals of government housing policy and are conscious of the limitations of an unregulated and atomistic market for housing services. Despite this, however, many of the authors are rather critical of the effects of policies which have been adopted and of the complexity of government regulation and subsidy.

It is the thesis of this book, however, that the functioning of housing markets is more likely to be improved through a detached analysis of the operation of existing institutions than from either an ideological commitment to replacing economic incentives with more enlightened government allocation or from a naive caricature of the virtues of free and unregulated markets.

2
THE SWEDISH HOUSING MARKET: DEVELOPMENT AND INSTITUTIONAL SETTING

Alex Anas
Ulf Jirlow
Björn Hårsman
Folke Snickars

INTRODUCTION

Sweden is the fourth largest country in Europe in terms of land area. However, only 10 percent of its land is cultivated; 50 percent is forest. The population is 8.3 million, with a density of only 20 inhabitants per square kilometer. The three largest metropolitan areas are: Stockholm (1.39 million), Göteborg (0.69 million), and Malmö (0.45 million), with populations amounting to 16.7 percent, 8.4 percent, and 5.5 percent of the national population, respectively (Statistics Sweden, 1983).

The low population density and the abundance of timber resources might suggest that large Swedish cities would be sprawling and consist primarily of spacious, wooden single-family homes. Yet the opposite is the case. Swedish metropolitan areas have a large share of compactly built, large multifamily buildings and complexes. The important factors in this regard are the need to conserve energy in heating and transportation, strong government control over building activity since World War II, and a national goal of making social services easily accessible to most inhabitants.

THE STATE, THE COUNTIES, AND THE MUNICIPALITIES

Sweden's national or central government (hereafter referred to as the state) consists of a number of ministries. One of these is the Ministry of Housing and Physical Planning, responsible for physical planning, housing provision, and construction. The country is divided into 24 counties which constitute a regional form of government. The County Administrative Boards coordinate state planning within the county and act in a supervisory capacity, hearing appeals and ratifying plans adopted by the municipalities. County Housing Boards come under the jurisdiction of the National Housing Board and administer State loans and grants for housing provision.

The country is divided into about 280 municipalities. Since 1945, the number of municipalities has been gradually reduced through consolidation, thereby increasing administrative efficiency in public service provision. In the County of Stockholm, for example, the number of municipalities has been reduced from 109 in 1945 to 25 in 1980. Greater Stockholm now consists of 22 of these municipalities, excluding three on the periphery. The largest municipality in Greater Stockholm is Stockholm City, which comprises the core of the region.[1]

HOUSING POLICY

The general principles of current Swedish housing policy were forged by the Parliament in a series of decisions in the years after World War II (1946 and 1947). These principles originated from the work of the Swedish economist Alf Johansson.[2] Johansson stressed the importance of achieving a state of "double equilibrium" in the building market and, simultaneously, in the housing market. Johansson's analysis calls for strong action by state and local government.

These policies were meant to provide all households with healthy and spacious buildings at affordable costs. Policy goals were to reduce occupancy to less than two persons per room (kitchen excluded) and rent burdens to no more than 20 percent of income. The State should be responsible for supplying "sufficient" mortgage funds to complement loans from the mortgage banks and for providing housing allowances to households with children.

---

[1] For a study of the interactions of state and municipal politics in the Stockholm region, see Anton (1975).

[2] Johansson was General Director of the National Housing Board and later Professor of Economics at Stockholm University. His work was presented in a series of committee reports. The most remarkable one, in 1945, is still considered the standard work in the field of Swedish housing policy.

Local governments-- the municipalities-- were assigned the responsibility of implementing programs to develop local housing supply, thereby ensuring sufficient and modern housing for the population. In order to accomplish this task, the municipalities were encouraged to create their own local housing associations (nonprofit companies). One of the primary duties of these enterprises was to initiate production of new rental dwellings for particular households (for example, those, with children, who often had difficulty obtaining adequate housing in the private market). The general and long-term objective of the nonprofit companies was to ensure that the entire population, regardless of income or social affiliation, had adequate housing. This goal has not changed.

The nonprofit companies were entitled to the most favorable terms with regard to state-subsidized loans, i.e., up to 30 percent of the production costs; a first mortgage loan at subsidized interest rates usually covered 70 percent. The state loans for cooperative associations and private builders of multi-family housing amounted to 20 percent and 15 percent, respectively. For owner-occupied single-family houses, the State loan was 20 percent of construction costs.

The municipalities were also given important roles as intermediaries for State loans and as distributors of housing allowances. Applications for loans would always be considered by the local authority before they were forwarded to county-level governmental bodies. Applications for housing allowances were evaluated by the local authority, which received part of the funds from the state. Finally, central responsibility over housing policy, and ultimate authority over the County Housing Agencies, was vested in a new body-- the National Housing Board.

These principles of modern housing policy had two antecedents which were undertaken during World War II. The first was rent control, aimed at preventing rent increases caused by a housing shortage. The shortage was caused by a breakdown in housing construction combined with relatively strong urbanization.

The other measure was the introduction of a guaranteed interest level for housing financed with state loans. The content of the guarantee was that the interest rate for the loans from the state and the mortgage banks would be stable at a low level for a relatively long period of time. The rationale was that temporary fluctuations in the interest level should not be permitted to disturb building activity and, of course, the demand for new housing. The guaranteed interest rate was fixed at 3.5 percent, which at the time corresponded to the rate for long-term loans. Interest payments above this level would be subsidized by the government. Also included was the provision that the level be adjusted if the long-term interest rate changed. This fundamental feature of the state housing policy still remains, though the details have changed over time. This guarantee did not involve any state expenditure worth mentioning until the 1950s.

THE PLANNING SYSTEM

Parliamentary decisions concerning the planning system accompanied the adoption of new principles for Swedish housing policy. The 1947 Building Act regulated the various types of plans that the municipalities could make. The main purpose of the Act was to enable the local authorities to decide not only where but also when dense development was to take place. The local planning power-- often called the "planning monopoly"-- was considered for implementation by the municipalities in light of desired and expected development.

This development would then be reflected in a long-range plan for the entire area within a large part of the borders of the community. The Building Act required each municipality to make a master plan showing the intended purposes for land and buildings. This master plan was to serve as a basis for more detailed town plans and, in rural areas, rural development plans. In areas where several municipalities had reasons to cooperate in their planning activities, they could make a regional plan together.

The master plan indicates the use of land for different purposes-- housing, traffic arteries, and public areas, for example. If vacant land is to remain undeveloped, the plan states this fact. The master plan is to be based on population forecasts and analyses of economic conditions and other special surveys.

The municipality's master plan is the ultimate determinant of land use. A master plan normally specifies the type of land use and amount of floor space to be built in each area. Private landowners must request approval for developing their land in a desired manner. If the municipality denies them permission, the private landowners do not usually have the right to go to court. Municipalities can refuse development requests for various reasons, including, for example, the high costs of supplying the land with public infrastructure, utilities, or public services. The regional plan shall be set up whenever two or more municipal systems, airfields, recreation areas, water supplies, sewage systems, or other services require a joint plan covering such common matters. The town plan regulates in more detail the boundaries for buildings, blocks, streets, and public places. This plan often specifies the number of buildings that may be put up on a lot, the height of the buildings, the maximum floor space, and other pertinent details.

After being adopted by the local parliament, the master plan can be used within the municipality as a general guideline for further planning activities. The town plan must be approved by the County Government Board to be valid as a legal instrument.

The procedure for adopting a town plan is regulated by law. The municipality prepares the town plans through the building committee, a political body appointed by the local parliament. Private interests wishing to develop a certain area may also submit proposals to the committee for examination. The planning decision rests solely with the municipality, through its building committee.

When a final draft has been presented by the building committee, it is published and offered for inspection by landowners and other interested parties. During this time of public inspection, all concerned parties are invited to give their points of view to the building committee which, after considering any objections, makes its final decision. The proposed plan is then brought to the local parliament for adoption. If adopted, the town plan is submitted to the County Government Board for approval. If approved, the town plan has a legally valid status. Then, in contrast to the master plan, anyone who is adversely affected by the plan-- primarily landowners in the neighborhood-- may appeal the decision. The ultimate decision then rests with the central government (i.e., the Cabinet).

Other key legislation that regulates the planning process and building activity are the following: the Building Ordinance regulates building permits and design standards; the Swedish Building Code regulates the detailed design and construction of buildings; the Pre-Emption Act enables the municipality to act as the buyer in an ongoing transaction by paying the price agreed upon between private buyers and sellers. The purpose of this law is to provide a mechanism for land acquisition in advance of urban development. The Expropriation Act makes it possible for the municipality to acquire land which is required for development. The Nature Conservancy Act regulates adverse effects from water, air pollution, and noise.

Drawing their powers from these legislative acts, Swedish municipal governments have strong control over land use and the housing stock. Municipalities own or can acquire substantial lands within their domain. Thus, they are the chief suppliers of land to developers. In addition, municipalities can designate the type and extent of development with binding master plans. (Another means of control is municipal ownership of nonprofit housing companies, which may build and manage a large part of a municipality's rental housing stock.)

LAND USE AND THE OWNERSHIP, SUPPLY, AND PRICING OF LAND

Swedish municipalities have been buying, selling, and leasing land for many decades. As a result, they now typically own most of the land to be used for urban development within their jurisdictions. They are in a strong monopoly position with respect to housing development, even more so due to a "land condition rule." This rule states that a builder of housing cannot receive a subsidized government loan unless the land on which he builds is acquired from the municipality. The most important exception to this rule concerns construction of single detached houses. Commercial and industrial development in Sweden is not subsidized, and builders must obtain a loan at the market interest rate. Builders of such developments are free to build on non-municipal land but must, of course, abide by the municipal guidelines specified in the master plan.

When selling land to developers, municipalities charge the cost of acquiring comparable land at the current time plus any administrative or land improvement costs. In the case of housing developers, the principle that the municipality should make no profit guides the transaction. In the case of nonresidential developers, no law exists against extracting the highest price the buyer is willing to pay. However, even if the municipalities do not sell land at very low prices (as a means of attracting local employment, for example), they seldom exceed a conservatively estimated price. One reason for this is, of course, that any sale price paid to the municipality can be used by private landowners selling to the municipality in the future-- or by others whose land is being expropriated by the municipality-- as an argument for equivalent compensation.

Expropriation with adequate compensation is a power of the municipalities, but they choose to exercise it with caution, as it can be challenged in court with the municipality being held liable for the legal costs of the property owner at the pre-appellate level. Often, municipalities choose to maintain land ownership by leasing land for development according to plan. This arrangement is known as a "lease-hold system:" The Stockholm municipality, for example, operates a large lease-hold system. Lease values can be changed at fixed time intervals which, over the years, have been gradually reduced from 60 to 10 years. This enables the municipality to extract from the lessee the current value of the land, although lease holders have legal recourse.

The primary effect of these Swedish land ownership institutions is that land speculation is severely discouraged and successfully curtailed. Developers can obtain land at low prices when buying from the municipality for purposes of subsidized developments such as housing. A segmented land market exists, since commercial industrial developments are free to occur on private land and at unrestricted prices as long as they are consistent with the municipal land use plan.

Municipalities rarely change their land use plans. This is in sharp contrast to American zoning specifications, which are frequently changed in times of development pressures. Since Swedish land-use plans are so stable, it is rarely possible for private landowners to profit from anticipating changes in these plans; and, conversely, it is equally rare that municipalities have to compensate landowners because of changes in the land-use plan.

Since land ownership is so highly centralized, the land "market" is not a competitive one. Municipalities can force housing development to occur in places which would not be developed by competitive forces. This type of pattern has appeared in some suburbs of Stockholm. One consequence of this is that turnover and vacancy rates in such places are unusually high.

THE HOUSING STOCK, HOUSING PRODUCTION, AND THE BUILDING SECTOR

Most housing in Sweden is built by private firms. The main exception is BPA, a construction firm owned by the trade unions. However, the owners of newly constructed multifamily dwellings are, in most cases, nonprofit companies owned by the municipalities or cooperatives.

The housing stock in Sweden can be grouped into three categories:

1. Single-family housing: These dwellings are generally owner-occupied by families and are mostly constructed by private builders. A striking aspect of these dwellings is that they are often planned to be spaced close together in a subdivision. There are precise building standards which apply to design and construction, and careful attention is paid to their proximity and relationship to public facilities, shopping, open space, and public utilities. A substantial part of the single-family stock is of older vintage and does not necessarily conform to current building standards.

2. Multifamily cooperative buildings: These dwellings are individual flats in multifamily buildings, and are tenant owned. Owners have the same rights as single-family dwelling owners in purchasing and selling these units, except that they are subject to some control by the cooperative association in the areas of repair and renovation. Also, the maintenance of common facilities in these buildings is financed by means of an assessment levied on the tenants by the association. The form of tenure is very similar to condominium ownership in North America. The Swedish cooperative market is dominated by large national cooperative associations. The largest are HSB and Svenska Riksbyggen, national associations with branch associations in counties, municipalities, and individual buildings.

3. Multifamily rental buildings: A large part of the housing stock in Sweden consists of rental flats in multifamily buildings. Approximately half of these buildings are owned and managed by private landlords. However, since World War II, the bulk of multifamily buildings has been built by nonprofit housing companies. These companies generally retain ownership and management of the buildings. Each municipality owns at least one nonprofit company. The Stockholm municipality owns a number of such companies, the largest being AB Svenska Böstader, with a holding of 50,000 flats.

Tenants who obtain a flat hold an irrevocable lease and have the right to

TABLE 2-1
Population and Dwelling Units, 1945-1980.

Year	Number of dwellings (in thousands)	Index (1945=100)	Population (in thousands)	Index (1945=100)
Sweden				
1945	2,102	100	6,674	100
1960	2,675	127	7,498	112
1965	2,876	137	7,773	116
1970	3,181	151	8,081	121
1975	3,530	168	8,208	123
1980	3,669	175	8,320	125
Greater Stockholm Area				
1945	292	100	895	100
1960	434	149	1,163	130
1965	482	165	1,258	141
1970	563	193	1,349	151
1975	645	221	1,358	152
1980	665	228	1,387	155

Source: National Bureau of Statistics.

remain in the flat indefinitely, as long as they conform to the conditions of their lease and continue to make rental payments. They also have the right to swap.

It is sometimes the case, and increasingly so in recent years, that some privately owned rental buildings are converted into cooperatives and turned over to a cooperative association for management. This is usually possible if the owner wishes to sell and a majority of the tenants in a rental building vote in favor of conversion.

Swedish multifamily buildings are generally compactly built and consist of small flats. There is visible differentiation in architectural features and in the number of stories, by vintage. A great deal of this differentiation can be explained by changes in the building code and construction costs over time. Building complexes constructed since World War II are generally carefully situated near transit stations and contain within them shopping facilities, recreational grounds, and schools.

From the post-war period until 1980, the population in Sweden increased by 25 percent and the number of dwellings for permanent use increased by 75 percent. In the Greater Stockholm Area, the increases in population and

TABLE 2-2

Dwelling Stock by Housing Type and Ownership Class in the
Greater Stockholm Area, 1960-1980.

	Number of dwellings (in thousands)	Ownership (percent)			
		Nonprofit companies	Coopera-tives	Private persons	Private companies
All dwellings					
1960	434	20%	15%	50%	15%
1970	563	26	16	41	17
1975	645	29	16	38	16
1980*	665	28	19	38	13
Multifamily houses					
1960	358	23	18	41	17
1970	454	31	19	29	21
1975	511	37	20	24	20
1980*	508	36	25	22	17
One- or two-family houses					
1960	76	4	0	93	3
1970	109	4	3	91	2
1975	134	3	1	94	2
1980*	157	3	2	93	1

Note: * Estimates.
Source: National Bureau of Statistics.

housing stock have been even greater, 55 percent and 128 percent, respectively (see table 2-1).

The ownership structure of the housing stock has changed considerably in the last two decades. The public sector (nonprofit companies, municipalities, etc.) and the cooperative sector have increased their share of the multifamily housing market, while the private sector has lost its former dominance. For one- and two-family houses, owner-occupancy is the predominant form of tenure.

The ownership structure in the Greater Stockholm Area is shown in table 2-2. Further information concerning the distribution of dwellings in this area and the household distribution in Sweden and in Greater Stockholm is given in tables 2-3 and 2-4. Housing expenditure as a percent of income for different households and tenure types is shown in table 2-5.

TABLE 2-3
Dwellings by Housing Type and Size in the Greater Stockholm Area,
1975-1980.

Housing type	Size*	1975		1980	
		Number	Percent	Number	Percent
Single-family houses	Small	2,787	2 %	2,952	2 %
	Medium	30,063	22	29,028	19
	Large	100,759	76	121,746	79
	Total	133,609	100	153,726	100
Multi-family houses	Small	156,428	30	147,415	29
	Medium	289,143	57	291,000	57
	Large	65,141	13	68,934	14
	Total	510,712	100	507,349	100
TOTAL	Small	159,215	24	150,367	23
	Medium	319,206	50	320,028	48
	Large	165,908	26	190,680	29
	Total	644,321	100	661,075	100

Note: A small number of dwellings of unknown size has been excluded.

*   Small dwellings are defined as one room plus kitchen. Medium-sized dwellings are two to three rooms plus kitchen. Those with four or more rooms plus kitchen are defined as Large.

Source: National Bureau of Statistics.

TABLE 2-4
Occupancy by Building Type and Household Size, 1960-1980.

	Number of households	Distribution of household size (percent)				
		1	2	3	4	5+
Sweden						
All dwellings						
1960	2,582,000	20 %	27 %	22 %	18 %	13 %
1965	2,777,000	23	27	21	17	12
1970	3,050,000	25	30	19	16	10
1975	3,325,000	30	31	17	15	7
1980	3,498,000	33	31	15	15	6
One- or two-family houses						
1960	1,216,000	14	27	22	19	18
1965	1,263,000	15	27	22	20	16
1970	1,309,000	15	29	21	21	14
1975	1,448,000	15	30	20	23	12
1980	1,616,000	15	31	19	24	11
Multifamily houses						
1960	1,366,000	26	28	22	16	8
1965	1,514,000	29	28	21	15	7
1970	1,741,000	33	30	18	13	6
1975	1,877,000	42	32	14	9	3
1980	1,881,000	48	31	11	7	3
Greater Stockholm Area						
All dwellings						
1960	423,107	25	29	20	16	10
1965	470,256	26	28	20	16	10
1970	540,114	30	29	18	15	8
1975	596,388	37	30	15	13	5
1980	628,271	39	30	14	12	5
One- or two-family houses						
1975	132,472	10	26	22	29	13
1980	155,805	11	27	21	29	12
Multifamily houses						
1975	463,916	45	31	13	8	3
1980	472,466	49	31	11	7	2

Source: National Housing Board.

TABLE 2-5

Housing Expenditure as a Percent of Income by Type of Household and Ownership Class in Sweden, 1973-1982.

| | | | Head of household less than 65 years | | | Head of household 65 years or older | | |
	One-person households	Couples	Couples with children 1	2	3	Adult w/ children	1-person households	Couples only
Rental units								
1973	13%	11%	13%	14%	14%	23%	16%	12%
1978	12	9	11	11	11	14	12	11
1982	16	12	13	14	13	18	15	13
Cooperative units								
1973	12	9	12	12	13	19	16	13
1978	11	7	8	9	9	11	12	9
1982	13	9	11	11	11	16	14	11
Owner-occupied units								
1978	16	11	12	12	11	16	13	12
1982	17	12	14	14	13	18	16	12

Definitions:

Income: For couples, the total income for both members is included; for other households, only the income for the head of household is included.

Housing expenditure: In rental and cooperative units, the rent less the housing allowances. In owner-occupied units (single-family houses), the total costs less tax reductions and housing allowances.

Source: National Housing Board.

The Parliamentary decisions in 1946 and 1947, which formed the basis for modern housing policy, have been regarded as key factors in the steady increase of housing production, at least until 1970. In the 1970s, the production of multifamily houses fell rather drastically from a level of nearly 80,000 flats per year to around 15,000 flats by 1976. Total new construction reached a peak in the late 1960s and early 1970s with 100,000 to 110,000 completed dwellings per year. Construction has since decreased to slightly over 40,000 (in 1983). Figures 2-1 and 2-2 indicate new production in Sweden and in the Greater Stockholm area since 1949.

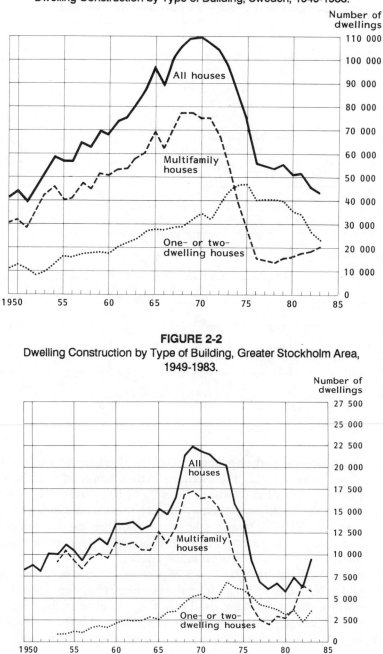

FIGURE 2-1

Dwelling Construction by Type of Building, Sweden, 1949-1983.

FIGURE 2-2

Dwelling Construction by Type of Building, Greater Stockholm Area, 1949-1983.

FIGURE 2-3

Total Production Cost of Dwellings and Nonresidential Premises, 1965-1985
(Current Swedish Crowns, SEK, per square meter of useful floor space).

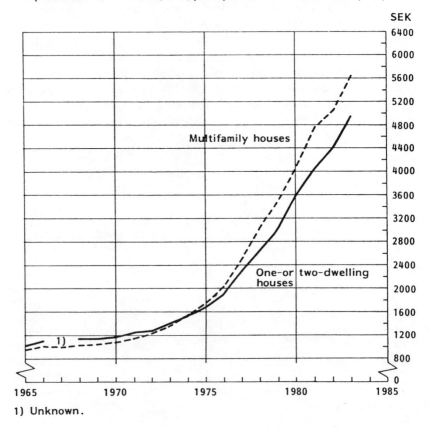

1) Unknown.

The overwhelming portion of housing construction since World War II has been financed by state loans. For dwellings in multifamily houses, the share financed by state loans has increased from 90 to 100 percent. For owner-occupied dwellings (mostly single-family houses), the share has varied between 72 and 99 percent. The differences in the financing of these two kinds of houses can be explained to a large extent by differences, over time, in the rules for subsidization and the nature of the taxation system.

In the time period from 1971 to 1975, 25 percent of owner-occupied houses were completely financed by loans from the mortgage and commercial banks. In 1983, only 1 percent of these dwellings were financed in this way. The combination of changes in the tax system which limited interest deductions (described below), skyrocketing costs for new production and historically high interest rates, made state-financed-- and subsidized-- dwellings the one and only option for households looking for new dwellings. The same is true for dwellings in multifamily houses. The general interest subsidy reduces interest rates to about 3 percent when market interest rates are 13 percent. This subsidy is about 600 Swedish Crowns (SEK) per square meter per year.

Between 1968 and 1984, the construction cost for multifamily housing increased from 1,025 to 6,162 SEK per square meter, an increase of 500 percent in nominal terms and approximately 45 percent in real terms. The costs of constructing single-family houses also increased substantially, though not at the same rate as for multifamily housing. This development is illustrated in figure 2-4.

These cost changes can be decomposed as follows: product changes, i.e., changes in the quality of the dwellings or buildings; changes in the factor prices; and changes in the production process, i.e., efficiency changes. A decomposition of this kind has been accomplished by Wigren (1986) for the period from 1968 to 1984. According to his findings, changes in factor prices were far more important in explaining the increase in current cost than changes in efficiency and quality. This is evident from figure 2-4 (based upon tables 2 and 3 in Wigren's study) below.

In real terms, the cost of construction per square meter for multifamily

FIGURE 2-4
Actual and Estimated Hypothetical Changes in Current
Production Costs per Square Meter, 1968-1984.

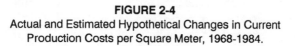

A= Actual, CQ=Constant Quality, CF=Constant Factor Prices, CE = Constant Efficiency

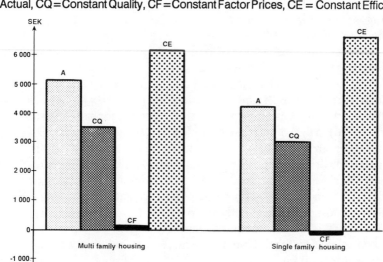

Source: Wigen (1986), Tables 2 and 3.

housing increased by 44 percent between 1968 and 1984. Quality improvements increased real costs by 35 percent and real factor prices by 25 percent. Technical progress and efficiency gains reduced real costs by 16 percent. The corresponding cost increase was 15 percent for single-family housing. In this instance, quality increases added 29 percent to costs and real factor prices added another 29 percent. These increases were approximately the same for multifamily housing. However, the cost savings obtained by greater efficiency was 44 percent, more than twice the gain for multifamily housing.

As a consequence of these cost increases, regulated rents in new production have risen substantially. In general, the relative price of rental housing increased gradually from the middle of the 1950s until about 1970. After this period, the development does not show any significant trend, as is illustrated in figure 2-5.

Partly as a result of reduced housing construction, investment in structures in Sweden has stagnated. As a consequence, almost all branches of the building materials industry have suffered losses in volume in the domestic market. Increases in exports have not compensated for these losses.

Although the pricing of all new housing is subject to the stringent controls discussed below, the Swedish industry of building contractors is competitive and free of government controls. There are between 10 and 15 large building contractors dominating the multifamily market, and a vast number of smaller contractors operating in the single-family sector. In the multifamily market during the 1970s, firms either carried losses or had small profit margins. Larger profit margins were made in the building of commercial and industrial developments, not subject to rent control measures.

According to Wigren (1986), the efficiency gains in the construction of housing would have been much higher if the size of building projects had remained the same as at the end of the sixties. Economies of scale appear in place, at least in the construction of multifamily housing. Other reasons for the relatively small efficiency gain in the housing construction sector are, according to Wigren, a lower capacity utilization and an increasing share of nonprofit investors. The latter result supports the hypothesis that cost pressures towards X-efficiency are higher among private than among nonprofit investors.

In contrast to the contractors, the industries for most building materials are highly monopolized. Rates of return on working capital in various building materials industries seem to be higher than the average for all of Swedish industry. For example, the ready-mix concrete industry (in which firms have great spatial monopoly power because of high weight-to-value ratios) and the wall paper industry, which is highly monopolized, have shown recent returns on working capital of 20 percent and higher.

One explanation for the rapid price increase of building materials-- which exceeds the general rate of inflation-- is that it is caused by the decline in new

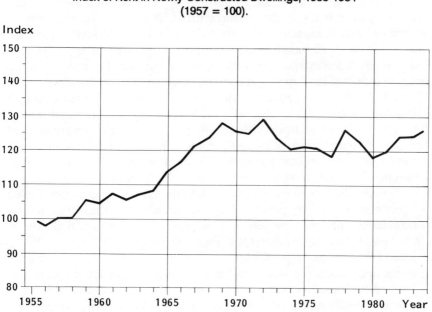

FIGURE 2-5
Index of Rent in Newly Constructed Dwellings, 1955-1984
(1957 = 100).

construction and the increase in housing rehabilitation. This shift has greatly reduced total building volume and might have forced these industries to raise prices to cover large fixed costs incurred in the past.

One disturbing aspect of the high degree of monopolistic market structure in the Swedish building materials industry is that price setting in this industry can defeat the purpose of cost-covering rent control. Profits, which in a free market would accrue to landowners, may simply be passed on to the suppliers of building materials whose price setting behavior is unregulated.

FINANCING OF NEW CONSTRUCTION AND MODERNIZATION

As emphasized above, the Swedish State subsidizes nearly all new construction in the housing sector. In contrast, other construction, such as commercial and industrial, is not subsidized. Government subsidies for housing take the form of guaranteed interest rates on both state loans and first mortgage loans. The effective interest rates for both kinds of loans are well below the market rate.

Developers are free to build with market loans, but the state subsidy is so large that any such construction is unprofitable. To qualify for a state subsidy, a private builder or nonprofit company must fulfill the following requirements: 1.) it must build on municipally owned land according to the master plan; 2.) it must conform to the building code; and 3.) it must apply for approval by the municipality, demonstrating that its estimated construction cost will not be much in excess of the "approved construction cost" for that locality.

To fulfill the last requirement, the builder files an application showing the calculation of the "approved construction cost" for the proposed building through the use of unit prices frequently published by the government. In addition, the builder also estimates the actual construction expense that will be incurred, this number being generally higher than the approved cost. If the difference is thought to be too high, a state-subsidized loan is denied.

The subsidized loan structure is as follows: For rental dwellings built by nonprofit companies, 100 percent of the "approved construction cost" receives a subsidized loan. For cooperatives, single-family dwellings, and privately owned rental houses, the corresponding percentages are 99 percent, 95 percent, and 92 percent, respectively. The unsubsidized portion and any excess over the approved construction cost must be covered by a market loan.

Given the subsidized loan structure above, the loans are actually disbursed as follows. A mortgage loan equal to 70 percent of the approved construction cost is obtained from a mortgage bank, and the state subsidy compensates the bank for the difference between market and loan interest rates. Recently, the market rate on these bank loans has been 12 percent, and it is adjusted at five-year intervals. The subsidized loan interest rate for multifamily construction is 3 percent in the first year and rises indefinitely by an increment of 0.25 percent a year. For single-family homes, the loan interest rate is 5.5 percent in the first year and rises at 0.5 percent yearly until it reaches the market interest rate. The pattern of interest rates for state loans and first mortgage loans and the guaranteed interest level for multifamily houses are shown in figure 2-6.

The remaining 30 percent, 29 percent, 25 percent, or 22 percent of the approved construction cost (for nonprofit rental, cooperative, single-family dwellings, and privately owned rental dwellings, respectively) comes directly from the State.[3] The subsidized interest rates and annual increments for this portion of the loans are the same as for the bank loans. A peculiar aspect of this subsidy program is the method of amortization for these loans. The government has stated the goal (or expectation) that the state portion of the loan be paid off in 30 years. However, for multifamily houses this may or may not come

---

[3] Since July 1985 State loans are financed by a new State-owned financing corporation outside the government budget.

FIGURE 2-6

Interest Levels for State Loans, First Mortgage Loans, and Guaranteed Interest Rate: Multifamily Houses, 1975-1983.

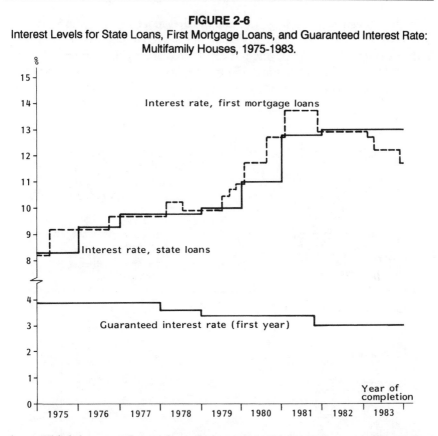

about. This is because the graduated payments on the state loan are not applied toward capital amortization until the interest rate reaches the market level. Thereafter, amortization proceeds normally. If, subsequently, the market rate increases above the subsidized rate, then amortization ceases. Conceivably, the subsidized rate may never exceed the normal rate and thus amortization may never begin. For single-family houses, amortization of the state loan starts immediately after the house is constructed and goes on for 30 years.

Starting in July 1985, new State loans for new construction are to be repaid in 35 years after an initial period of five years without amortization. The bank portion of the loan for multifamily houses is subject to more rigid rules of amortization. It is guaranteed to be amortized in 50 years with principal payments graduated in ten-year intervals. The equivalent time for single-family houses is 40 years.

The state and subsidized bank loans are in principle assumable by all future owners. However, the first buyer of a single-family home normally relieves the builder of a construction loan at market rates. The first buyer pays the difference between the selling price and the first mortgage plus the State loan as a down payment. The same procedure applies to cooperative associations. In the next step, the down payment is distributed among its members, i.e., the households living in the building. Figure 2-7 shows the institutional structure of the housing financing system.

FIGURE 2-7
The Institutional Structure of the Swedish Housing Finance System.

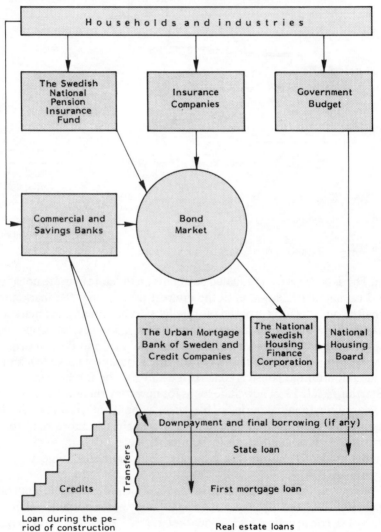

As noted above, in recent years new construction activity in Sweden has diminished substantially, and has been replaced, in large measure, by rehabilitation and modernization activity. Modernization refers to major upgrading of a building, addition of facilities, repairs, and, frequently, merging flats within a building to create a smaller number of larger flats. The state subsidizes modernization by loans repayable within a maximum of 30 years. These are also subject to approval by the municipalities; excesses over approved costs must be covered by market loans.

Beginning in 1984, the state began subsidizing loans for repairs and maintenance in multifamily houses. The loans are given by certain banks, and the subsidy has the form of an interest guarantee. The subsidy is available for nonprofit companies, cooperatives, and private owners of multifamily rental dwellings. This subsidy system is quite different from the general interest subsidy system and is effective for 10 to 20 years depending upon the specific improvements made in a building.

PRICING, RENT CONTROL, RENT POOLING, AND RENT NEGOTIATIONS

Rents are regulated by a so-called "use-value system" where the rents for dwellings owned by the municipal nonprofit housing companies are used as a yardstick for privately owned rental housing. Furthermore, the municipal housing stock is priced according to the principle that it should not generate a profit, which in practice means a cost-related rent setting system.

For newly built single-family (owner-occupied) dwellings with state loans, a similar principle is enforced. A builder sells completed dwellings at the approved price, which is set at the time of the subsidized loan application. These prices are set to cover precisely the builder's estimated construction cost plus a small profit (assuming these estimates are not too high to qualify for a subsidized loan). When a builder sells at this price, the buyer, usually a household, makes a down payment equal to the unsubsidized portion of the builder's loan and assumes the subsidized state and bank loans. If such a buyer (the initial owner) wishes to resell the dwelling within three years, he cannot sell at a profit if the state loan is to be kept. Thereafter, prices are entirely free and subject to the forces of supply and demand. For cooperative dwellings, the tenant can sell at any time and at any price.

Rent control is a very important feature of the Swedish housing market and has been the focal point of study, debate, and reform (Kemeny, 1981; Turner, 1982). Again, the principle is to set rents throughout the lifetime of a dwelling in such a way as to cover the construction, maintenance, and operating costs of the dwelling so that the owner-- a nonprofit company or private owner-- does not make a profit.

We now turn to an examination of the nonprofit company, which is essential to understanding the concept of rent pooling. A nonprofit company contracts with a building firm to construct rental housing. Thereafter, the nonprofit firm owns and manages the rental units. The zero profit principle applies at the company level. Annually, each company determines the total cost of its entire stock. This cost includes that year's loan payments plus an estimate of maintenance, operation, and any new construction costs. Also included are any funds needed to replenish the company's reserves. Dividing this total cost estimate by the number of rental dwellings in the company gives the average rent per dwelling in the company. This average rent is then adjusted for various dwellings in the company according to size, age, quality, and other factors.

This process of rent pooling and adjustment is resolved in annual negotiations between representatives of each nonprofit company, representatives of the tenants of that company (who are members of the National Tenants' Association), and regional or municipal representatives of the tenants' association. During these negotiations, the tenants' association examines the company's books and requires documentation of interest income and other investments of the nonprofit companies.

Tenants are often opposed to pooling and new construction by the company because, in times of rising construction costs, pooling increases the rents of sitting tenants. Additionally, the companies' efforts to adjust rents by size and quality do not resemble a market adjustment. In 1972, a national committee composed of representatives of the nonprofit companies' association (SABO) and the tenants' association recommended the use of a point system. This system issued points to buildings according to their age, and then made adjustments for, for example, location, social services, and commercial services. This point system is not used in any formal way nor does it seem to have any scientific or statistically valid rationale. In any event, such a point system would only work to bring relative rents within a company more in line with a free market rent structure; it would not correct the discrepancy in rents among companies.

Clearly, different nonprofit companies must charge dissimilar average rents if they have significantly different construction profiles over time (different vintage mixes). For example, new companies which were set up in the 1960s to build housing in the new suburbs of Stockholm would charge much higher rent for flats identical to those held by older companies which built in Stockholm during the 1940s and 1950s. A consequence of this rent pooling scheme is that the rent for the same type of flat increases with distance from the city center, contrary to what would normally be observed in a free market.

Another effect of rent pooling is observable in Stockholm, where the municipal companies of the city of Stockholm have built housing in the past on land bought or leased from suburban municipalities. The costs of these relatively new outlying buildings are then pooled with the older and centrally located buildings owned by the same company. Thus, tenants in these newer buildings end up paying rents much lower than the rents paid by tenants in the stock built by the suburban company.

Negotiations are held annually to set rents for the following year. The tenants' association negotiates separately with each company and also with the local association of private landlords. If a specific set of negotiations with a nonprofit company is deadlocked, the case is appealed to a National Committee on the Rental Market, which consists of officials elected from SABO and members of the tenants' association. This committee then decides on a compromise rent level for the coming year. The associations of private landlords cannot appeal to this committee, but instead must seek recourse in the courts.

One issue which figures prominently in the negotiations is the carrying cost of vacancies in the stock, particularly any newly built stock. SABO believes that the municipalities should subsidize the cost of vacancies in excess of 1.5 percent of the potential total rent income. This is negotiated with each municipality, and most have agreed to follow this practice.

It appears that there is substantial variance in the negotiating powers of different nonprofit companies and their respective tenants. Even though they are nonprofit, a few companies have accumulated reserves, while most of them have survived on much tighter budgets. The recent rent development in the Greater Stockholm Area is shown in table 2-6.

THE PUBLIC QUEUE: THE CASE OF GREATER STOCKHOLM

Sweden has adopted a conscious policy, followed by localities with various degrees of consistency, to ration new dwellings by municipal queues. In Greater Stockholm, this is accomplished by a consolidation of the 22 local municipal housing agencies (the Stockholm Federation of Municipal Housing Agencies, KSB), thus creating a single public queue at the metropolitan level into which all dwellings available for rationing are pooled.

There is a complicated set of rules governing the rationing of dwellings by KSB. By law, all dwellings built since 1968 with government loans (including rental, cooperative, and single-family homes) can be claimed by KSB whenever there is a vacancy. However, KSB chooses to exercise this right differentially: it does not exercise the right to sell newly constructed single-family homes, but will lease them if they are rental single-family homes.

In the case of cooperatives, there are special agreements between KSB and particular cooperative associations. The agreement with HSB (a major Stockholm cooperative) is that the cooperative itself should sell all of its new flats.

TABLE 2-6

Average Monthly Rent for Dwellings in the Greater Stockholm Area:
Multifamily Structures Financed with Government Loans and
Owned by Nonprofit Companies, by Size of Dwelling, 1975-1983.*

	Size of dwelling, excluding kitchen					Rent for three-room unit, index	CPI index
Year	One Room	Two Rooms	Three Rooms	Four Rooms	Five Rooms	(1980=100)	(1980=100)
1975	539	658	756	899	1,093	44.8	60.7
1976	506	708	810	961	935	48.0	66.9
1977	631	874	931	1,010	1,973	55.2	74.6
1978	723	1,071	1,356	1,622	1,769	80.4	82.1
1979	768	1,215	1,511	1,807	1,968	89.6	87.9
1980	1,051	1,432	1,685	2,002	2,312	100.0	100.0
1981	1,281	1,587	1,861	2,220	2,443	110.4	112.1
1982	1,459	1,819	2,182	2,514	2,944	129.4	121.7
1983	1,547	1,864	2,308	2,658	3,063	136.9	132.6

Note: * Rents for first year only, in Swedish Crowns (6.25 crowns = $1 U.S., in 1990).

Source: National Bureau of Statistics.

Riksbyggen, on the other hand, gives all of its cooperative units to KSB for rationing by queue. Agreements with other associations provide, for example, an assignment of 50 percent of their new cooperative units to specific banks. Banks, in turn, ration these units to those customers who raise down payments by participating in the banks' savings programs for cooperative tenant ownership.

In addition to all the newly built rental dwellings, KSB also handles approximately 50 percent of the vacancies in the existing stock. The remaining half is available for rental directly from private landlords.

It is estimated that approximately 15 percent of the total mobility in Greater Stockholm is handled through KSB. On the supply side of the queue, there is a rule that KSB has approximately three months to fill a flat. If a flat is not filled in this period, it is returned to the landlord or nonprofit company, who generally prefers to do its own leasing.

To obtain a flat through the public queue (KSB), a household fills out an application describing its current dwelling, its desired dwelling, and a maximum rent it is willing to pay. This application must be renewed annually if the household remains in the queue a year or longer. A household is entitled to receive a maximum of three rental offers and is ejected from the queue if it rejects those offers. It rarely happens that a landlord or nonprofit company will object to a tenant assigned by KSB. In the rare cases when this occurs, KSB can go to court on behalf of the tenant. Another rule is that if a tenant is assigned to a dwelling by KSB, that tenant's vacated dwelling must be turned over to KSB for reletting.

Out of the total number of flats that KSB handles, roughly 20 percent are allotted to households with severe medical or social problems and households that must be evacuated because their flats are being reconstructed. For the remaining 80 percent of the flats, KSB uses a six-level priority classification of households according to assessed need. Priority One includes households in emergency circumstances (e.g., fire) and families in heavily overcrowded flats. Priority Two consists of households with children, with their parents or in substandard flats. Priority Three covers households without a flat but with children who are able to live on their own (as occurs after a divorce when children can stay with one parent). Priority Four mainly includes households, without children, who live in a substandard flat. Priority Five covers households wanting to swap flats. Also in this priority level are those who have a cooperative and want to move to a rental unit. Finally, Priority Six consists of households which do not currently live in Greater Stockholm but desire to move there.

These assessments of need take precedence over the time an applicant has been waiting in the queue. However, when need is equal, then time in the queue is the deciding factor. The time a household spends waiting in a queue can vary enormously depending on the location, type, and price of the desired flat.

In the beginning of 1985, the number of applicants registered by KSB was about 103,000. The number of dwellings assigned to applicants in the queue was 23,000 in 1983. The majority of households (70 percent) assigned dwellings through the agency consisted of one or two persons. Fifty-five to 60 percent of the assigned dwellings were small flats of no more than two rooms and a kitchen.

The total number of individuals who were affected by the assignments of dwellings through the agency in 1983 can roughly be estimated at 44,000. This figure could be compared with total individual mobility in 1983, which amounted to at least 245,000. This comparison suggests that 15 to 20 percent of household location changes in Stockholm are facilitated by the intermediary functions of KSB.

SWAPPING, BLACK MARKETS, MOBILITY, AND HOUSEHOLD FORMATION

The public queue is extremely important because it is the only means by which new rental dwellings are leased, and it is a very vital means of entering the market for some households. As mentioned above, however, it only amounts to about 15 to 20 percent of mobility in Greater Stockholm.

The predominant, and legal, means of relocation is the swapping of one dwelling for another without any side payments. Such swaps can occur between two tenants or between an owner and a tenant. This form of relocation is generally believed to be responsible for 75 percent of total household mobility. Swappers find each other through newspaper columns, through the services of realtors, or through friends and acquaintances. Two households getting married will often swap their two units for the one unit occupied by a household undergoing a divorce. In general, there are no restrictions on the nature of the swaps.

It appears that Swedish regulations are unclear about what constitutes legal pricing during a swap. For example, it is legal to swap one's cooperative unit with a tenant's apartment. If the apartment is attractive and well located, the owner of the cooperative may substantially lower the selling price. The question arises: Does this constitute a fair or black market transaction?

Swapping differs from what might be called a "direct" black market transaction, which is clearly illegal. While it is not illegal to pay to get a rental contract, it is illegal to receive payment with financial penalties and jail sentences enforced. Black market transactions are believed to be significant but not very large.

It is obvious that these institutions of swapping, black markets, and the public queue have a pronounced impact on household formation and mobility. New households with young members do not have a flat to swap nor the income to buy; they are thus restricted to entering the public queue. Since this queue is not as efficient or fast as a free market, it is reasonable to conclude that it retards household formation, forcing these young households to remain with their parents longer or to join into other forms of co-tenancy.

Swapping and the black market also retard mobility because they involve processes of matching and search which are much more cumbersome and risky than those of a free market, where vacancies can be rented directly from the landlords on a first-come, first-serve basis at the market rent.

HOUSING ALLOWANCES

The Swedish state and municipalities jointly administer a system of housing allowances designed to improve the housing consumption of certain household groups. The percentage of rent to be covered by the housing allowance is determined on the basis of household income and wealth, the rent or price to be paid by the household, and the number of children. There is also a special municipal allowance system for pensioners. Households are eligible for allowances regardless of dwelling type and tenure.

In 1981, total housing consumption expenditures amounted to 20 percent of total private consumption, a percentage which has remained stable over time. In the same year, about 9 percent of total housing consumption expenditures were paid as rent allowances and another 12 percent as interest subsidies. Thus, 22 percent of total housing expenditure was subsidized (not taking into account interest deductions by homeowners).

In summary, even though the intent of rent control in Sweden is to keep down the average cost of housing, the state and municipalities recognize the needs of many groups. Public subsidies contribute significantly in an effort to improve the housing consumption of needy households relative to the rest of the population. A large number of households receives such allowances, although the bulk of the payments are concentrated on pensioners and those "underconsuming" housing.

In 1980, about 52 percent of the pensioner households (a head of household who is 65 years or older) received housing allowances. The corresponding share for non-pensioner households was 13 percent. For the latter households, the average figure conceals a wide variance, from 5 percent for households without children to 60 percent for households with three or more children. (A child is defined, in this context, as an individual under 18 years.)

HOUSING AND INCOME TAX[4]

Sweden has an extremely high rate of personal income taxation. Thus, income tax subsidies to homeowners, landlords, and nonprofit companies that own housing are of special significance. The state income tax is progressive for individuals. The municipal income tax is not progressive and, although it varies somewhat by municipality and is set annually, is generally about 30 percent of income. The proceeds are divided roughly equally between the county and the municipality. The total income tax rate for the average industrial worker is about 40 percent, and the marginal income tax rate is about 60 percent. For companies, the income tax is about 52 percent of net taxable income.

The treatment of housing within the Swedish income tax system relies on "assessed (or taxation) value." In Sweden, buildings are assessed every five years, and the assessed value is defined as 75 percent of the estimated fair market value.

Housing is an asset from which income is imputed. Nonprofit companies and cooperative associations impute a flat 3 percent of assessed value. Owners of single-family homes must impute as income a percentage that increases with

---

[4] This section contains a description of the taxation system effective at the end of 1988. The system is in constant change. However, the main structure is still as described.

assessed value. At present, this percentage starts at 2 percent and increases to 8 percent. From the imputed income, the owner subtracts interest payments. If, in this calculation, the dwelling generates a loss (as is usually the case for owners of single-family housing), the loss can be netted against other income.

Recent rule changes will modify this. The new rule limits the taxes saved from the ownership of single-family housing-- by the deduction of loss due to interest payments-- to no more than 50 percent of the loss. This rule, in fact, applies to all losses due to interest payments. Independent of imputed income calculations, all housing owners pay a flat-rate national property tax of 1.5 percent of assessed value.

In Sweden, income from the sale of an asset is ordinary taxable income, but housing is afforded special treatment, as in the United States. In the case of housing, the taxable capital gain is the real capital gain, adjusted for inflation. Starting in 1981, to discourage short-term speculation in home ownership, the law was changed to prohibit the use of the inflation adjustment for sales that occur within five years of the purchase of housing. Thus, unlike the U.S. tax system which taxes only nominal capital gains, the Swedish system nominally taxes only short-term capital gains. As in the United States, capital gains for homeowners are postponable under certain rules.[5]

A capital gain realized from a cooperative dwelling is fully taxable only if the dwelling was held less than two years. The percentage of the capital gain which is taxable falls to 25 percent when the ownership period exceeds five years. Assessed values for cooperative buildings are pro-rated to specific units on the basis of their share in floor space. Interest is paid directly by the association and is deducted in its income tax calculations, whereas capital gains and losses are taken by the individual tenant-owner. (An income tax feature that concerns owner -occupiers and renters alike is that housing allowances are tax-free.)

The deductibility of interest payments has a substantial effect on the net housing expenditures of the owners of single-family homes. In 1981, the total foregone tax revenues from owners of single-family houses corresponded to 20 percent of total housing consumption expenditures by all households in that year.

Since 1983 a special tax has been levied on many rental and cooperative houses.[6] The tax for 1983 was 1 percent of the assessed value and was raised to 1.5 percent and 2 percent for 1984 and 1985, respectively. The tax is somewhat inaccurately called the "rental-house-fee" and is motivated on parity

---

[5] These rules require that the gain exceed a minimum amount, that the owner must have been the occupant for at least three out of the five years immediately preceding the sale, and that a more expensive house be bought within one year of the sale.

[6] Specifically, the tax is levied on those built before 1975 with the exception of those built or reconstructed with the support of state loans after 1957.

grounds since the guaranteed interest rate for the subsidized housing is continuously raised by 0.25 percent per year, compared to 0.5 percent per year for single-family housing.

According to a parliamentary decision, the rental-house-fee was replaced in 1985 by a new national property tax motivated by fiscal needs. For privately owned rental houses, the tax rate is 2 percent of the assessed value, and the tax is deductible. For nonprofit companies and cooperatives, the rate is 1.4 percent of the assessed value and the tax is nondeductible. For single-family houses, the tax rate for 1985 is 0.5 percent of one-third of the assessed value. For 1986 and 1987, the tax rate for these houses increases to 1.0 percent and 1.4 percent, respectively. For single-family houses, the tax is not deductible.

In 1984 another new state tax was introduced, the so-called "profit-sharing-tax." The proceeds of this tax are funnelled into five wage-earners' funds. It is, however, unclear how this tax will affect private landlords. (Nonprofit companies and cooperatives are excluded, as are private persons.)

CONCLUSIONS

The overall impression of the development of the Swedish housing market is that a relatively rapid improvement has taken place since World War II. The prewar problems of unsound and unhealthy dwellings and of overcrowded conditions have almost vanished. Evidence of this development is given in figures 2-8 and 2-9. It is also evident that the general quality of buildings and neighborhoods is much higher today than it was 40 years ago.

The guidelines for housing policy and the instruments used for its implementation have aimed at improving housing conditions, not just for certain social groups with special needs, but for all households. Thus, the U.K. concept of so-called "social housing" has not been accepted in Sweden. Swedish policy also seems to have been successful in so far as it has eliminated slums, at least those of the U.S. stereotype. Residential segregation by income class also seems to be much less pronounced than in other countries. In terms of basic equity, the distribution of housing has become more even, more so than even the income distribution.

Although this general view is embraced by a vast majority of Swedish people, there are distinct differences in opinion as to the cost and effectiveness of the institutions and policy instruments that are used to achieve the different policy goals.

A number of criticisms of Swedish policies follow from the preceeding analysis.

The total amount of housing subsidies has increased substantially. Today, cash subsidies and tax expenditures constitute approximately thirty percent of

FIGURE 2-8
Room Units per Person in Sweden, 1945-1980.

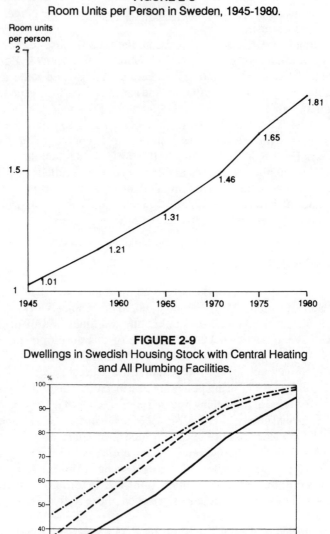

FIGURE 2-9
Dwellings in Swedish Housing Stock with Central Heating
and All Plumbing Facilities.

total housing consumption. This has created serious problems for a government facing huge budget deficits.

The complexity of the various institutions, laws, codes, and systems for taxation and subsidies affecting the housing market has made it almost impossible to comprehend the system. It is very difficult to estimate the effect of a given policy change. As a result, it is often the case that policy is revised in order to mitigate unexpected consequences of previously introduced policy measures.

The rent setting system has led to an inefficient use of the housing stock. Black market activities in the central parts of the major cities, as well as high vacancy and turn-over rates in newly constructed housing areas, attest to this inefficiency.

Nonprofit companies appear to be less efficient and cost conscious than private companies. One indication of this is that their operating costs, per square meter of equivalent dwelling, are higher as a rule than those of private and cooperative companies. Another is that the increased cost of new production seems to be related to the increased production share of nonprofit companies.

The system used for deciding whether or not to approve state loans for a proposed building project may lead to unnecessary cost increases. The system provides no incentives to estimate costs below the approved cost. And as soon as most builders make offers exceeding this cost, there seems to be a general tendency for pressure groups (such as the National Associations of Tenants and the National Association of Nonprofit Private Investors) to opt for increased subsidies. Another indication of unwanted effects in this respect is the relatively high profit level in the building materials industry.

In conclusion, it is unclear that the equity benefits of current Swedish housing policy fully outweigh the direct and indirect costs of these programs. In our opinion, some reforms toward less control should be taken to increase efficiency, to decrease the overall subsidy level, and to make the system less difficult to comprehend. If well-designed, such changes need not necessarily conflict with ambitious social goals. On the contrary, we believe that the potential efficiency gains to be made will reduce the need for subsidies and will reduce the need for such a complex system of subsidies.

We have conducted a variety of policy simulations aimed to identify the potential benefits of reducing compexity. These simulation experiments suggest that there are, indeed, substantial potential benefits from reforming the search and transaction-related complexity in the Stockholm market.

REFERENCES

Anton, T. 1975. *Governing greater Stockholm: A study of policy development and system change*. Los Angeles and Berkeley: University of California Press.

Kemeny, J. 1981. *Swedish rental housing: Policies and problems*. Birmingham: Centre for Urban and Regional Studies, University of Birmingham.

Statistics Sweden. 1983. *Yearbook of housing and planning statistics 1983*. Stockholm: Official Statistics of Sweden.

Turner, B. 1982. The future of public rental housing in Sweden: Rent pooling and production. The National Swedish Institute for Building Research, Gävle. Mimeo.

Wigren, R. 1986. Efficiency, quality change and trends in housing construction costs in Sweden. The National Swedish Institute for Building Research, Gävle. Mimeo.

3
THE FINNISH HOUSING MARKET: STRUCTURE, INSTITUTIONS, AND POLICY ISSUES

Christer Bengs
Heikki A. Loikkanen

INTRODUCTION

This chapter examines the structure, institutions, and policy issues important to the Finnish housing sector. Special emphasis is given to institutional constraints and public intervention on both the demand and supply sides of the housing market. The institutional description presented in the chapter applies in many respects to the whole country, but we give particular emphasis to the market in Helsinki, the national capital. Empirical material is presented and interpreted for the country as a whole and also for those elements characteristic of the Helsinki metropolitan area. Figure 3-1 indicates the location of Helsinki in the southern tip of Finland.

Most countries share similar housing objectives and institutions. Despite common elements, differing historical developments and distinct social values and attitudes underlie some noteworthy differences across countries. Among the Scandinavian countries, there has been a deliberate aim to unify policy measures in different functional areas. This applies especially to social policy where harmonization has gone furthest. In addition to this, there has been a general tendency in Finland to imitate Swedish reforms (but with a lag), and quite a few Finnish policies are motivated by the "Swedish model."

These considerations might suggest that housing is an area where dissimilarities among Scandinavian countries are rare. However, this is not the case.

FIGURE 3-1
Finland and the Helsinki Metropolitan Area.

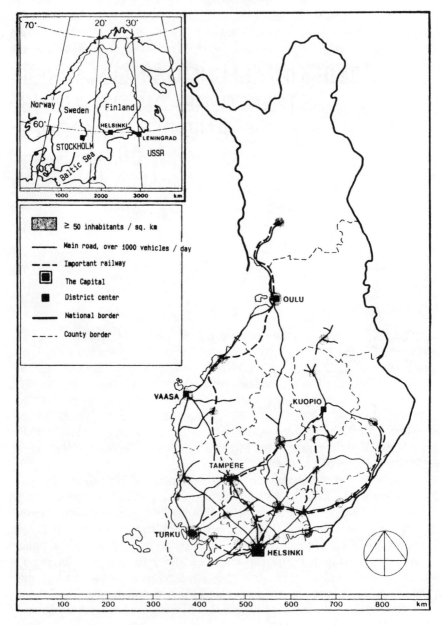

There are important differences, partly due to historical developments, and partly resulting from conscious policy choices and unequal economic structures.

This chapter is organized as follows. First, we briefly describe the historical background. We then examine the nature of urban land and land policy and describe the administrative apparatus of public housing policy and urban planning. Next we discuss housing production, including the links between housing materials, land acquisition, planning, and construction. We then describe the dwelling stock, tenure forms, and types of housing finance. We analyze price and rent formation in the housing market and the operation of nonprice allocation mechanisms. The relationship between housing, mobility, and household formation is the topic of next section, while housing allowances and taxes are described subsequently.

HISTORICAL BACKGROUND

Until the latter half of the nineteenth century, the economy of Finland was almost entirely based on primary production and barter. The two sectors employed 90 percent of the total labor force. The distributional pattern of natural resources determined regional employment levels. The south, including Helsinki, and the west had the highest natural resource densities.

Industrialization began in the 1860s. The new export industry, located on the coast, was based mainly on forest resources. Accordingly, seaside towns represented a major part of urban growth. In the 1870s, birth and death rates began to decline almost simultaneously, resulting in net population growth. At the same time, town populations began to grow exponentially. In Finland population growth did not slow down until the 1930s, later than elsewhere in industrialized Europe.

After Finland became independent in 1917, the number of people employed in agriculture and forestry continued to increase until the 1940s, rendering a fairly even regional demographic development throughout the country.

The major changes in the regional and community structure in Finland have occurred since World War II. The mechanization of agriculture and forestry has reduced the need for labor in primary production substantially, though this decrease is offset by an increase in employment in manufacturing and services. The share of people employed in agriculture dropped from 50 to 15 percent over a 30-year period, starting in the mid-1940s-- some 40 to 60 years later than in other Nordic countries. This resulted in large-scale, extremely rapid urbanization and migration from the North and East to the South and West, as well as emigration, primarily to Sweden.

From 1840 to 1970, the total population of Finland tripled to its current level of almost 5 million people. During the same period, urban population increased thirtyfold (Peltonen, 1982). The Helsinki metropolitan region has developed especially rapidly. In 1880, the region had a population of 55,600 (with the municipality of Helsinki accounting for 43,000). One hundred years later, the figure was 783,000 (with Helsinki having 483,000). Development has also been rapid in terms of employment. In 1960, the region had a labor force of 305,700, while the figure was 409,300 20 years later (see figure 3-2 and table 3-1). About three-quarters of the total population increase during the 1970s (123,300 persons) occurred in the provice of Uusimaa, which includes the Helsinki region.

During the 1970s, population increased from 4.6 million to 4.8 million, yielding an average population density of 16 persons per square kilometer for the whole country and 113 persons per square kilometer for the most developed South coast region of Uusimaa. A considerable change has occurred in the age structure of the population as well. The proportion of the population under 14 fell from 24.3 percent in 1970 to 20.2 percent in 1980. There has also been a steady decline in the average size of households from 3.2 in 1970 to 2.6 in 1980.

URBAN LAND

History

The total area of Finland is 337,000 square kilometers of which 2.2 percent is developed, about 10 percent is agricultural land, and the rest is covered by forests, swamps, and water systems. With the emergence of industrialization in the 1860s, the traditional facilities of the industrial centers, notably Helsinki, became inadequate. Most of the land within municipal boundaries was owned by the municipalities themselves. By law, this land alone could be exploited for new construction. The expanding population did not fit into the planned areas within the city and did not have the economic resources to do so. The prevailing notion was that a town would only incorporate nonmunicipal land already in its possesion but outside its borders. Outside the borders, private landlords could lease or sell land to newcomers. This private land could be freely exploited without any kind of restrictions from this side of the town. During this period, around the turn of the century, land speculation companies emerged, acquiring large areas, carrying out plot subdivisions, and selling single plots. This combination of municipal land ownership and uncontrolled private land exploitation resulted in two totally different urban fabrics -- the suburbs and the planned city centers (Vuorela, 1979).

In 1925, the cities acquired the legal right to incorporate suburbs, and the Town Plan Code of 1931 gave municipalities the privilege of planning the use

TABLE 3-1

Development of Labor Force in Finland's Largest Metropolitan Areas, 1970-1980.

Metropolitan area	Total population (in thousands) 1980	Economically active population (in thousands) 1970	1980	Manufacturing as a percentage of total 1970	1980	Building as a percentage of total 1970	1980	Services as a percentage of total 1970	1980
Helsinki	901.1*	411.5	448.1	25 %	20 %	8 %	6 %	64 %	72 %
Turku	229.8	101.3	110.0	36	32	9	7	50	56
Proi	99.5	42.2	46.4	42	38	8	6	43	48
Tampere	243.9	107.0	116.9	44	38	8	7	44	51
Lahti	125.0	54.9	59.0	46	41	8	7	40	47
Kuopio	89.7	34.2	40.7	24	20	11	10	55	62
Jyvaskyla	110.4	45.5	51.0	34	30	9	8	48	56
Vaasa	67.5	26.3	30.7	37	34	7	7	50	53
Oulu	124.0	45.0	54.8	23	22	12	8	59	65

Note:: * Extended metropolitan region includes eight municipalities in addition to Helsinki, Espoo, Vantaa, and Kauniainen.

FIGURE 3-2
Population and Employment in the Helsinki Metropolitan Area,
1880-1980.

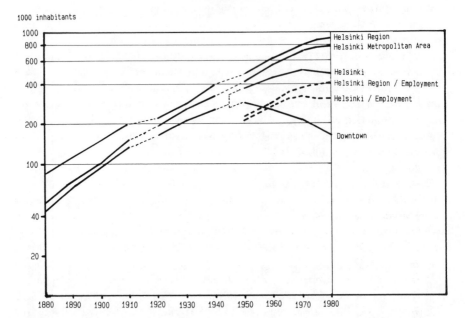

of privately owned land. In addition, the municipalities continued to use the traditional means of buying or expropriating land to be zoned for development. The Building Code of 1958 extended these principles and possibilities. These laws can be seen as an extension of public rights at the expense of private interests. They could also be assessed in quite an opposite way. Under these regulations, private land within a municipality could be exploited legally and in an orderly fashion, reinforcing the externalities inherent in urban land. The correct interpretation to be chosen is not a theoretical issue, but a question of historical development since the 1920s.

In most cities, the land obtained under historic royal charters was fully developed by the 1950s. The expanding cities then had two options: to acquire new land, or to inhibit the direction of growth. The municipalities began buying vacant land in the 1950s, as did private speculators-- mainly construction companies. By 1974, when the strongest urbanization boom was already past, the total amount of raw land planned for development in municipal possession could have housed some 600,000 inhabitants. The amount of raw land planned for development in private possession could have housed approximately 1 million more inhabitants-- roughly 60 percent of the total city population at that time. During the period from 1975 to 1981, the area covered by detailed plans increased by 36 percent. Of the total area of land planned for development, about 60 percent was located in the four southernmost provinces. Table 3-2 presents some summary features of land planned for development in Finnish towns.

TABLE 3-2

General Features of Zoned Land in Finnish Towns, 1975 and 1981.

	1975	1981
Planned land area (in thousands of hectares)	119	156
Percentage of planned land area zoned as:		
Residential areas	30 %	29 %
Industrial and commercial areas	13	15
Public buildings	6	6
Parks, sport amenities, and outdoor recreation areas	24	24
Other areas	7	6

Source: Ministry of Interior and the National Housing Board (1982, p. 17).

The Development of the Helsinki Metropolitan Area

The Helsinki metropolitan area consists of four municipalities: Helsinki, Espoo, Vantaa, and Kauniainen. The regional planning body actually includes nine municipalities and the regional influence of the capital is even wider (see figure 3-3). The growth of the Helsinki metropolitan area since 1950 has been rapid. Between 1951 and 1984, some 260,000 dwellings were produced and about 175,000 jobs were created. Additionally, within the Helsinki metropolitan area, the boundaries of the capital have expanded over time (Schulman, 1984). The municipality of Helsinki incorporated adjacent, built-up areas in 1906 and 1912, and other very large areas in 1946 and 1966.

FIGURE 3-3
Helsinki Metropolitan Area.

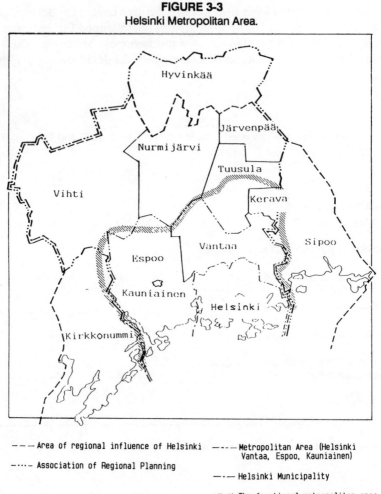

——— Area of regional influence of Helsinki   ———— Metropolitan Area (Helsinki
                                                        Vantaa, Espoo, Kauniainen)
—·····— Association of Regional Planning
                                               —·— Helsinki Municipality

                                               \\\\\\\ The functional metropolitan area

The urban structure in 1950 was characterized by a strong concentration of the building stock in the traditional core, the peninsula of Helsinki, and along the two railway lines running west and northeast. Construction of new multistory blocks of flats occurred in the late 1950s, mainly at the urban fringe of the Helsinki municipality. The main radial freeways were also constructed during this period. During the most extensive construction period, from 1960 to 1975, the whole area was a scene for the construction of huge housing blocks, offices, and industrial facilities. From 1975 onward, housing construction activities have been scattered and relatively small-scaled. Figure 3-4 indicates the pattern of development since 1950.

FIGURE 3-4
Urban Development in the Helsinki Metropolitan Area, 1950-1985.

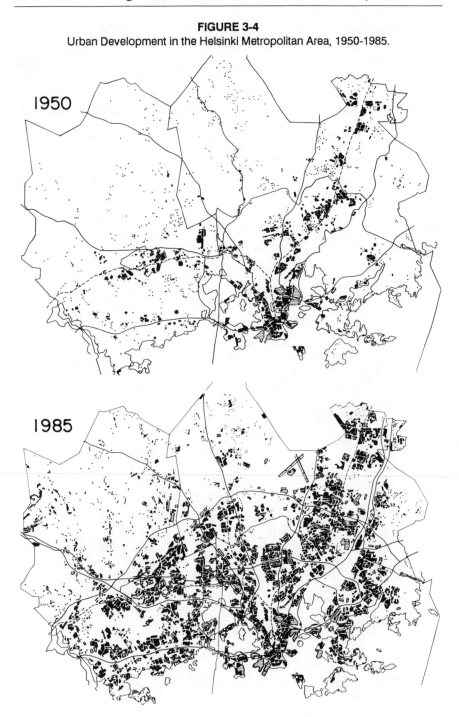

A glance at the situation in 1985 shows a very scattered urban structure. The old city center is still of great importance, providing nearly 50 percent of metropolitan jobs, but housing only 20 percent of the population in 1985 (compared with 72 percent in 1950). Construction activity during the 1950 to 1985 period took place not only within areas adjacent to the largest concentric traffic routes, but in areas in between as well. From a functional point of view, the urban sprawl seems to have created a haphazard urban fabric. The scattered structure has resulted in a substantial increase in traffic congestion and cross-town commuting (see figure 3-5).

FIGURE 3-5
Principal Commuting Patterns in Helsinki, 1950-1980.

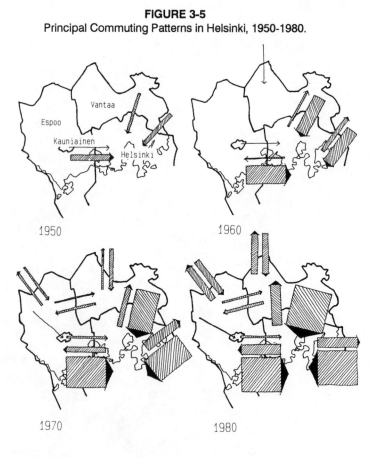

20 000 ┐
10 000 ┘   Number of Commuting Persons and
                  Direction of Commuting

Expectations during the 1960s of the continued growth of the Helsinki metropolitan area, by both developers and the municipalities, turned out to be overly optimistic. Much of the allowed building volumes have not yet been constructed because of a sharp decline in the rate of urbanization. If the present construction rate continues, the Helsinki metropolitan area is now supposed to possess enough raw land already zoned for housing purposes for many years. Within the municipality of Helsinki, however, there is a lack of subdivided land. This is especially a problem for state-financed housing since a prerequisite for getting public finance is that the land price does not exceed a given upper limit per square meter.

ADMINISTRATION OF HOUSING AND URBAN PLANNING

Administration and Planning of Towns

The Finnish governmental system is divided into central and provincial administration of the state, as well as local self-government. The central state administration comprises a number of ministries and subordinate national boards exercising wide executive power. The Ministry of the Environment handles housing and planning matters and, in cooperation with the National Housing Board (NHB), prepares Council-of-State decisions related to housing.

The Ministry also acts as a ratifying authority for plans made at lower levels, provided this task is not delegated further. A national physical plan is not included in the framework of land-use plans, but provision for such a plan has been made in the ongoing preparatory work for the revision of the Planning and Building Act.

The main task of the NHB is to implement housing policy drawn up by the Ministry. The board also supervises the granting of state loans for housing. Through this mechanism, the NHB exercises control over the design and costs of state-financed housing construction.

Twelve provincial governments, responsible for any physical planning delegated to them by the central government, carry out regional administration. In addition, they act as ratifying authorities for certain local plans and have appellate jurisdiction for decisions by the local authorities. Finally, they control and supervise housing within their province.

At the intermediate administrative level there are 20 regional planning associations corresponding to regional physical planning areas. The municipalities of the area jointly form these municipal federations in order to formulate regional physical plans according to the guidelines of the Ministry of the Environment.

The regional plans are overall land-use plans covering the area of several municipalities. This type of plan is generally compiled and approved in a series of stages. At present, regional planning involves a so-called comprehensive plan and a confirmatory plan. The comprehensive plan covers the whole regional planning association area and is of a development policy character. It is revised every fourth year. The confirmatory regional plan is legally binding upon municipal authorities. So far, regional plans primarily concerning recreational areas and nature reserves have been prepared.

Most local administration falls within the sphere of local self-government, which includes 84 towns and 377 other municipalities. The municipality is responsible for master planning and detailed planning, and holds a so-called planning monopoly. No dense development can take place without detailed plans drawn up by the municipality. The municipal authorities also draw up an annual housing program and take a direct hand in the production of rental housing financed by the NHB. The local authorities allocate state housing loans to eligible applicants, supervise the use of the state-subsidized housing stock, and dispense demand-side housing allowances.

A master plan is approved by the municipal council and ratified by the Ministry. The legal force of unratified master plans is limited to the right of the local authority to acquire land under specified circumstances and to have the first claim on the purchase of land.

Ratified town plans are legally binding. They confirm the right to build but do not directly require it. They do affect implementation indirectly, however, because tax revenues are affected by the value of land, which is influenced by the plan itself. The municipality has the supreme right to draft detailed plans; the provincial offices of the Ministry scrutinize and sometimes reject these plans, but they are not entitled to alter their contents.

Every municipality is also obliged to maintain an up-to-date plan concerning the development of the municipal administration, finances, and investment in infrastructure over a five-year planning horizon.

The main provisions for the participation of citizens in the planning and programming of human settlements are stated in law. Landowners have considerable influence on planning. According to the Planning and Building Act, they must be heard at various stages of the planning process and their interests are safeguarded by a two-stage appeal procedure.

Planning versus Market Forces

The relationship between market forces and the formal urban planning system seems to be quite immutable. In the long run, the planning system has always been malleable, and restrictions on economic activities have seldom been significant. For example, during the last 100 years, the urban structure of the Kallio city sector in Helsinki has been reconstructed three times. The first generation buildings were one- and two-story wooden houses. The second generation consisted of three- to five-story stone buildings, and the latest generation is 7- to 12-story concrete blocks of flats and offices. In all phases, the building ordinances were valid until the moment they became binding, after which they were changed to accommodate demands for larger building volumes. Similarly, extensive construction of higher density buildings has been accomplished by changes in plans and "exceptional" building permits (Kuoppamäki-Kalkkinen, 1984).

The nature of master planning in Finland has changed; initial master plans were quite detailed in regulating the physical shape of each building. According to present day master plans, the physical shape of buildings is not restricted in any way. Rather, modern planning involves regulating quantities such as construction volumes and balancing the fiscal interests of landowners. This has reinforced the character of planning as a means of conciliating diverse economic interests.

The system of "site development contracts" is important in order to understand the character of Finnish planning (Bengs et al., 1989). According to an agreement between the municipality and a private developer (construction company), the town zones the land owned by the developer to permit construction. In return, the developer agrees to undertake the construction of public utilities for the area (which according to law should be a concern of the municipality). Ultimately, this infrastructure is financed by prospective buyers of dwellings. This system was established during the initial phase of the postwar urbanization. The system has actually been much more than just a "planning matter," because it provides the mainstream political parties with funds and contributions for political activities from construction and developer interests. The system has important implications for municipal democracy.

HOUSING PRODUCTION

Organization of Construction

Housing production can be distinguished by the actors in the production process: landowners, public agents, and final users. The process can also be structured according to phases: land acquisition, subdivision, financing and credit access, construction, selling or leasing, etc. According to the first categorization scheme, organization of production, we may distinguish several typical cases:

1.   The developer, builder, and user are the same person. Under these circumstances, production is undertaken for a specific user.

2. Developer, builder, and user are all distinct. Since the goal of the production is not a specific user, dwellings are geared for average market demands.
3. Developer and builder are the same entity, while the user enters the process to buy the ready product. This is a form of production where some market transactions are eliminated by vertical integration.

The historical development of Finnish housing production follows this typology. The first production mode has always characterized rural housing production and remains a small part of urban housing production. The second mode was rather important urban production form from 1900 until the end of the 1950s. The vertical integration of production was established during the extensive phase of urbanization and is now dominant.

The absence of legal constraints has permitted nearly any kind of company to act as a developer. In other Scandinavian countries, developers have been subject to public ownership and control, and limited profits. In Finland, however, few developers or associations of developers are so controlled because of intermingling developer and contractor interests. In Finland, there are only a few developer associations whose owners are not essentially the same as those of the largest construction firms. In addition, real estate agencies representing the largest banks have also entered the development sector.

Integration and Concentration in Construction

When discussing housing production, the role of construction companies is often emphasized. However, firms in the construction materials industry play a central role, particularly the only two large firms producing concrete. Some 50 percent of all multi-story building in Finland is constructed of prefabricated concrete elements, and some 25 percent of all concrete produced is used in prefabrication (see also table 3-3).

The integration of construction firms and enterprises producing building materials, especially precast concrete products, is relatively advanced. The largest firms producing construction materials have their own construction companies, subsidiaries, or joint ventures. Some of the largest construction firms also own plants that manufacture windows, doors, bathroom fixtures, and other housing materials.

According to 1980 estimates, the total number of Finnish firms carrying out year-round construction work is some 850 to 900. (When very small firms acting as subcontractors are included, this figure rises considerably.) Most firms are privately owned joint stock companies. One of the largest firms is a cooperative owned by labor union interests. Many of the largest firms are owned by commercial, industrial, and banking institutions.

Concentration in the construction business has followed a path similar to

TABLE 3-3
Buildings Completed by Mode of Construction and
Material Used, Finland, 1975-1980.

	1975	1980	1985
Completely prefabricated			
Wooden	1,980	3,180	5,557
Concrete	1,016	1,526	1,511
Other stone material	639	615	812
Partly prefabricated			
Wooden	1,919	3,047	5,880
Concrete	675	557	982
Other stone material	486	571	860
Fabricated on site			
Wooden	38,220	41,369	39,648
Concrete	1,628	1,456	1,600
Other stone material	3,933	2,563	258
Total bldgs. completed	50,496	54,884	59,431

Source: Building construction statistics.

that of other sectors of the economy. The share of the total labor force of the 20 largest companies was 29 percent in 1973 and 46 percent in 1979. In 1982-1983 alone, some 30 construction firms were incorporated into larger firms. All the largest firms operate throughout the entire country.   Subsidiary companies have been acquired regionally, through the purchase of local firms. A second feature is the diversification in large firms, which construct buildings as well as infrastructure and public utilities. These concentration trends are re-inforced by the "site development contracts," noted above, which often exclude small contractors from competition (Junka and Loikkanen, 1975; Junka, 1988).

Prices and Costs

Nominal prices of free market (not state-financed) dwellings in the Helsinki metropolitan area increased over tenfold during the 1961-1985 period. The real price increase has also been considerable, rising nearly 60 percent. When compared with the increase in construction costs, the relative price increase was of roughly the same magnitude during the period from 1961-1985 (see figure 3-6). The corresponding figure for state-financed housing is about 20 percent. During this time period, real disposable income grew by nearly 80 percent, suggesting that acquiring an owner-occupied dwelling of a given size in the Helsinki region was almost as difficult in 1985 as in 1961, despite a considerable increase in construction productivity and GNP. More recently, prices of owner occupied dwellings have skyrocketed after liberalization of financial markets in 1987 (Bengs, 1989; Loikkanen, 1988).

There is certainly no clear and direct correspondence between the development of construction costs and prices for owner-occupied dwellings. The rise of construction costs in the Helsinki metropolitan area, in comparison with the country average, is largely due to an increase in construction material prices. In the Helsinki region, the prices of materials have increased some 25 percent per year during booms and stayed even during depressions. These

FIGURE 3-6
The Development of Housing Prices and Costs,1961-1985.
(1961 = 100)

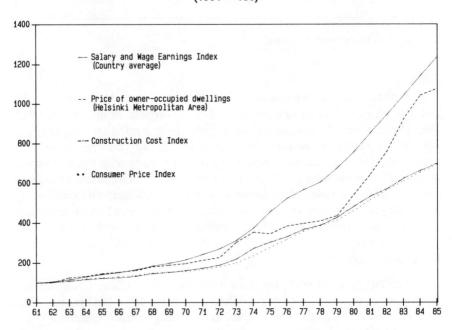

figures are suggestive of the relatively strong monopolization of the construction material producing industry.

The reasons for the price increases and relatively large fluctuations have not been investigated in great detail, but the strong urbanization and demographic changes have certainly caused demand pressures over and above the pressure arising from increases in wealth and disposable income. Furthermore, credit markets directly influence demand volumes, thereby indirectly affecting construction activity. In addition, rent regulations have caused the private rental housing stock to diminish precipitously, causing increased pressure on the demand side.

Horizontal integration in the construction industry has led to price increases (Bengs and Rönkä, 1990). High concentration alone, however, would not necessarily indicate monopolization provided that construction firms could be easily established. In the Helsinki metropolitan area, free entry is limited by present land ownership, existing development contracts, and planning practice.

The Role of Financial Markets

The Finnish financial markets have often been characterized as undeveloped because of the central role of banks and the small role played by specialized financial institutions. Incurring bank loans rather than issuing shares in the thin stock market has been the most important source of external finance for business firms, and there are no specialized private institutions for funding housing. Funding is carried out by private or cooperative banks as a normal part of their business activity.

Until the early 1980s, these financial markets were thoroughly regulated. The regulatory framework included interbank agreements on deposit rates, exchange control, regulation of bank lending rates, regulation of bond issues, preferential tax treatment of deposits, and finally, a quota system for the banks' central bank borrowing at the discount rate. This financial structure has important implications for the housing sector.

First, in a variable interest rate system, changes in the discount rate cause corresponding changes in the entire outstanding stock of loans. This regulation caused the decisions on the rate of interest to be highly politicized, especially where income distribution and housing matters were involved. Second, the regulated interest rates were typically below any conceivable equilibrium level. Thus, the actual tightness of the financial markets was manifested in fluctuations in the availability of credit instead of in its price. Credit availability naturally caused corresponding fluctuations in prices of unregulated owner-occupied dwellings and in the volume of construction.

From the household's viewpoint, the combination of regulation and the tax deductibility of interest payments resulted in negative real rates of interest.

TABLE 3-4
Development of the Housing Stock in Urban Areas
and Provinces, Finland, 1970-1980.

	Housing stock (in thousands)		Growth (% change)
Region	1970	1980	1970-1980
Helsinki Metropolitan Area	279.5	378.3	35.4%
Rest of Uusimaa Province	72.3	93.8	29.8
Turku Metropolitan Area	76.0	99.1	30.4
Pori Metropolitan Area	29.8	39.5	32.4
Rest of Turku and Pori Province	125.2	149.2	19.1
Ahvenanmaa (Åland) Province	7.2	9.3	28.5
Tampere Metropolitan Area	76.2	101.8	33.7
Lahti Metropolitan Area	37.5	49.9	33.0
Rest of Häme Province	100.5	118.3	17.7
Kymi Province	110.0	131.1	19.7
Mikkeli Province	64.3	78.0	21.3
Pohjois-Karjala Province	51.6	63.5	22.9
Kuopio Metropolitan Area	23.1	34.2	48.0
Rest of Kuopio Province	49.4	56.0	13.5
Jyväskylä Metropolitan Area	31.3	42.3	35.2
Rest of Keski-Suomi Province	42.0	48.1	14.4
Vaasa Metropolitan Area	19.8	27.3	38.1
Rest of Vaasa Province	108.7	127.6	17.4
Oulu Metropolitan Area	31.1	45.9	47.6
Rest of Oulu Province	75.3	95.0	26.3
Lapland Province	52.7	66.7	26.6
Finland	1,463.2	1,855.0	26.8

Source: Ministry of Interior and the National Housing Board (1982, p. 15).

Under these circumstances, most people attempted to take out the largest housing loans they could, in the face of rationing by the banks. Banks, offering typically negative real deposit rates, required customers to save heavily in order to qualify for a loan later. This "barter system" has been essential in maintaining the predominant role of bank saving in the household sector.

In the early 1980s, the central bank withdrew from the forward exchange markets. Bank borrowing at unregulated rates of interest-- the so-called money market-- has grown quickly. Alongside these trends toward a more market-oriented system, many elements of the old regulation remain intact. The former discount rate (now called the "base rate") still plays a role in determining interest rates in the old stock of loans, whereas the so-called "call money rate" now reflects more closely the cost of funds in the unregulated markets. The interbank agreement on retail deposit rates and the supporting legislation on tax exemption are still in force.

Clearly, the present situation in the financial markets is one of transition and further deregulatory innovations are taking place all the time. As for housing finance, interest rates, rather than credit rationing, have already become more important in the allocation of funds. In addition to the role of interest rates, banks have begun to compete with each other in the terms of housing loans; many, for example, offer amortization periods more than twice as long as the previous average.

The last major phase of deregulation occured in 1987 when controls on companies' long-term borrowing from abroad were lifted and interest rate regulation of loans came to an end. Occuring at a time of unexpectedly rapid growth and expansionary economic policy, led to skyrocketing housing prices and a boom in the construction industry.

DEVELOPMENT OF THE DWELLING STOCK AND HOUSING FINANCE

The Dwelling Stock

There were 1,855,000 dwelling units in Finland in 1980, 1,735,000 of which were occupied. Table 3-4 shows the distribution of this stock throughout the country, and the pattern of growth during the 1970s. Housing production was strong during the mid-1970s, peaking at 73,000 dwelling units (15.6 per thousand inhabitants) in 1974. Since that year, there has been a steady decline in housing production (see tables 3-5 and 3-6 and figure 3-11) until the recent boom. Furthermore, the housing stock is very young, as more than three-quarters of it was constructed during the postwar period. Not surprisingly, the quality standards of dwellings have improved considerably since the end of World War II (see figure 3-7).

Larger dwelling types accounted for the greatest increase in the housing stock in the 1970s. Despite the increase in large dwellings, however, there are still, relatively speaking, more small units in the Finnish housing stock than in most other European countries. In 1970, a majority of the dwellings in Finland had fewer than four rooms, kitchen included (see figures 3-8 and 3-9).

By 1980, however, the average floor area per dwelling was 69 square meters, representing an increase of nine square meters in one decade. Conditions of extreme crowding were expected to disappear almost completely

TABLE 3-5
Housing Production, Finland, 1976-1985.

Year	Dwellings* completed	Units per 1,000 in- habitants	Average net floor space in sq. meters	Percentage of units in detached, semidetached row and terrace houses	Percentage of units state- subsidized
1976	57,498	12.2	73.5	47.1	66.6
1977	56,966	12.0	76.0	50.2	59.3
1978	55,287	11.6	78.9	55.7	61.8
1979	50,301	10.5	79.4	57.7	60.9
1980	49,648	10.4	82.2	61.4	54.7
1981	46,988	9.8	82.7	63.2	50.2
1982	47,997	9.9	82.7	66.6	47.9
1983	50,500	10.4	81.1	66.6	48.6
1984	50,337	10.3	78.8	64.2	37.4
1985	50,306	10.2	78.2	64.7	35.9

* This total does not include seasonal dwellings, which were built at an annual average rate of 8,700 in the 1970s.

Source: Construction statistics and the National Housing Board.

TABLE 3-6
Investment in Housing, Finland, 1976-1981.

Year	Housing as a percentage of all investments	Housing as a percentage of investment in buildings	Housing as a percentage of GNP
1976	25.5%	55.7%	7.2%
1977	27.9	56.2	7.6
1978	30.3	58.1	7.4
1979	29.4	57.5	6.9
1980	28.4	56.2	7.2
1981	27.2	56.0	6.9
1982	27.6	55.2	7.0
1983	27.0	51.8	6.9
1984	27.1	53.1	6.4
1985	25.8	52.4	6.1

Source: National accounts.

FIGURE 3-7
Vintage and Quality of Dwellings, Finland, 1985.

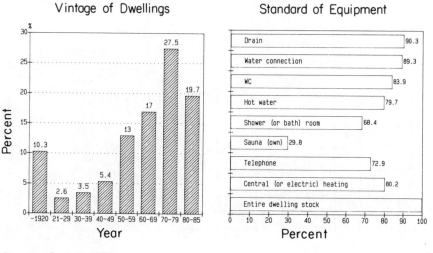

Source: Census 1985.

during the 1980s. Figure 3-10 presents some comparisons of housing conditions among the Nordic countries.

Development of Housing Policy

The system of state-financed housing in Finnish urban areas was established in 1949. Initially, the state granted loans at low interest rates (one to three percent) which covered 60 percent of the estimated costs of rental housing. The corresponding figure for one-family houses was 40 percent. In the early 1950s, the major portion of state-financed housing consisted of owner-occupied flats. Initially, eligibility for state loans was not restricted by income, resulting in a situation in the 1950s during which about half of the population in state-financed condominiums belonged to the highest social class.

The goals of the initial housing production legislation were not, however, of a social welfare character; they were aimed more narrowly at increasing production. The program reflected a belief in the so-called filtering process; as wealthier people are supported in housing, their dwellings will trickle down to the poorer part of the population. This housing policy diverged from those adopted in many other European countries at that time. By the 1950s, many

FIGURE 3-8
Structure Type and Dwelling Size, Finland, 1973-1983.

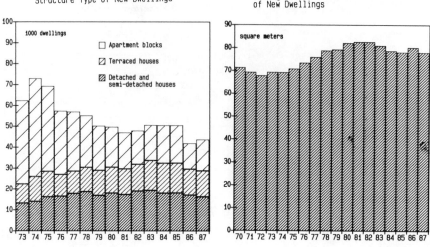

Source: Construction statistics.

FIGURE 3-9
Dwelling Size and Overcrowding, Finland, 1950-1980.

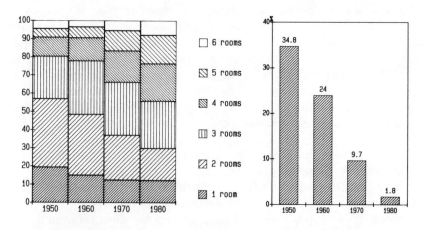

Source: Census 1950-1980.

European countries had initiated housing construction programs in conjunction with economic policy and developed a selective housing support system. For instance, in the 1960s, about 150,000 households received housing allowances in Sweden, while the corresponding number in Finland was 600.

In absolute terms, housing production did not grow in the 1950s in Finland (see figure 3-11). During this period, housing loans were largely directed toward rural areas. Especially during the early 1950s, the forestry industry had a constant excess demand for labor. The state encouraged regionally scattered, small-scale farming where the farmer was a part-time lumberjack to provide this labor force. As the mechanization of forestry rapidly proceeded, beginning in the late 1950s, the need for forest labor diminished, encouraging urbanization. Altogether, the proportion of state-financed housing loans remained rather small, covering as little as about one-quarter of the total housing production in the early 1960s.

During the 1960s, emphasis was placed on savings incentive programs for housing. In the early 1960s, this strategy was formalized in government studies concluding that saving for one's home is the most efficient form of "forced" capital investment. At that time, tax exemptions granted to individuals investing in rental housing were still in effect and covered both income and property taxation. These were gradually eliminated by 1972, when any kind of housing investment, except that for owner-occupied dwellings, was fully taxable. In 1963, the last year of total tax exemption, production reached a level of 44,000 dwellings, which was surpassed only in 1970.

During the 1960s, new construction each year, except for 1963, was nearly constant. The state-financed share increased substantially during this period, however. Eligibility for state loans was broadened. In the mid-1960s, a goal of producing half a million dwellings between 1966 and 1975 was set. Although the Finnish program was mainly a policy statement, the goal was met much as a result of the boom preceding the first oil crisis in 1973. Also the absolute amount of state-financed housing began to grow steadily in the mid-1960s, reaching a peak in the mid-1970s. The number of state-financed dwellings was approximately 32,000 per year during the 1970s, of which 15,000 were rental dwellings. The average total production was roughly 53,000 dwelling units annually.

Beginning in 1971, the repayment period for state loans for rental housing was reduced from 45 to 25 years. (It was subsequently extended to 27 years in 1982). The interest rate level for state loans had long been kept low, but starting in 1975, it was gradually increased, even for existing loans. As the state share of financing declined in the late 1970s, suggestions were made to replace the current system by interest support loans.

During the 1980s, privately financed housing construction increased. In 1979, the share of completely privately financed housing production was about

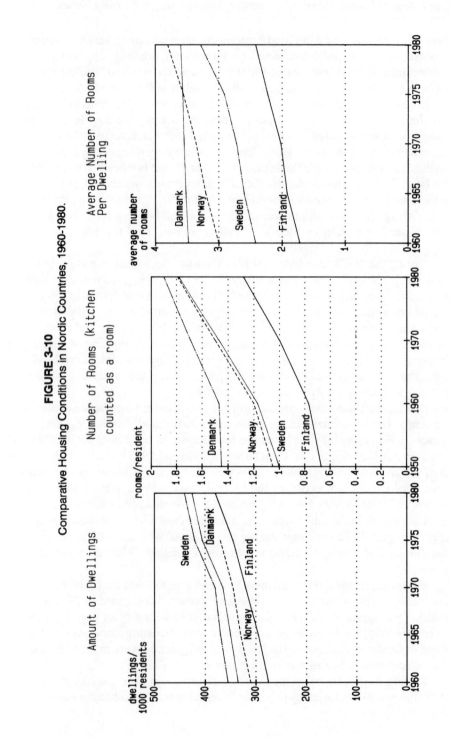

FIGURE 3-10

Comparative Housing Conditions in Nordic Countries, 1960-1980.

one-third, but by 1984 it was nearly two-thirds. Figure 3-11 summarizes the course of subsidized and unsubsidized housing construction during the past 37 years.

Tenure Forms

Two types of tenure dominate: owner-occupancy and tenancy (see figure 3-12). There are very few dwelling cooperatives, accounting for less than 0.5 percent of the total housing stock. This is a remarkable difference compared to the rest of Scandinavia. In Finland, the owner-occupancy rate was 69 percent in 1985, an internationally high number. There are two kinds of owner-occupied dwellings; one type consists of those held in "fee simple" (generally detached houses), while the other is a particular form of condominium ownership. In the latter case, the owner of an individual apartment or condominium is a shareholder in a housing company, which manages the property and is a self-governing economic unit. Decisions are taken jointly at meetings of

FIGURE 3-11
Housing Production and Financing, Finland, 1950-1987.

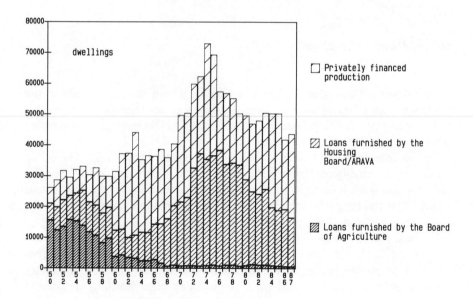

Source: National Housing Board.

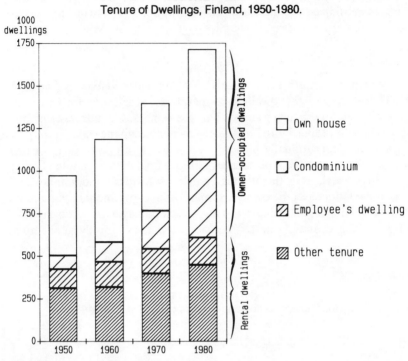

FIGURE 3-12
Tenure of Dwellings, Finland, 1950-1980.

Source: Asuntotoimen pääpiireet (1984).

shareholders. Each shareholder may decide about matters affecting the control and use of the apartment designated by the shares owned (e.g., whether to let or sell it). In state-financed owner-occupied dwellings, the ownership rights of shareholders are more restricted.

Most condominium housing is built by construction companies who set up a joint stock housing company in the initial phase of construction. When the construction work is completed, the developer generally sells the apartments to private individuals who then become shareholders in this company. Except for state-subsidized housing, the prices are not regulated.

A real estate company is a joint stock enterprise established to build and own rental dwellings. The shareholders in such a company can be different kinds of corporate bodies including municipalities, foundations, insurance companies, and others. Real estate companies offer housing services to various sections of the population or to associations and companies.

To give an idea of the importance of public financing, the cumulative production of state-financed owner-occupied and of all rental dwellings during

1950-1980 was about 13 and 27 percent of the total dwelling stock, respectively.

The total number of private rental dwellings diminished during the last decade, and there has been a substantial drop in state financing of rental dwellings. State-financed rental production fell from nearly 20,000 new rental dwellings in 1972 to less than 10,000 during the 1980s.

Forms of Housing Finance

Housing production may be broken down into two categories according to source of finance: the partially state-financed (so called ARAVA) production, controlled and regulated mainly by the National Housing Board (NHB); and privately financed production, usually bank financed and unrestricted in nature (see figure 3-13).

The NHB finances rental housing and condominiums as well as one-family houses. In 1982, out of a total of 17,000 state-financed dwellings, the shares of these three housing types were 37, 30, and 33 percent, respectively. The overall financing of state-subsidized dwellings consists of state loans, primary loans, and secondary loans furnished by banks, as well as personal savings. The terms of state loans and the structure of finance in ARAVA production are included in table 3-7.

FIGURE 3-13

Sources of Mortgage Credit and Distribution of Housing Finance, Finland.

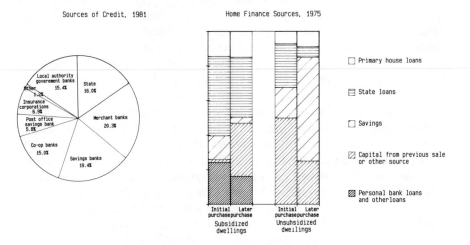

TABLE 3-7

Financial Structure of State-Financed ARAVA Housing Production, Finland, 1982
(in percent).

	State Loans				Other	
Share of total estimated housing price	Share in realty (1981)	Interest rate	Amortization period (in years)	Savings (own capital)	Primary loans	Secondary loans
Rental houses						
60 %	56 %	0.5-9.75 %	27	11 %	33 %	--
Condominiums						
25-60 *	41	0.0-9.5	18	18	14	27 %
Single-family houses						
25-60 *	41	0.0-9.5	18	23	36	--

Note: * Depends on family size and income.
          -- Not available.
Source: National Housing Board

Amortization of state loans starts in the fourth year for rental housing or the fifth year for owner-occupied housing. The amortization rate, as well as the interest rate, increases towards the end of the period. The nominal amortization amount is supposed to grow at 7 percent per year.

In ARAVA production, the proposed construction costs and associated plans must be approved by the NHB. The individual dwellings are entitled to state loans, which are received by the buyer of a flat. The eligibility of a recipient for a state loan is determined according to income, household size, and property. The lending process, including the qualification of mortgage applicants, is administered by the municipality, although the marketing and selling of state-financed condominiums is also undertaken by private banks.

The loan distribution criteria and the restrictions on maximum approved land prices have promoted social segregation in these devlopments. State authorities have tried to cope with the problem by approving a mixture of state-subsidized and free market dwellings within the same building.

The terms of primary bank loans in ARAVA projects must meet the requirements of the NHB. In 1987, the amortization period for the purchase of a rental dwelling was 20 years, and the interest rate was 9.5 percent. For condominium and single-family housing purchases, the interest rates were at 10 percent, while the amortization periods were 14 and 15 years, respectively.

Amortization is cumulative, starting at zero percent and ending at 12 percent of the loan value. The state administration and the financing institutions annually negotiate the total amount of primary loans and the shares of respective financing institutions.

The terms of second mortgages are determined by normal bank financing procedures and, therefore, depend upon the bank in question, the customer, and the saving period. The average amortization period is 8 to 10 years and the interest rate varies from 8.0 to 10.0 percent. Recently, as a result of deregulation of financial markets, new loans have been offered with much longer amortization periods and relatively high interest rates.

The terms of finance for totally private dwellings differ substantially from those with state financing. In the case of new private condominiums, primary loans (which are taken by the housing company and are assumable) cover some 5 to 10 percent of the total price. The rest is covered by personal (nonassumable) secondary loans, bank savings, and the sale of assets. In the case of single-family houses, assumable mortgages also typically cover some 5 to 10 percent of total price.

In 1980, a new law was introduced to assist young persons (18 to 34 years old) in acquiring their first owner-occupied dwelling. A state premium subsidizes bank savings, increasing the interest rate on savings to 8.25 percent. This program has almost collapsed recently due to deregulation of financial markets and the related housing boom.

The NHB also appropriates funds for renovation of rental and owner-occupied dwellings. The size of the loan for rental dwellings is 60 percent of approved construction costs. For owner-occupants, the loan varies from 30 to 60 percent of such costs. In 1985, these loans covered the renovation of some 8,000 dwellings.

PRICING OF HOUSING

In Finland, the determination of housing prices differs from one sector of the market to another and affects the very functioning of the housing market. Distinct pricing rules apply according to the form of tenure and also within the rental and owner-occupied sectors. We shall proceed below by considering the pricing principles applicable to the private and partly state-financed (ARAVA) owner-occupied sectors. Then we shall turn our attention to rent formation.

Pricing of Private Owner-Occupied Dwellings

In the owner-occupied sector, new dwellings constituting shares in housing companies and financed without public assistance can be sold by the construction firms or developers at unregulated market prices (see figure 3-6). The same applies to privately financed single-family houses. In both cases, the land occupied by the new units is typically owned privately, not by the state or the municipality.

Analogously, the prices of all types of privately financed owner-occupied units in the old housing stock are also determined by the market.

Pricing of Partly State-Financed (ARAVA) Dwellings

Public financing of housing is mainly channeled through new construction. State housing loans are obtained by the builder to carry out the project and subsequently by the prospective (first) buyers. These are the so-called "ARAVA dwellings," partly financed by state loans and supplemented by bank and personal loans. To obtain state financing for "ARAVA dwellings," the land need not be publicly owned; indeed this is seldom the case. There is, however, a limit on the price of land on which publicly financed (ARAVA) housing can be built. Since price formation on privately owned land is unregulated, and publicly owned land is not abundant (at least in the large cities), this has meant that new publicly financed housing is built predominantly at the outskirts of cities, despite the availability of undeveloped private land closer to city centers.

New ARAVAs.

The pricing of owner-occupied ARAVA housing-- new houses and dwellings or shares in multifamily buildings constituting housing companies-- is strictly controlled by the National Housing Board (NHB). The procedure is as follows. The developer (a single-family house builder or a construction firm) must submit an application to the NHB in order to qualify the project for the state financing which will later be channeled to the ultimate purchasers. The construction plan must abide by the quality standard of the NHB and must satisfy the general building code restrictions. In addition to land price control, construction price bids are supervised by the NHB. A separate cost estimate, based on the plans, is made by the NHB to judge whether the tendered price is reasonable.

When the builder also owns the land, much depends on the ability of the NHB to make cost calculations. There is some evidence that the procedures followed have been imprecise and that large land owning developers have been at a strong informational advantage relative to the NHB (Loikkanen and Suokko, 1972). Thus the NHB has changed its policy of the mid-1970s so that regardless of the owner of the land, preference in state financing is given to projects which have been subject to competition among at least three separate construction firms. In any case, the NHB makes the final decisions, given its housing finance budget, on the number of state-financed new units to be produced annually and their prices.

Under these circumstances, one may wonder what interest private construction firms have in participating in state-financed projects. First, despite price control, such projects have been generally profitable and they have helped firms to survive during periods of low construction activity. Second, the share of all ARAVA dwellings has been sizeable (see figure 3-11). Third, given that state financing provides housing loans with long maturity to prospective buyers, there have been no problems selling dwellings in otherwise unattractive locations. Thus state-financed production has been a way of selling the first dwellings in new and less desirable areas and of initiating citizen demands for transportation and services. Thereafter, land owning firms have continued with privately financed housing not subject to price control (Manninen, 1989).

New owner-occupied ARAVAs in the Helsinki metropolitan area are being built primarily in the surrounding municipalities of the capital, that is, in Espoo and Vantaa, where the biggest construction firms own sizeable amounts of raw land. Within the city of Helsinki, the production of partly state-financed owner-occupied dwellings has ceased almost entirely due to the land price limit applied to ARAVA projects. Unlike the situation in remotely located new suburbs, there is no need for builders to use ARAVA dwellings in the city area as a marketing device.

Old ARAVAs.

Owner-occupied ARAVA dwellings are subject to price controls. Until 1980, as long as the owner still had an outstanding state loan, the dwelling could be sold with the loan to a buyer approved by local authorities at the original price (the construction cost accepted by the NHB) adjusted by the construction cost index. Alternatively, the owner could pay off the state loan and then sell the dwelling at the market price. As housing price inflation, especially in metropolitan areas, exceeded that of construction costs, the latter procedure offered a capital gain. The only disadvantage of the latter procedure was that after repaying the state loan and selling on the free market, the seller no longer had immediate access to the state-financed sector. The main motive for selling the dwelling with the state loan at a controlled price was the possibility that the seller could qualify for a new state-financed dwelling.

In 1980, the terms of reselling old ARAVAs were tightened, and the option of paying back state loans and selling at an uncontrolled market price was eliminated for owner-occupied ARAVAs built after that year. New ARAVA units were to remain subject to regulated prices for 27 years even if state loans were repaid. Partly as a result of this, the number of applications for state-financed single-family projects diminished by 50 percent over the next five years. Not surprisingly, the regulations had to be changed again. Since 1987, ARAVA owners have been allowed to pay back state loans plus the accumulated interest subsidy and to sell their units at unregulated prices after five years of possession time.

Between 1949 and 1985, about 535,000 ARAVA owner-occupied dwellings were produced. Somewhat surprisingly, there are no statistics on the number of ARAVAs sold under the alternative terms. Thus, we do not know the number of ARAVAs in the housing stock which still have outstanding state loans.

Price Formation for Houses Built on Land Leased by the Municipality

The pricing of owner-occupied housing has also been affected by the terms under which municipalities have provided their own land for housing purposes. At the beginning of this century, the City of Helsinki rented its land for 50 to 60 year periods to families who built houses on the public (leased) land. Originally, the leases meant low constant annual rents which were not tied to any index. Furthermore, in most cases there were no restrictions on selling the properties with the land lease contract. When the house was sold, the prospective land rent subsidy was capitalized into the sale price. Accordingly, nearly the entire subsidy accrued to the first owner, first as a flow of reduced land rent, then as a capital gain.

A second major capitalization wave occurred in the City of Helsinki in the 1970s when the old leases, dating from the beginning of the century, expired and had to be renewed. This time, the rents were deliberately set approximately 30 to 40 percent below the estimated market level in order to continue subsidizing houses on municipal land. Additionally, the rents became indexed to the consumer price index (CPI) so that full (100 percent) indexation followed the partial indexation in effect for the first five years of the lease contract. The extension of land leases for another 50 to 60 years with no resale restrictions meant that the entire rent subsidy was enjoyed by those who possessed the properties at the time of lease renewal. Currently, municipal land in the city of Helsinki is leased for housing purposes through the HITAS system.

HITAS System. The HITAS municipal land management policy was started in Helsinki during the 1970s. Land was offered for housing purposes with subsidized (and indexed) rents, but the resale prices of the housing units were controlled in a fashion similar to owner-occupied ARAVA dwellings. Accordingly, the price obtained from the sale of a privately financed owner-occupied HITAS dwelling is limited to the original approved price corrected for inflation (using the national construction cost index, CCI). The owner may sell his or her unit to any buyer, but the municipality has the right to intervene as a buyer and offer the unit to a buyer of its own choosing. Prices of HITAS dwellings remain regulated without time limit.

The HITAS system aims at low cost housing and at preventing the capitalization of land rent subsidies into selling prices. There are some obvious implications and problems with this system. First, in the case where the municipality does not intervene as a buyer, the seller may be able to capitalize (at least part of) the rent subsidy in the form of an undocumented "side payment." Secondly, since housing prices in the Helsinki metropolitan area have increased faster than the national construction cost index, many HITAS occupants who would otherwise want to move to a different dwelling are "locked into" their HITAS units. Furthermore, the HITAS market (which consisted of about 6,000 dwellings in 1987, half of which are ARAVAs and half privately financed) is too small for extensive intrasector swapping. Not surprisingly, there have been continuous demands from HITAS residents to renew the pricing rule. Recently a new index rule has been adopted where alongside CCI, prices of owner-occupied dwellings have one-third weight. Furthermore, HITAS units must be sold to a City Office which runs a queue for buyers in which each applicants' order is drawn by lot.

Rent Formation in the Private Rental Stock

Most of the rental stock in Finland has been privately owned, although the share of public rental units has increased over time. After the war, rents were controlled through the 1950s, except in the biggest cities where rent control lasted until 1962. Additionally, the distribution of dwellings was the responsibility of public housing offices for some time after the war.

In the spirit of liberalization of foreign trade and a general deregulation of the Finnish economy, rent control in private units was lifted in 1963. To increase the supply of rental housing, special tax relief was given to new rental housing investments by both private and institutional investors in 1963 and 1964. Awareness of the short-term nature of the tax rebates on rental income created a construction boom at that time (note the sharp peak in figure 3-11).

Rent control was reintroduced as a component of the extensive stabilization policy package that followed a massive currency devaluation (of 27 percent) at the end of 1967. Rents were frozen at the level prevailing on February 29, 1968. This state of nominally fixed rents continued for six years. Since 1974, the government has made annual decisions on acceptable rent levels for different types of rental units. These decisions are based on the proposals of a rent board with tenant and landlord representatives. A tenant who claims to pay "excessive" rent or a landlord "deserving" to increase the rent above the approved level can take the case to court. In the large cities, there are special housing courts which handle rent and eviction disputes.

It is worth noting that these rent controls applied, until quite recently, to private rental units only and left public (ARAVA rental) units unregulated. During 1968 to 1973, owners of units which were rented for the first time could also set the initial rent freely, but could not adjust rents upward. Sublets and furnished dwellings have always been exempt from rent control.

The strict rent control policy, with new units outside control, caused rent dispersion in the privately owned stock. Rent dispersion also results from government decisions about acceptable rental levels because few housing characteristics are taken into account when determining acceptable rents. Specifically, only approximate age, size, housing type, and location within the country (city size) determine the acceptable rent level. As for the courts' procedures for solving rent disputes, an analysis of the decisions of the Helsinki Housing Court indicated that the resulting relative rent structure differs markedly from that of market-determined rents. Court decisions about rents, for example, seem to be unaffected by the distance from the city center when controlling for other factors (Kiiski, 1978).

During the period from 1962 to 1968 when rents were not controlled, the housing component of the consumer price index increased by 30.1 percent, while the increase in the overall CPI was 44.2 percent. During the rent controlled and regulated period (1968-1983), the housing component of CPI increased by 184.8 percent, while the increase in the overall CPI was 308.0 percent.

The most severe shortage of rental housing has been in the Helsinki metropolitan area, and it is far from ameliorated. With an exceptionally rapid immigration from the countryside starting in the late 1960s, the only options for many movers were either to buy owner-occupied dwellings or to move to Sweden which had a better housing and employment situation. During the 1960-1975 period, close to 40 percent of the population of rural areas moved to cities and more than a quarter-million Finns moved to Sweden.

Table 3-8 illustrates changes in the housing stock and the population of the Helsinki metropolitan area between 1950 and 1985. Largely as a result of the rent policies noted above, the number of private (non-ARAVA) rental dwellings was only 8,000 more in 1985 than in 1950, and the private rental share of total dwellings decreased from 74.4 percent to 26.8 percent. During the last period of rent control and regulation, the absolute number of private dwellings decreased by 11,300 units between 1970 and 1985 as many rental dwellings were converted to owner-occupancy.

The negative effects of the rent control and regulation policies on the development of the private rental stock have come as a surprise to many decision makers, and only during the last few years has this problem been openly addressed. This unexpected shortage explains why rent control was not accompanied by a marked increase in the supply of public rental housing, and accordingly, why the share of all rental units in the housing stock has decreased.

Rent Formation in the Rental ARAVA Stock

We now consider rent formation in the partly state-financed (ARAVA) rental stock, where the units are owned either by municipalities, nonprofit associations, or firms (ARAVA employee dwellings).

These ARAVA rental dwellings are predominantly flats in big multi-story buildings and are organized as real estate companies. Each company is

TABLE 3-8

Number of Dwellings by Tenure Form and Population
in the Helsinki Metropolitan Area, 1950-1985.

Number of dwellings
(percentage shares in parentheses)

| | ---- Rental* ---- | | | | | |
	ARAVA	Non-ARAVA**	Total rental	Owner-occupied	Total dwellings	Population
1950	500	88,000	88,500	29,800	118,300	414,000
	(0.5%)	(74.4%)	(74.9%)	(25.1%)	(100.0%)	
1960	8,600	90,700	99,300	75,900	175,200	556,000
	(4.9)	(51.7)	(56.6)	(43.4)	(100.0)	
1970	24,100	107,300	131,400	116,700	248,100	694,000
	(9.7)	(43.4)	(53.0)	(47.0)	(100.0)	
1980	51,200	93,900	145,100	176,400	321,500	759,000
	(15.9)	(29.2)	(45.1)	(54.9)	(100.0)	
1985	59,000	96,000	155,000	203,100	358,000	787,000
	(16.5)	(26.8)	(43.3)	(56.7)	(100.0)	

Notes: * Includes all dwellings other than owner-occupied.
          **Includes empty dwellings and tenure unknown.

Sources: Census 1950-1985 and National Housing Board.

managed on a nonprofit basis so that rents cover maintenance and other operating expenses, as well as the repayment of state and private loans according to their maturity structures. Additionally, an 8 percent return on the owner's own capital investment is included in the rents. Since the down payments of loans are tied to historical construction costs, the ARAVA rental stock is characterized by rent dispersion by age of the building, and according to the payment terms of primary (bank) and secondary (state) loans. With increasing construction costs and rent regulation of the private rental stock, public housing emerged as one source of increase in the CPI rent index. Quite a few rental ARAVAs have rents higher than "acceptable," according to rent regulation directives, and tenants have taken their cases to the housing courts. Faced with this situation, postponements of interest payments on state loans have been selectively allowed, more as an emergency policy than as planned action.

A summary of the rather complex pattern of housing price and rent formation is offered in table 3-9. Only privately financed HITAS owner-occupied dwellings (built on land leased from municipalities) are not included in the table. They are similar to owner-occupied ARAVAs built after 1980 except that their prices are "indexed" without time limit. Note the question marks in the table. The pricing rule applied to ARAVA rental units after the primary and secondary loans have all been paid off is simply unknown. If the mechanical cost-based rent calculation applies, rent dispersion will become an even more prominent characteristic of the rental stock. The first state loans from the end of the 1940s with 45-year maturities will be paid back in the mid-1990s. This is the same time that the amortization of the first shortened state loans from the 1970s with 25 years, maturity will be paid back. The outcome remains to be seen.

OBTAINING SHELTER IN THE HELSINKI METROPOLITAN AREA

This section describes the nonprice allocation mechanisms that operate both in the rental market and in the market for owner-occupied housing. There are several submarkets with their own special features affecting the allocation of households to dwellings. Most of this discussion is related to the situation in the Helsinki metropolitan area, although many features also apply to other major cities.

Private Rental Sector

After the Second World War, public housing boards directly affected the allocation of housing space. With different types of standards, owners of rental property as well as owner-occupants with ample living space in the cities were obliged to accept tenants (or subtenants). Direct intervention was regarded as necessary to solve the acute housing problem of returning war veterans and of the residents of areas lost to the Soviet Union in World War II. Given the housing shortage in the cities, quite a few of these people were given land in rural areas. This is one of the main reasons behind the aforementioned out-migration in the early 1970s, when the new postwar generation moved to the cities and to Sweden from the rural areas.

The termination of rent control in late 1962 left the allocation of private rental housing entirely market determined. When rent control resumed at the end of 1967, the government maintained its policy of nonintervention in the allocation of private rental units. The excess demand for rental housing in the biggest cities prompted the emergence of typical "black market" phenomena, however. In some cases, private landlords demanded "key money" or other

TABLE 3-9
Summary of Housing Price and Rent Formation in Finland.

Private Financing

Owner Occupied:	- Free Market Prices
Rental:	Until 1962 Rent Control
	1963-1967 Free Rent Control
	1968-1973 Rent Control
	- Rent Increases Negotiated Annually
	- Housing Courts Handle Rent Disputes

ARAVA* Financing

New: Housing Board set quality constraints and controls the construction cost and sets maximum land price limits

Owner Occupied: - Controlled Prices

Rental: Rents are determined as operating expenses + capital costs covering interest payments and down payments of private and state loans
- Rent Dispersion by Age of Building

Old: State loan still in effect

Owner Occupied: - Sales price = initial controlled sale price x CCI**
Rental: ?

Old: State Loan paid off

Owner Occupied: Before 1980
- Free market prices
Between 1980 and 1986
- Free market prices if built before 1980
- Otherwise price=initial price x CCI**
Beginning 1987
- Units less than five years old: Price = initial price x CCI**
- Five years old or older: Free market prices

Rental: ?

Notes: *ARAVA is a name for dwellings in which state loan financing is involved.
**CCI = Construction cost index.
? unknown

forms of extra compensation. Alternatively, landlords screened potential tenant candidates on the basis of personal characteristics, or the landlords' relatives and acquaintances recommended their preferred tenants. As a result, families with children often found it difficult to obtain accommodations.

Information sources on the availability of private rental units have shifted from public sources, such as newspapers and housing agencies, to informal channels, such as through relatives and acquaintances. Only big institutional owners of private rental housing (like insurance companies) have applied an open queue system. Institutional owners have reallocated their investments away from rental housing. However, many institutional owners have faced an increasing demand for their remaining rental properties by their own employees. Thus, the number of vacant units available to outsiders from these sources has decreased. Private rental housing agencies have disappeared altogether from the market in the Helsinki area, with the exception of a "religious people's agency" and a students' agency, both of which deal predominantly in sublets.

A study of the intra-urban mobility behavior of housing allowance recipients in Helsinki, Tampere, and Turku found that market search methods (ads or answers to ads in newspapers and housing agencies) were related to only 15 percent of all moves, whereas public housing offices and employer-related mechanisms represented 33 percent and 16 percent, respectively (Loikkanen, 1982).

Rental ARAVA Sector

As for public rental units, each of the owners allocates his or her dwellings through a publicly advertised queuing system with the allocation criteria of the Housing Board serving as a constraint. The allocation criteria state the family size and income constraints that must be satisfied in order to be eligible for ARAVA rental units. Family size also determines the size of an ARAVA rental unit an applicant can obtain. In this fashion, the system strives to prevent "overconsumption" of housing by setting official norms for living space. In practice this means, for instance, that a family of four can apply for an ARAVA rental apartment with four (but not five or more) rooms and a kitchen. These allocation norms are applied in connection with every move into an ARAVA rental unit. This system obviously causes "signalling" behavior among applicants with respect to changeable characteristics; for example, an applicant may deliberately delay entering the job market in order to qualify for an ARAVA dwelling on the basis of low income.

Most big cities have a queue managed by a special housing office whose purpose is to allocate tenants to those ARAVA rental units owned by the municipalities. In Helsinki, applications must be renewed annually, and there is a priority system favoring evicted households, single heads of families with children, and so on. No explicit point system is applied, but a lengthy stay in the queue is not necessarily a guarantee of getting an ARAVA rental unit. Single adult men have little chance of getting a dwelling through the queuing system. For many of them, alternatives are also limited. In addition to the municipal queue, the Students' Housing Foundation, and the rental housing cooperative have queues of their own.

The average number of applicants per vacant rental ARAVA dwelling in all urban municipalities was 2.9 in the year 1985. The corresponding figure for the ARAVA rental stock owned by the city of Helsinki was 5.7.

Privately Financed Owner-Occupied Dwellings

In the case of owner-occupied housing, privately financed units are allocated via market-determined prices. In this submarket, the only nonprice criteria are related to the terms of finance. As noted previously, one consequence of housing finance in an interest rate controlled capital market is that many households face quantitative credit rationing. In addition to the savings requirements necessary for getting a loan in the first place, loan amounts and their maturity are tied to savings in banks. It is not unusual for banks to impose the requirement that saving deposits must equal 30 to 40 percent of the value of a house or apartment in order to qualify for a mortgage. Moreover, the maturity of the housing loans offered has been 8 to 10 years on the average.

Recently, the financing situation has undergone an important change. First, to increase the opportunities for young people to become homeowners, the government has reached an agreement with banks about savings plans. After having met the savings requirement, interest payments are subsidized by the state. Second, and more importantly, partial deregulation of the banking sector has changed the terms of available housing finance. As the system of controlled interest rates has become less strict, the banks have begun to compete on the terms of housing loans. New customers are offered loans with maturities of 18 to 25 years but with high interest rates. But many old customers still have loans with the previous less liberal terms. The variety of terms and the great range of interest rates will probably diminish after some period of transition to this new regime.

Owner-Occupied ARAVA Dwellings

Because the terms of finance in the owner-occupied sector are so variable, there has been excess demand for partly state-financed (ARAVA) units. The allocation of new ARAVA dwellings typically takes place through the banks that supply first mortgages. Accordingly, each bank, or its local office, may establish its own queue for financing. In allocating the units, the bank needs only to ensure that accepted families fulfill the income and family size constraints placed by the National Housing Board on owner-occupied ARAVAs.

(Recall that in addition to general eligibility, family size also determines the acceptable maximum size of a dwelling for each family, while the income level affects the share of a state loan received.) These eligibility constraints must be fulfilled only at the time of application, and the terms of finance are also fixed at that time. Thus the timing of application is of utmost importance. For instance, the gain from being a last-year medical student instead of a first-year general practitioner is decidedly nontrivial. The penniless student with a high permanent income can get the best terms, whereas the practicing physician is probably ineligible for state finance.

In general, the allocation system of new owner-occupied ARAVA apartments leaves enough room for choice so that the supplier (bank) interests can greatly affect the outcome. Preferred customers may bypass the queue when vacant units appear due to cancellations. In the case of old owner-occupied ARAVA units, many movers paid back the state loan and sold the unit at market price before restrictions prohibited it. Between 1980 and 1986, the law dictated that ARAVA dwellings built after 1980 could be sold at market prices only after 27 years. Before that, they could be sold only to a buyer named by the municipality either from the housing office queue or through an application procedure. The municipality also calculated a maximum acceptable price based on the original construction costs and the value of land occupied, adjusted by the construction cost index.

As discussed above, the ARAVA law has been changed again as the demand for owner-occupied ARAVAs has decreased greatly in response to the selling price regulations that applied between 1980 and 1986. Beginning in 1987, the resale prices of ARAVAs will be regulated for only five years after construction. Thus, the housing offices of municipalities currently apply the family size and income constraints of the NHB to all ARAVAs younger than five years old and also to those sold without first paying off the state loan and the cumulative interest subsidy.

The nonprice allocation mechanisms operating in the different sectors of the housing market are summarized in table 3-10. The only missing category from the table is the HITAS owner-occupied dwellings existing in the city of Helsinki. Privately financed HITAS units built on municipally owned land are allocated through banks that are involved in the financing of construction and the provision of first mortgages. There is excess demand for these units due to both the smaller amount of capital needed to buy HITAS dwellings built on leased land and the subsidized land rents. Customers with savings plans in banks financing HITAS projects typically queue for both these and ARAVA projects even before the construction has begun. The queueing system, however, is rather informally arranged, permitting preferential choices by the banks or their officials. To get a new HITAS (or ARAVA) dwelling, the key elements are often knowledge of emerging opportunities and of the appropriate contact.

TABLE 3-10

Summary of Nonprice Housing Allocation Mechanisms in Finland.

<u>**Private Financing**</u>

Owner Occupied: Credit Rationing
Until 1984
- Regulated interest rates
- 8 to 10 year loans, on average, from banks
Deregulation begun in 1984
- 20 to 30 year loans offered with high interest rates

Rental: Excess demand with controlled rents in biggest cities
- Rationing by landlords' preferences
- Nonmarket information channels predominate. Illegal key money or bribes emerge
- Housing courts handle disputes
- No swapping

<u>**ARAVA* Financing**</u>

New:

Eligibility & state loan terms based on income & family size
Rationing of space: maximum number of rooms = No. of persons in family

Owner Occupied: Alocation by banks
Rental: Allocation by queues of muncipal offices & employers

Old: State loan still in effect

Eligibility is checked & space constraint (Max no. of rooms = no. of persons)
is applied at each entry of new inhabitants following a sale of the dwelling

Owner Occupied: Allocation and/or inspection by municipal offices
Rental: Allocation by queues of municipal offices, employers, nonprofit organizations

Old: State Loan paid off

Owner Occupied: Before 1980
- Same as private
Between 1980 and 1986
- Control planned to apply for 27 years
Beginning in 1987
- Municipal control only for first five years if state loans are paid off

Rental: Allocation by queues of municipal offices, employers, nonprofit organizations

Note: * ARAVA is a name for dwellings in which state loan financing is involved.

MOBILITY, HOUSEHOLD FORMATION, AND THE HOUSING MARKET

The many allocation mechanisms in effect in Finnish housing markets affect intra-urban mobility and household formation. As a matter of fact, many life-cycle choices, such as labor supply decisions, are affected as well. Although definitive research is lacking, the following issues seem important.

Given the general excess demand for rental housing, possibilities for adjusting housing demand through mobility in the rental stock are very limited. Within the rental ARAVA or HITAS stocks, direct swapping between two parties is not possible. The NHB eligibility and dwelling size constraints apply in connection with each move into ARAVA dwellings, so an ARAVA tenant must join the queue in order to move within the ARAVA stock. Even if a matching partner is found such that both parties fulfill all requirements, the transaction must still take place through the municipal housing office. Similar procedures apply for swapping within HITAS rental stocks.

Swapping private (rent regulated) rental units does not take place because the old tenant cannot legally choose the next tenant. The options are restricted to participating in the various queues, searching by placing ads in newspapers, or using informal channels (inquiring of employer, relatives, friends, etc.). Since there is generally not much to be expected from these rental search procedures for ordinary families without pressing problems, many renter households are in disequilibrium. Some are underconsuming housing relative to their current demands, and others are overconsuming. As mobility is retarded, the locational pattern of households within the rental stock becomes rigid, with the further result of some remarkably long commutes.

Given the limited opportunities for intra-urban mobility within the rental stock, more and more households are "forced" to the owner-occupied sector. More precisely, if there were a more balanced rental market, some people would not enter the owner-occupied sector at all.

Tables 3-11 and 3-12 present information on the mobility rates in Finland and the Helsinki metropolitan area. Table 3-11 presents the number of movers per 1,000 inhabitants. In the Helsinki metropolitan area this mobility rate is 152, that is, 15.2 percent of the population moved during 1981. Table 3-12 indicates that mobility rates from employer-related rental dwellings are higher than from other rental dwellings, while owner-occupiers are least mobile.

Unless a household entering the market for owner-occupied housing has sufficient initial wealth, it faces an interest rate regulated banking sector with heavy savings requirements and a short repayment period as conditions for obtaining a mortgage. This situation has caused a life-cycle mobility pattern where the first owner-occupied dwellings are often quite small. Over time, dwelling size and quality are upgraded by moves, but the pattern is such that often the initially desired housing conditions (i.e., the ideal housing in the

TABLE 3-11

Mobility Within and From Municipalities, by Type of Municipality, Finland
(Moves per 1,000 Inhabitants).

	I. Intra- municipal	II. From municipality	III. All moves (I+II)	IV. Mean population
Entire country	83	40	123	4,800
Urban municipalities (Cities)	103	42	145	2,873
Rural municipalities	51	39	90	1,927
Helsinki metropolitan area	130	22	152	763
Helsinki	117	42	159	483
Espoo	81	58	139	139
Vantaa	75	69	144	133
Kauniainen	62	65	127	7

Source: Valkonen et. al. (1984, p. 44).

TABLE 3-12

Intra-Urban Mobility Rates by Tenure Type in the Helsinki Metropolitan Area, 1981.

	Moving persons per 1,000 inhabitants			
	Changes of dwelling	Other moves	All moves	Households changing dwelling per 1,000 households
Owner occupiers	54	32	86	55
Tenants	100	56	156	107
Employer-related dwellings	123	57	180	132
In all	76	42	118	81
Numbers of moves	53,900	30,200	84,100	24,500

Note: Tenure type refers to the dwelling from which the move took place.
Source: Valkonen et. al. (1984, p. 89).

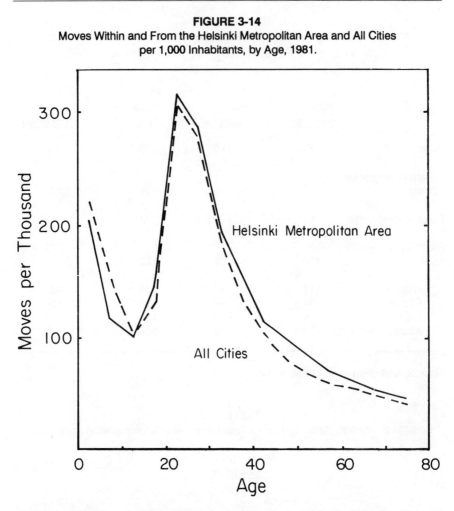

FIGURE 3-14

Moves Within and From the Helsinki Metropolitan Area and All Cities
per 1,000 Inhabitants, by Age, 1981.

absence of credit rationing) are attained only when children of the families are
at the age of entering the housing market themselves. The consequences of the
very recent changes in the terms of housing finance resulting from the deregulation of the capital market remain to be seen.

The age profile of mobility rates is illustrated in figure 3-14. Adults in their
mid-twenties to mid-thirties have the highest mobility rates. The Helsinki
metropolitan area does not differ in mobility rates by age from the other
Finnish cities.

To fulfill the savings requirements imposed to obtain a housing loan,
lifetime labor supply is often adjusted. The high labor force participation rate
of women may be partly a result of the housing finance system. In 1965, during
the time when the massive relocation from rural areas to cities began, the

women's labor market participation rate was 65 to 70 percent. By 1981, the participation rates were in the 80 to 85 percent range. The necessity of two-career incomes as a means of purchasing an owner-occupied dwelling may affect the size and age structure of families by postponing the birth of first children and by reducing the size of families in general.

HOUSING ALLOWANCES

In Finland, there is a housing allowance system aimed at improving the housing consumption of certain household groups and diminishing their housing expenditure to income ratios. In addition to housing allowances to students, there are three distinct systems. A pensioners' housing allowance system is administered by the National Pensions Institute (KELA). The other two systems, which apply to tenants and owner-occupants, are administered by municipalities. Eligibility and allowance payments are determined on the basis of household income, wealth, family, size, and a rent or price constraint. Housing allowance recipients are not allowed to have subtenants, a condition which has restricted the supply of this form of housing.

The housing allowance system applicable to a nonpensioner tenant family defines a subsidy structure such that no allowance is received for the smallest housing units. Starting from a lower housing size limit, the marginal subsidy rate is 80 percent of rent up to an upper size limit, and zero thereafter. Accordingly, the transfer is maximized at the upper size limit, which varies with family size.

The structure of this system provides a strong incentive for adjusting housing consumption to the target size level. However, adjustments typically take place through moves, and as stressed above, the opportunities for moving in the Helsinki metropolitan area are quite limited. Thus, the targets of the detailed allowance system cannot easily be realized. The combination of an extensive housing allowance system stimulating demand and a regulated rent market presents a real paradox. If the aim of government policy is to continue with the present rent regulation policy, then instead of making the housing allowance system more generous and increasing the number of eligible families, one would expect to see measures undertaken to increase the supply of public rental housing. Otherwise, newcomers to the rental market face the present dilemma: rent regulation and the available housing allowances make decent housing conditions affordable, but there is too little rental housing available (Loikkanen, 1988).

Owner occupants became eligible for housing allowances in 1974, and eligibility is limited to those living in a dwelling built after that year (in addition to other constraints). In principle, this allowance system is similar to that of an 80 percent marginal subsidy rate applied to housing expenditures beyond a limit which depends on family size and income. However, this system treats equal families differently depending on whether they have bought a new or an old dwelling. Those purchasing dwellings built before 1974 are not eligible for allowances at all.

In 1985, 16 percent of all households received housing allowances through one of the three systems. There were 159,000 pensioner, 85,000 nonpensioner, and 94,000 student allowance recipients. Average housing expenditures in that year were 17.3 percent of total private consumption (excluding light, power, and heating costs totalling 3.5 percentage points), and the recipients of housing allowances spent about 15 percent of income on housing. Without housing allowances, the latter share would have been 26 percent.

HOUSING AND THE INCOME AND WEALTH TAXES

In Finland, the share of public expenditures in GNP was 41.1 percent in 1985. This is higher than in the United States but lower than in other Scandinavian countries. For individuals, the state income tax is progressive whereas the municipal income tax is basically proportional, varying from one municipality to another. (The average municipal income tax rate in 1985 was 16 percent.) The overall average income tax rate for wage and salary earners was about 30 percent and the marginal tax rate was about 50 percent in 1985. When income transfers, housing allowances, and child care subsidies are taken into account, the marginal tax rate becomes high at rather low levels of taxable income.

For companies, the state income tax in 1986 was 43 percent of net (taxable) income. Adding municipal taxes makes the overall rate about 60 percent. However, because of various ways of (legally) manipulating net taxable income, companies actually pay very little in taxes. Company income taxes accounted for only 4.5 percent of all taxes collected in 1982, whereas the share of household income taxes was 44.5 percent.

The treatment of housing within the Finnish income tax system varies according to tenure and type of owner. For owner-occupied housing, the imputed income from housing assets has, in principle, always been taxable. Before 1973, this housing income was calculated as the difference between comparable (regulated) market rents and operating expenses of the dwelling involved. Since 1973, the imputed income has been calculated on the basis of assessed values. Until quite recently, however, assessments have been low relative to market prices. There has also been a high deductible value allowed, and only that part of assessed values above the limit (215,000 FIM; 1 U.S.$ = 4.5 FIM in 1989) has been subject to the calculation of imputed rental income. Thus, until quite recently, very few owner occupiers have paid tax on imputed income. In 1981, there were 38,000 taxpayers with imputed income from housing amounting to 970 FIM on the average. Later, the assessed values have been increased to resemble more closely market values, and in 1985, more than 100,000 taxpayers paid tax on the imputed income from their housing assets.

Owner-occupied dwellings are also included in taxable wealth, but again low assessed values are applied. In addition, a 40 percent deduction from assessed values (up to 50,000 FIM in 1985) is permitted.

Interest payments on housing loans were fully deductible from taxable income before 1974, but since then there has been an upper limit on deductibility (25,000 FIM in 1987). In 1985, 34 percent of all households (about 700,000) took mortgage or housing loan interest deductions, and less than 1 percent of all taxpayers reported interest payments above the 25,000 FIM limit. All other nonhousing interest expenses are tax deductible up to a limit of 10,000 FIM.

Although there is no municipal property tax on housing in Finland, assessed values have lately become the basis for user charges applied to municipal services; these assessments are often tax-like unavoidable expenses.

The treatment of capital gains and losses in taxation is also noteworthy. In Finland, income from the sale of an asset is taxable at different rates, depending upon the holding period. The tax rate also depends on the nature of the asset involved. If an apartment in a housing company is sold (that is, its shares are sold) within five years of purchase, the nominal capital gain is fully taxable unless the owner lived in the dwelling and purchases another owner-occupied dwelling within a year. After five years, however, the entire capital gain is tax exempt. The corresponding time limit for single detached houses is ten years.

CONCLUSIONS

The Finnish housing market is characterized by a mixture of market processes and strong government intervention. The analysis in this chapter can only outline this market, its institutions, and its outcomes, but it is fair to claim that the operation of the market and its relation to the rest of the economy have never been thoroughly analyzed.

Finnish housing policy can perhaps be best understood as a historical process where additional policies have been initiated successively as an answer to short-run economic problems with little consideration of the system as a whole.

Contrary to the United States, where a great deal of resources are devoted to analyzing the effects of alternative policy measures, but where very few are actually undertaken, Finland is a more typical European case. The parliament has been active in legislating new policy measures based largely on faith in their efficacy. This approach has been one of "wishful thinking," since little has been done to evaluate the expected effects or to study the results after policies have been adopted.

A reading of the official reports and committee papers on housing policy gives an impression that there is a great deal of planning involved, or at least an enlightened steering of the process. The analysis in this paper concludes that the reality has been quite different. Municipalities have a monopoly on land use planning, but they do not use it as one might expect. This may be explained by the fact that the extremely rapid urbanization of Finland came as a surprise to public authorities. As for housing, the easiest, but irresponsible, way to get a quick response in housing construction was to give building incentives to large construction firms operating in the expanding cities. These firms were quick to buy raw land, creating a situation where land ownership and "good relations" with municipal decision makers became essential in order to secure projects without competition. In general, municipal planning and building codes became subsidiary to construction interests.

Given the multiplicity of policy targets and instruments in housing, coordinating them has never been thoroughly considered. For example, the effectiveness of quite a few other housing policy measures will depend on whether there is rent control, or whether the capital market is characterized by interest rate controls. In none of the official committee reports or similar documents can one find a systematic policy analysis which would recognize these alternative "policy regimes." This may explain, for example, why the rental housing allowance system has been expanded in terms of eligibility and government appropriations, thereby increasing the demand for this form of tenure, while at the same time, rent control and rent regulation caused a steady conversion of rental units into condominiums, and few resources have been allocated to increase the supply of public rental housing. Ultimately, the reaction of many households who may have preferred accommodations in the rental sector has been to join the savings programs of banks in order to become owner occupiers. This combination of rent control, which reduced dwelling availability in the rental market, and credit rationing in the capital market has created an ideal opportunity for banks to increase profits through forced savings plans.

Current housing policy issues in Finland do include ways of increasing the availability of rental housing, however. The measures recently undertaken to promote the supply of rental housing have been restricted to special tax relief for non-institutional owners of rental housing. On the owner-occupied side, further measures to limit the right to deduct interest on housing loans from income have been discussed. Suggestions have been made to tie the deductible amounts to household characteristics, or in contrast, to convert deductions to tax credits. Limitations on the right to interest deductions seem to be a substitute for increasing the taxation of imputed income from owner-occupied housing. Little thought has been devoted, however, to studying how the burden of taxation is distributed or how the structure of housing consumption is affected by these alternatives.

To conclude, we shall briefly note the future challenges of Finnish housing policy. Finland has clearly lagged behind the other Scandinavian countries in housing consumption despite of having narrowed the difference in terms of per capita income. In 1960, there were 76 rooms per 100 inhabitants in Finland whereas the average of Norway (126), Sweden (121), and Denmark (140) was 129. By 1980, the figures were 128 for Finland and an average of 186 for the others (Norway 184, Sweden 176, and Denmark 198). The latter gap is smaller in relative terms but larger in absolute terms compared to 1960. As for the form of future housing subsidies, one institutional change that should cause some rethinking is the deregulation of the capital market. Under the market conditions associated with credit rationing, it was not necessarily a bad idea to supply state loans for housing construction. As the deregulation of the banking sector continues, the role of state finance and the forms of housing subsidy must be reevaluated.

REFERENCES

Asuntotoimen pääpiirteet. 1984. Asuntohallitus.

Bengs, Christer, 1989. Pääkanpunkiseudun asuntojen hinnat vuosina 1965-1988. VTT, Tiedotteita 1007. Espoo.

Bengs, C., V. Lehtimäki, and K. Rönkä. 1989. Pääkaupunkiseudun aluerakentamissiopimusalueiden maanomistus ja -hinnat vuosing 1950-1985. VTT, Tiedotteita 1006. Espoo.

Bengs, C., and K. Rönkä. 1990. Kilpailu asuntotuotannossa. Kilpailuvirasto, selvityksiä 2B/1990. Espoo.

Junka, Teuvo, 1988. Kilpailu ja keskittyminen talonrakennusalalla, Taloudellinen suunnittelukeskus. Helsinki.

Junka, Teuvo, and Heikki Loikkanen. 1975. Talonrakennustoiminnan keskittymisaste. Taloudellinen suunnittelukeskus. Helsinki.

Kiiski, Liisa. 1978. Vuokrarakenne Helsingin asunto-oikeuden ja vuokratoimikunan päätoksissa, kansantaloustieteen pro gradu tyo. Helsingin yliopisto.

Kuoppa-mäki-Kalkkinen, Riitta. 1984. Kaupunkisuunnittelu jarakentaminen Helsingin Kalliossa 1880-1980 TKK. A-os, yhteiskuntasuunnittelun laitos, A 30.

Lampinen, H., and A. Seppälä. 1985. Pääkaupunkiseudun alueellisen rakenteen muutoksisa. H VTT. Tiedoteita 996. Espoo.

Loikkanen, Heikki. 1982. *Housing demand and intra-urban mobility decisions: A search approach*. Helsinki: Commentationes Scientiarum Fennica.

Loikkanen, Heikki. 1988a. *Housing demand and mobility of Finnish housing allowance recipients*. Scandinavian Housing and Planning Research 1988: 3.

Loikkanen, Heikki. 1988b. Rahoitusmarkkinoiden muutoksen vaikutus kotitalousksien taloudellisiin toimintaedellytyksiin - mikrotarkastelu. *Kansantaloudellinen aikakauskirjq* 1988: 4.

Loikkanen, Heikki, and Seppo Suokko. 1972. Asuinkerrostalojen rakennuskustannukset, Tilastomatemaattinen analyysi. Rakennustalouden laboratorio, Tiedonanto 4, Espoo.

Manninen, U. 1989. Aravarakentaminen pääkaupunkiseudulla vuosina 1950-1985. VTT, Tiedotteita 1068. Espoo.

Ministry of the Interior and the National Housing Board. 1980. Current trends and policies in the field of housing, building and planning in Finland.

Ministry of the Interior and the National Housing Board. 1982. Finland -- Monograph on the human settlements situation and related trends and policies, UN ECE.

National Housing Board. 1983. *Housing in Finland.* Helsinki: National Housing Board.

National Housing Board. 1984. *The financing and taxation of housing in Finland.* Helsinki: National Housing Board.

National Housing Board. 1985. *Housing finance policies and support to housing in Finland*. Helsinki: National Housing Board.

Peltonen, Arvo. 1982. *Suomen kaupunkijarjestelman kasvu 1815-1970.* Helsinki: Societas Scientiarum Fennica.

Schulman, Harry. 1984. Paakaupunkiseutu, suunnittelumaantieteellinen aluetutkimus. YTV B, 6 Helsinki.

Valkonen, Tapani, Tuija Martelin, and Hilkka Summa. 1984. Muuttoliike ja asunnonvaihdot pääkaupunkiseudulla. Pääkaupunkiseudun julkaisusarja B 1 Helsinki.

Vihriälä, Vesa, and Samuli Skurik. 1985. Housing Prices: An emperical analysis of the determinants of the price level in metropolitan area of Helsinki. *Scandinavian Housing and Planning Research* 1985: 2.

Vuorela, Pentti. 1979. Kaupunkimaan omistus ja maankäyttörakenne Suomessa. YJK A1. Espoo.

4

THE FUNCTIONING OF THE HOUSING MARKET IN AMSTERDAM

Leo van Wissen
Peter Nijkamp
Annemarie Rima

INTRODUCTION

This chapter describes the development and basic structure of the Amsterdam housing market, its submarkets, the nature of supply and demand, and prices. The chapter also analyzes in some detail the institutional-economic framework of the housing market in Amsterdam. From the large set of housing market instruments used in the Netherlands (86 in number, according to Conijn, 1984), we concentrate on the following policy instruments:

- planning and programming of residential buildings;
- price controls, subsidies, financing, and taxes on housing expenditures; and
- housing distribution and allocation.

One consequence of this regulated market is the phenomenon of a black market. This is discussed subsequently.

To set the stage, the usefulness of the institutional-economic structure is explained, followed by a brief description of the geographic and economic position of Amsterdam within the Netherlands. This is followed by an historical overview of the development of the housing system in Amsterdam and the role of the government. Both local and national factors are important in this respect.

AN INSTITUTIONAL-ECONOMIC FRAMEWORK

Housing markets-- the interaction of supply and demand for dwellings-- can be subdivided into competitive and regulated markets. In competitive markets, the prices of dwellings and their quantities are the result of actions of groups of buyers and sellers, whereas in regulated markets, prices and quantities are determined or influenced by institutions governing all or part of the housing market. Since a regulated market price need not reflect allocative efficiency, the allocation of the dwelling stock among households (as well as the construction of new dwellings or the renovation of the existing stock) is an important task for those public institutions operating in the housing sector.

With the transition from a representative democracy to a participatory democracy (at the local and regional level) in many countries, citizens' desires to be more involved in the decision-making process are often expressed in the housing arena. This has led to changing power relationships in the local and regional political system and, after some time, to an institutionalized housing market.

In the analysis of housing markets, the emphasis has always been placed on the conditions under which supply might equal demand for dwellings, but very often the institutional-economic aspects of the housing markets have been neglected (see, for instance, McGuire, 1981). Since institutional arrangements in a regulated housing market may exhibit great diversity, it is clear that difficulties may arise in terms of causal explanation, evaluation of performance, and predictive ability of housing market analyses (see also Stahl and Struyk, 1984). In this section, some elements of an institutional-economic approach to the housing market will be noted.

From this perspective, the analysis of a regulated housing market should not only address the microeconomic behavior of individual decision makers or groups but also the impact of interventions and actions by institutions on the housing market. In this context, the institutional-economic approach seeks to provide an explanatory framework in which the actions and interests of decision agencies, interest groups, and/or individuals are related to group and individual values and behavior. In addition, this approach also attempts to relate these actions and strategic interests to economic, social, and technological factors (see Lambooy et al., 1982).

Specifically, housing market analysis in an institutional context has to consider many diverse endogenous variables that influence housing construction, consumer choice, and demolition of dwellings. Consequently, in addition to monitoring conventional indicators like prices (housing rents, sale prices, etc.) and quantities (including size and location), much more attention has to be devoted to the following factors:

- the institutional segmentation of the housing market, particularly the rules allocating dwellings in the regulated segments of the housing market;
- government subsidy programs;
- rent control mechanisms in specific market segments;
- tax regulations affecting the housing market (e.g., the impact of mortgages and transaction costs);
- the competence of various private and public institutions operating on the housing market;
- housing policies at the local and national level;
- the legal framework of the planning process;
- the economic organization of the building sector; and
- the phenomenon of the black or grey markets for dwellings.

In the specific context of the Netherlands, a variety of economic motives can be identified for public intervention in the housing market:

- The merit good principle, which holds that, in the view of the government, households consume too little housing. It suggests that subsidies should be used to stimulate higher housing consumption.
- The development principle, which suggests that subsidies and tax exemptions should be used to achieve the long-range goal of satisfactory housing for the vast majority of the population.
- The externalities principle, which indicates that high quality housing may exert positive external effects on the whole society, justifying an active housing policy meant to improve social welfare.

In the Netherlands, an array of policy instruments has been developed in order to fulfill these various policy objectives and to achieve a satisfactory and differentiated supply of dwellings at reasonable prices, affordable to all income groups, and based on an acceptable distribution of dwellings.

The Dutch housing market is characterized by several distinctive features, including specialized housing corporations, an administered price setting mechanism in the rental market, and control by regional authority. In this latter context, the Amsterdam municipal authority has probably the highest degree of control and organization over its housing sector of any regional authority in the Netherlands. In addition to national political instruments, many local instruments, usually in the form of housing bylaws, are in effect. This chapter analyzes the historical development and the impact of these policies in the specific context of Amsterdam.

THE CITY OF AMSTERDAM

Amsterdam, the capital of the Netherlands, has a population of 675,570 or about 4.8 percent of the Dutch population. The area occupied by the city is 20,760 hectares (85 square miles). The municipality of Amsterdam is part of the province of North Holland (see map 4-1). At the east side, it is bordered by the interior lake, the IJsselmeer; at the west side, the North Sea Canal connects the city with the North Sea. Ships weighing up to 100,000 tons can reach the ports of the city. Historically, overseas trade was the main stimulus for the development of Amsterdam, but since the end of the 19th century, Rotterdam has taken on the position as main port of the Netherlands. Today, Amsterdam is an important service center, noted particularly for commercial trade, banking, and financing. It is also the main cultural center of the Netherlands.

Amsterdam is also part of the Rim-city, a large conurbation that includes cities like Rotterdam, The Hague, and Utrecht. The Rim-city has a total population of approximately 6 million people. Amsterdam is the center of the northern wing of the Rim-city. The Rim-city also includes the industrialized area around the North Sea Canal (IJmuiden, Velzen) and some major urban centers (Haarlem, Zaanstad, Hilversum). In addition, a number of suburbs have developed since the 1950s-- Amstelveen and Uithoorn to the South, Purmerend to the north, and Lelystad and Almere to the east.

The major foci of economic development are the southeast (Bijlmermeer), the area around Schiphol airport, and the connecting railway south of the city. New population development is also taking place in the southeast, and will occur in the west in the near future.

THE DEVELOPMENT OF THE HOUSING SYSTEM

Introduction

The evolution of the housing stock in Amsterdam can be divided into a number of distinct development periods. The characteristics and the position of these development periods can only be understood in the light of the economic, social, and institutional setting of each individual time period. This historical overview provides a background for the more detailed description of the institutional framework of the present housing market situation, which is presented in the following sections.

MAP 4-1
Amsterdam and Environment.

Before 1900

Amsterdam was a thriving city in the Golden Age of the 17th century when it dominated international trade and the financial world. Prosperity led to a ring of expensive housing and other activities emerging around the medieval city, resulting in a planned development of canals and radial streets that gave the city its characteristic concentric form (map 2). However, in the 18th century economic decline set in, resulting in an almost complete cessation of building activities for more than a century. In 1870, the shape of the city was essentially the same as that at the end of the 17th century, but the population was now poorer and its housing conditions in an alarming state. Because the housing stock could not even keep up with the slow rate of population growth in the course of the 19th century, this situation only worsened. Although the government had previously followed a policy of strict nonintervention in the housing market, after 1870 the ruling class felt more and more that poor housing conditions could have negative external effects on other aspects of society, particularly on public health. Consequently, some form of government intervention was proposed by the more radical liberals at the end of the 19th century.[1]

The year 1870 represented a turning point in Amsterdam's economic position. Growth occurred in a number of sectors, and this marked the Netherlands' transition from a preindustrial to a capitalist society. This new growth took place mainly in the cities, and a population flow from rural to urban areas occurred. Together with rising incomes among some groups in society, a new urban market for housing emerged. Between 1870 and 1910, tens of thousands of houses were built, almost exclusively by the private sector. Although the quality of this housing stock was very low (due to the inferior organization of the industry, low quality materials, corruption, and the high speed of production), it was an improvement over the existing stock. Most of these houses were rented by either the lower middle class or the elite of the labor class. However, the majority of those in the lower classes still lived in cellar or internal dwellings in very high densities. This largely unplanned growth of the city constitutes what is now called the 19th century ring and is the source of present-day urban renewal problems (see map 4-2).

The 1900-1940 Period

The arguments in favor of government intervention resulted in the National Housing Act of 1901. This act enabled local and central governments to intervene in the housing market. Its intention was not only to end the existing miserable housing conditions (through slum clearance, directives to landlords to improve and maintain their property, expropriation, and clearance orders), but also to prevent future inferior housing (through building codes, building inspections, and town plans). A very important element of this Act was the provision for intervention on the supply side of the housing market. Local governments, nonprofit housing corporations, and building societies could qualify for low interest rate loans to buy land or build houses for the working class (Van Weesep, 1982). In principle, houses had to be rented at the market price, but in special circumstances, some subsidies could be given temporarily to renters. Amsterdam played an important role in the implementation of the

---

1   The Socialist party was not very important before the 20th century (Van der Schaar, 1984).

MAP 4-2
The City of Amsterdam.

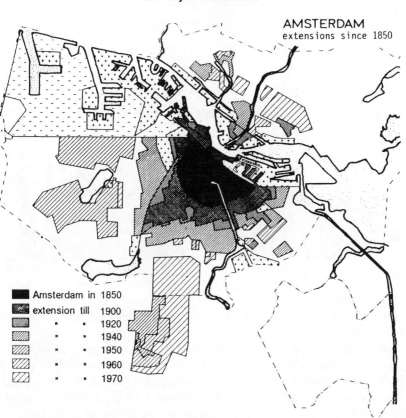

AMSTERDAM
extensions since 1850

Amsterdam in 1850
extension till 1900
"   "   1920
"   "   1940
"   "   1950
"   "   1960
"   "   1970

Act. The building bylaws set up in Amsterdam were very strict, and many municipalities followed this example.

Active intervention on the supply side did not start before 1910. Although the more socially oriented Amsterdam administration was eager to build a significant nonprofit sector, it was financially dependent on the national government. The First World War caused an almost complete collapse of private construction (see figure 4-1), however, and the central government was forced to play an active role on the supply side by allocating more funds for construction and operating subsidies. In addition, rent control was introduced through a Vacancy Act and a succession of Rent Acts, described below.

Nonprofit houses were indeed built, mostly by the housing corporations. It was generally felt by the central government of the Netherlands that the idea of government-owned housing was too socialistic, although Amsterdam (with

FIGURE 4-1

Housing Completions in Amsterdam by Financing Sector, 1906-1984.

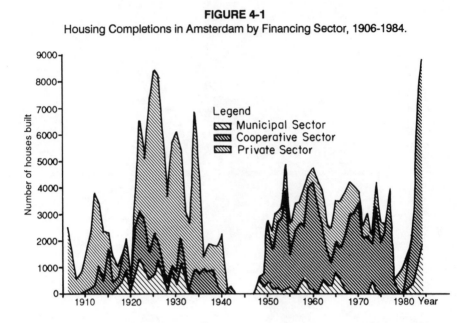

strong socialist participation in the local government) advocated municipal ownership.

After 1920, the building industry benefited from a general increase in economic activity, and the national government soon terminated the operating subsidy program and rent controls. Public housing funds were diminished in favor of construction grants to private investors, and this marked a return to a free market in which the nonprofit sector played only a marginal role. The nonprofit sector provided housing only for the lower-income segment of the housing market, which had been unprofitable for private investment. The economic crisis of the 1930s did not lead to a significant change in this situation, and as a result, financial problems arose for many housing corporations (Van der Schaar, 1984, p. 68). The Second World War marked the end of this period.

The housing stock that was built in the period from 1900 to 1945 was clearly of a higher quality than that from the 19th century construction period. Furthermore, the housing supplied by the nonprofit sector (less than 30 percent in Amsterdam between 1900 and 1945) was of a higher quality than that of the private sector, and many innovations were tried (Jobse 1980). This approach influenced housing quality in all sectors. Despite this trend, many private dwellings remained of an inferior quality, and part of this housing stock has since been demolished and renewed in the 1970s and 1980s (e.g., the Indische Buurt).

The municipal housing stock had a position different from the coopera-
tively owned housing stock. The former category afforded accommodation to
groups that could not afford to live in a cooperative house. The private sector
was mainly active for middle-class households.

Many houses were built during this period in Amsterdam (118,668 in total),
of which 71.9 percent belonged to the private sector, 18.8 percent were part of
housing societies and corporations, and 9.3 percent were municipally funded.

The 1945-1965 Period

The stagnation in the housing construction sector after 1935 and the
subsequent World War resulted in an enormous national housing shortage
after 1945. The shortage was estimated to be 300,000 units, with Amsterdam
accounting for 31,000 dwellings. Furthermore, limited national resources were
allocated predominately to productive economic sectors, while the building
industry had lower priority. This situation persisted until 1950, by which time
housing production had fallen to its prewar level-- far too low to reduce the
housing problem.

The national government-- a socialist administration that remained in
power until the end of the 1950s-- adopted a policy focusing on limited growth
of personal incomes and consumption. Correspondingly, rents also had to be
kept at a low level (see figure 4-2). To achieve this objective, various housing
market laws were adopted. The Housing Allocation Act (1947) provided the
local government with an instrument for establishing a fair housing distribution, (i.e., a housing permit system and the authority to requisition vacancies for
residential purposes). Although this law was suspended in some parts of the
country in 1969, it is still an important allocation instrument in Amsterdam.
Additionally, the Rent Act (1947) fixed the rents of all dwellings at their 1940
level, and renters were given extensive tenure protection. This law was
suspended in 1969 and replaced by a number of new Acts (see below). A third
law was the Reconstruction Act, which provided the central government with
instruments for a national construction program and regional construction
quotas.

A number of problems arose in this period. First, the imposition of rent
control made it virtually impossible to attract investment funds to the housing
sector. In order to bridge the gap between demand and supply, the nonprofit
sector, mainly housing construction societies, was allocated sizable investment
funds. Operating subsidies were also provided in order to keep rents below
market level. In short, the prewar condition of limited intervention changed
into a situation of full public control over the housing market (figure 4-3).

A second problem was the dramatic increase in construction costs of
housing (figure 4-4). This was partly due to increasing factor costs -- materials
and labor -- but was even more the result of higher quality standards adopted

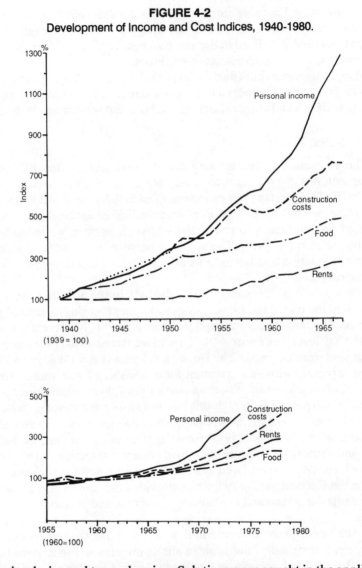

FIGURE 4-2
Development of Income and Cost Indices, 1940-1980.

in housing design and town planning. Solutions were sought in the application of industrial methods in construction and prefabrication. These new techniques were particularly suited for the construction of multistory apartments, and this became the dominant housing type in the new urban districts. The so-called "garden cities," in the western part of Amsterdam, were built in the 1950s and the first half of the 1960s, and were predominantly high-rise apartments. The Bijlmermeer, built around 1970 to 1975, was 90 percent high-rise multifamily houses.

FIGURE 4-3

Housing Construction in the Netherlands by Financing Sector, 1910-1980.

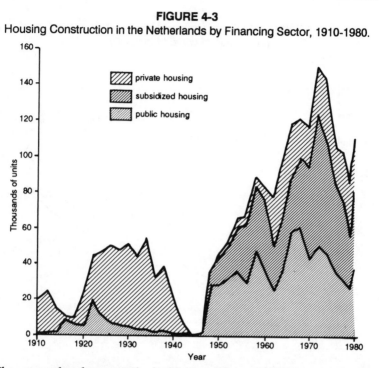

These new developments had a highly uniform character with much open space and a relatively high quality of housing. The character of the neighborhoods, however, was not always preferred by consumers and, when combined with high rents, especially in the Bijlmermeer, resulted in vacancies in some parts of the new housing stock.

Rents in the nonprofit sector were not the only ones controlled. In the older, predominantly private housing stock, the same controls were applied. At the same time, aging and deterioration became major problems, especially in the 19th century housing stock of Amsterdam. This was also the case in the low quality parts of the ring constructed in the 1920 to 1940 period. Consequently, many landlords deferred maintenance. Renters who could afford more expensive dwellings migrated to other, higher quality districts, and the vacancies were taken by new groups whose primary motivation for location in these areas was the low rent. The process of downgrading, which had already begun in the 1920s when higher quality houses were built in the 1920-1940 ring, became a major problem in these neighborhoods.

From 1960, the municipality of Amsterdam promulgated a number of policy documents on urban renewal and slum clearance. The first priority was the clearance of inferior houses. It was estimated that as a result of this process more than 2,000 households per year would have to be moved. But, for a

FIGURE 4-4
Development Cost of New Public Housing Units, the Netherlands,1953-1978
(thousands of current Florins, Dfl.).

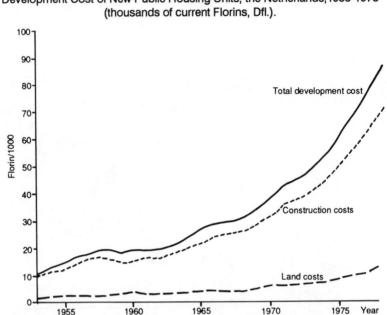

number of reasons, hardly any action was taken in the 1960s. First, the local planning and housing departments (with a long tradition of physical planning and construction of new residential areas on vacant land) had to adjust themselves to reconstruction and maintenance of existing neighborhoods, a process that involves physical, legal, social, and economic aspects.

Second, the residents of these neighborhoods demanded active participation in the planning process, consequently, many conflicts concerning the type, quality, and rents of the new houses arose between the active residents and the planning department. The city policy was to construct high quality housing in the lower density areas ("housing for the future"). However, the residents, who usually could not afford the resulting high rents, demanded simpler and cheaper houses in higher density areas. In the city's view, the replacement of the worst part of the housing stock by new high quality houses would guarantee a general improvement in housing conditions through the adjustment process of upward filtering; however, this filtering process did not work.

A third problem in the urban renewal process was caused by the conflicting views of the various local departments that were involved in the housing planning process, and the resulting impediments to their cooperation. Finally, a fourth major problem was the lack of legal instruments and financial resources provided by the central government. Although the negative effects of rent control on housing maintenance were recognized at the national level, urban renewal was not an important political issue in the 1960s.

After 1965

In the second half of the 1960s a national policy of liberalization and harmonization was adopted in order to return to a free housing market and to obtain a more rational rent structure. The Housing Allocation Act was suspended in 1969 in those parts of the country where the quantitative housing shortage was solved, but not in Amsterdam. This should have induced filtering in the housing market through a "natural" distribution of residents over the housing stock (with higher-income households in better houses, and those with lower incomes in lower quality houses). Additionally, a system of so-called "subject subsidies" (demand-side housing allowances) was proposed in order to keep reasonable housing conditions affordable to all dwellers. In contrast, the center-left administration implemented an "objective" price-quality standard in the 1970s, instead of relying on the free market to accomplish rent harmonization.

The legal instruments and the numerous regulations and controls that emerged in the housing market have met with much criticism in recent years. In general, the growth of the welfare state and the trend toward "institutionalism" in Dutch society have caused a shift toward decentralization and "deregulation" since 1980. At the same time, an effort was made to reduce the growing expenditures for housing in the national budget. Figure 4-5 shows the evolution of the share of housing in the government budget in the Netherlands, including both subsidies to households and other public expenditures in the housing sector.

Table 4-1 presents total expenditures for supply- (object) and demand-oriented (subject) subsidies for the period 1971-1980. Since the 1980s, an extensive cutback policy by the government has led to a reduction of both object and subject subsidies, despite the enduring quantitative housing shortage at the national level.

In Amsterdam, the housing shortage increased in the 1960s, despite the decrease in total population since 1957 and the huge housing construction program. This increase was mainly due to the overall reduction in family size and to urban renewal (see figures 4-6 and 4-7). The clearance of inferior houses in a tight market is problematic, and in order to produce more housing units, a solution was found in extended suburbanization. A number of municipalities at a commuting distance to Amsterdam (e.g., Amstelveen, Purmerend, and Zaandam) were able to build houses for the Amsterdam population. These units were charged to the Amsterdam construction quota. Thus, the housing market was extended to the regional level.

TABLE 4-1
Subsidies in the Housing Sector, the Netherlands, 1971-1980
(in Millions of Dfl.).

	1971	1975	1976	1977	1978	1979	1980
Object subsidies	340	960	1,230	1,500	1,620	1,560	1,720
Subject subsidies	20	230	530	630	790	880	965
Total	360	1,190	1,760	2,130	2,410	2,440	2,685

Source: Van der Schaar (1984).

Urban renewal and planned suburbanization were viewed as complementary processes. From 1965 onward, a growing number of people left the city; this outflow reached a peak of 51,000 in 1973 (see figure 4-8). These migrants were mainly young and relatively affluent families with children, whose relocation contributed to a growing spatial imbalance between the central city and the surrounding suburban communities.

The consequences of this suburbanization process are well known: a reduction of the threshold level for public and private services, an insufficient local tax base in the central city to cope with the negative spillover effects of suburban municipalities (i.e., traffic and central facilities), and so forth. This suburbanization process was also encouraged by the central government. The Second Memorandum on Physical Planning (Tweede Nota Ruimtelijke Ordening, 1966) introduced the principle of "bundled deconcentration": a controlled outflow of population from the central cities to a limited number of growth centers. The Third Memorandum on Physical Growth (Derde Nota Ruimtelijke Ordening, 1973) stressed the negative consequences of suburbanization for both the central cities and the rural areas.

Amsterdam enlarged its city area through the incorporation of formerly rural land in the southeast. Here, the city built a large-scale new high-rise housing district, known as the Bijlmermeer, containing more than 90 percent multistory apartments. It was planned as a high quality residential zone for approximately 100,000 people, with much open space and high quality (split-level) traffic and transportation services. However, the houses were too expensive, and despite the housing shortage, many houses were left vacant. In order to avoid exploitation problems, the housing corporations that owned these houses allowed nonmembers and noncitizens to rent apartments in this area, and thus a large group of residents entered the housing market who would otherwise never have obtained a dwelling unit in Amsterdam.

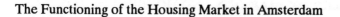

FIGURE 4-5
Share of Public Housing Costs in Total Budget, the Netherlands, 1964-1984.

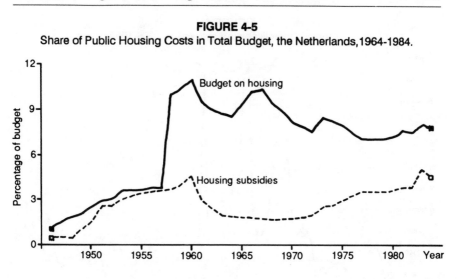

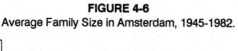

FIGURE 4-6
Average Family Size in Amsterdam, 1945-1982.

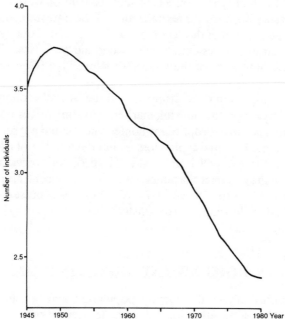

FIGURE 4-7
Housing Demolitions in Amsterdam, 1906-1984.

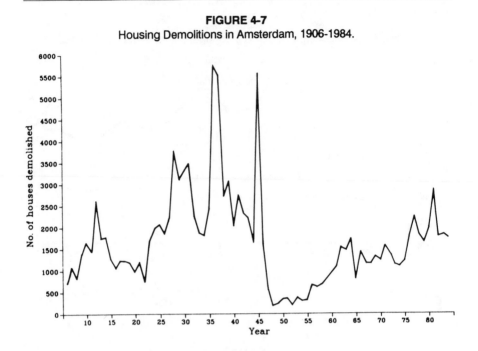

In the 1970s, the negative effects of suburbanization were felt, and by the end of the decade, the need for revitalization of the city was manifested at the local level in the concept of the "compact city"-- the use of open spaces within the city boundaries for residential and economic purposes. This concept formed the leading theme of the Urban Structure Plan (Concept Struktuurplan, 1984).

After 1973 migration rates dropped, and the overall economic recession had a severe impact on the housing market. Housing prices reached a peak around 1978 and began to drop. Many homeowners could not sell their houses without realizing substantial capital losses, and the number of transactions on the housing market dropped dramatically. The economic recession seemed to work in favor of the compact city policy, and in 1985, the central city population increased for the first time since 1957. Whether this represents a structural change in the urban development of Amsterdam or a temporary shift is unclear at the moment.

POPULATION, HOUSING, AND MOBILITY IN AMSTERDAM

This section analyzes the current population and housing situation in Amsterdam. Also, some attention is devoted to occupational structure and its consequences for residential mobility. Finally, the transactions occurring on the housing market (i.e., inter- and intra-urban mobility) are described. A later section provides more descriptive information concerning the regulated (distribution) sector of the Amsterdam housing market.

Population

Figure 4-8 depicts the basic components of population development in Amsterdam since 1945. Despite the decrease of population in the city of Amsterdam, the population of the metropolitan agglomeration has been continually growing in size (table 4-2).

Population growth in the Amsterdam agglomeration since 1960 is 11 percent, which is relatively low when compared with the national rate of 27

FIGURE 4-8

Population and Components of Demographic Change in Amsterdam, 1945-1984.

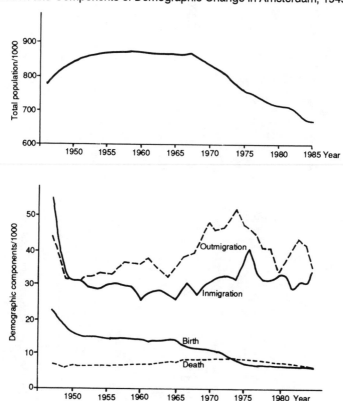

TABLE 4-2

Population in the Amsterdam Agglomeration, 1960-1985.

	1960		1971		1976		1981		1985	
	Pop.	% of Total	Pop.	% of Total	Pop.	% of Total	Pop.	% of Total	Pop.	% of Total
Amsterdam	864,747	75 %	807,100	66 %	751,156	61 %	711,982	56 %	675,570	53 %
Ring 1	218,159	19	294,200	24	322,370	26	335,268	27	339,801	26
Ring 2	71,161	6	128,896	10	166,199	13	214,383	17	271,013	21
Total Agglomeration	1,154,067	100	1,230,196	100	1,239,725	100	1,261,633	100	1,286,384	100

Source: Central Bureau of Statistics.

percent. Due to the aforementioned migration to the suburbs, the city of Amsterdam's population share has dropped since 1960. Additionally, the share of population in the first ring (closest to Amsterdam) has also dropped since 1981, although in absolute terms there is still some growth. The second ring shows the fastest growth, featuring major growth centers in Purmerend (to the north) and Almere and Lelystad (to the east).

Closer examination of the demographic statistics reveals some remarkable differences in age structure between Amsterdam and the rest of the region (figure 4-9). Elderly people and adults under 35 years of age are overrepresented, and children and middle-aged households are underrepresented in Amsterdam. This is a direct result of the out-migration of young families to the suburban rings.

Differences in age structure are also reflected in the types of households, but here differences are even more dramatic (table 4-3). In 1981, almost 40 perent of Amsterdam households were single, compared to less than 20 percent in the rest of the agglomeration. Approximately 30 percent of Amsterdam households contain three or more persons, compared with more than 50 percent in the rest of the agglomeration. Again, this seems attributable to the migration of young families to the suburbs, leaving Amsterdam as a haven for the unlikely combination of young singles and the elderly.

FIGURE 4-9

Age Structure of Amsterdam and the North-Holland Province, 1981-1984.

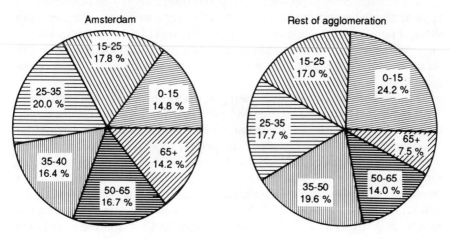

TABLE 4-3
Household Structure in the Amsterdam Agglomeration, 1981.

	Amsterdam		Rest of agglomeration	
Household category	Number	Percent	Number	Percent
One person < 35 y.	51,346	15 %	7,325	4 %
One person 35-64 y.	38,243	11	11,162	6
One person 65 + y.	39,556	12	11,940	6
Two persons < 35 y.	35,173	11	18,100	10
Two persons 35-64 y.	33,894	10	19,286	10
Two persons 65 + y.	29,340	9	12,414	7
Three persons, One Child < 18 y.	25,372	8	18,303	10
Three persons, One Child 18 + y.	16,452	5	10,294	6
Four+ persons, All Children < 18 y.	31,470	9	49,819	27
Four+ persons, One Child 18+ y.	20,061	6	21,544	12
Other	13,648	4	4,153	2
Total	334,555	100	184,340	100

Source: WBO, 1981.

The Housing Stock

In 1985, there were approximately 320,000 dwellings in Amsterdam; this is approximately 60 percent of the stock in the agglomeration. Amsterdam's share of housing production compared with the rest of the agglomeration has increased sharply since 1982, while its population has decreased (figure 4-10). As noted in the last section, this is not without consequences for the development of the population.

More details concerning the housing stock can be found in figures 4-11 and 4-12. Figure 4-11 presents the size distribution of dwellings in Amsterdam and the agglomeration. Almost 60 percent of all dwellings in Amsterdam have four or fewer rooms (kitchen included) compared to less than 25 percent in the agglomeration. Around 1970, the city of Amsterdam had a policy of building for a "balanced" population structure, (i.e., increasing the number of larger dwellings for families with children). However, the housing demand was quite different, and in the course of the 1970s, it was recognized that the city represented a special living environment chosen by a specific population category. The accompanying shift of policy is reflected by Amsterdam housing production since 1970 (table 4-4).

FIGURE 4-10

Housing Production in the Amsterdam Agglomeration, 1971-1984.

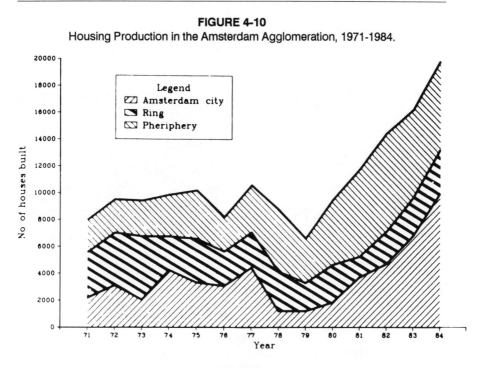

FIGURE 4-11

Size Distribution of Dwellings in Amsterdam and the
Rest of the Agglomeration, 1971.

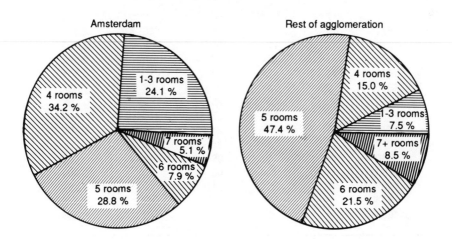

FIGURE 4-12

Year of Construction of Dwellings in Amsterdam and the
Rest of the Agglomeration, 1981.

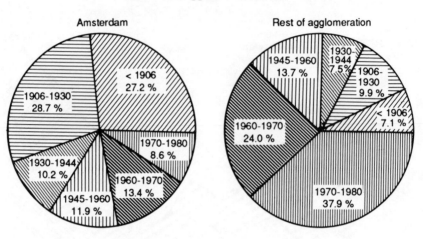

TABLE 4-4

Construction and Reconstruction in Amsterdam by Number of Rooms,
1970-1984.

Year	Number of rooms (in percent)				Total
	<u>1-2</u>	<u>3</u>	<u>4</u>	<u>5+</u>	<u>Total</u>
1970	17 %	25 %	50 %	8 %	3,845
1971	15	22	50	13	2,540
1972	22	11	55	12	3,096
1973	38	11	42	8	2,024
1974	35	12	43	10	4,237
1975	50	14	29	8	3,312
1976	29	25	35	10	3,056
1977	31	22	37	10	4,434
1978	41	16	24	18	1,203
1979	17	34	35	14	1,205
1980	18	35	39	8	1,853
1981	14	30	43	13	2,983
1982	36	25	31	9	4,261
1983	38	25	29	7	6,375
1984	44	29	24	3	8,843

Source: Central Bureau of Statistics

Another difference between Amsterdam and its surroundings is the age of the housing stock, noted in figure 4-12. More than half of the houses were built before 1930, and new construction (since 1970) amounts to less than nine percent of the total number of dwellings. In the rest of the agglomeration the reverse pattern is true: almost 40 percent of the total housing stock was built after 1970.

Dwelling Occupancy

Table 4-5 indicates the occupancy of dwellings by household categories in Amsterdam in 1983. Figure 4-13 presents similar data. It relates the number of rooms per dwelling to the number of persons living in the dwellings. It is clear that more than 90 percent of the one- and two-room dwellings are occupied by one or two persons. It is also apparent, however, that about 40 percent of large houses (five or more rooms) are occupied by two or fewer persons.

TABLE 4-5
Occupancy of Dwellings by Household Categories in Amsterdam, 1983.

| Dwelling size No. of rooms | Percentage of households occupying dwelling Household category | | | | |
	Family 0 child	Family, 1+ child	1 Parent family	Single	Other
1-2	21 %	7 %	10 %	45 %	27 %
3	44	32	37	29	35
4	26	44	38	13	22
5+	9	17	15	5	15
Total number of households	54,320	57,896	20,457	97,561	53,285

Note: Columns may not sum to 100 because of rounding.
Source: *Werkgroep Koppeling Vastgoed-Bevolking* (1983).

The structure of housing occupancy can be translated into "potential demand" for housing, assuming that there is some normal relation between household structure and dwelling size. One method of doing this is by using the same housing criteria used by the municipality for allocating households to dwellings. This "distribution sector" is the subject of another section, but for

TABLE 4-6
Percentage of Overcrowded Households in Amsterdam, 1983.

Household type	Urgency criteria	Permit criteria	Total households
Family, 0 child	1.2%	21.3%	54,320
Family, 1+ child	22.8	45.5	57,896
One parent family	20.5	52.1	20,457
Single	-	39.0	97,561
Other	23.8	52.5	53,285
Total	10.8	40.5	283,519

Source: Yearbook of Municipal Service of Housing, 1983.

the moment we note that there are two important sets of criteria that govern the (controlled) allocation of households to dwellings. The first set determines if a household is in "urgent" need (and thus is allowed to enter a queue for distribution of dwellings). The second set determines whether a household can get a housing permit (that is, if a specific dwelling is of "the right size" for the household). If we define the "urgency" criteria as a lower boundary, and the "permit" criteria as an upper boundary of potential demand for new dwellings, we arrive at the results in table 4-6.

These percentages can be interpreted as rough estimates of the propensity to move because of inadequate housing. One-parent families and the category "other" (more than one family in the house, two singles, etc.) have the highest relative number of overcrowded households, but in absolute terms singles are the dominant group, according to these permit criteria.

Mobility

As noted in figure 4-8, there has been an annual net out-migration from Amsterdam. In 1973, this outflow reached a peak of more than 50,000 persons, but since then the figures have dropped considerably. In 1984, in- and out-migration nearly balanced.

Compared to intra-urban moves, the magnitude of inter-urban migration is much smaller. This can be seen from figure 4-14, where both intra- and inter-urban migration since 1971 are displayed. Also included is the number of people in households that were allocated to a new dwelling in Amsterdam by means of a housing permit. Thus, the size of the distribution sector relative to the total number of transactions is represented. In 1984, approximately 80,000

FIGURE 4-13
Dwelling Size by Number of Persons per Dwelling in Amsterdam.

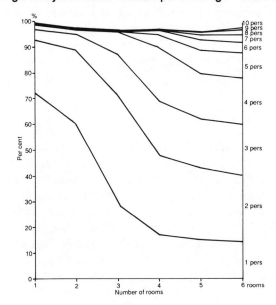

FIGURE 4-14
Intra- and Inter-Urban Mobility in Amsterdam and Total Persons Allocated
Through the Municipal Distribution System, 1971-1984.

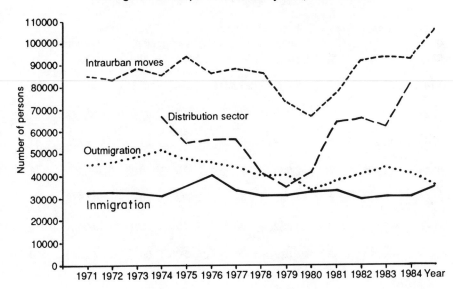

of the 140,000 people who moved within Amsterdam or immigrated found housing through government-controlled housing distribution.

The age composition of movers is quite different from that of the overall population (table 4-7). In general, movers are relatively young compared to the total Amsterdam population. Of all movers, the out-migrants are most like the total population, with the in-migrants being the youngest mover group. Almost three-quarters of in-migrants are under 30 years of age.

THE PLANNING SYSTEM

There are three spatial planning levels in the Netherlands: state, province, and municipality. The physical planning process, as described in the Physical Planning Act, and the programing of housing construction are important elements in the housing sector. The former provides the legal framework to control future land use developments. The latter lacks a well-described legal background (the Reconstruction Act was withdrawn in 1969), but is still used to control the total number of newly constructed dwellings and housing maintenance by type and municipality. In this section both planning processes will be described briefly.

TABLE 4-7
Age Composition of Migrants and Amsterdam Population.

	Intra-urban movers		Inter-urban movers immigration		out-migration		Amsterdam population	
Age	No.	%	No.	%	No.	%	No.	%
0-19	22,988	22 %	8,559	25 %	7,704	22 %	134,774	20 %
20-29	42,835	41	16,430	47	11,207	31	142,587	21
30-39	18,288	17	5,419	16	7,595	21	115,706	17
40-49	7,305	7	2,094	6	2,856	8	71,453	11
50-64	6,731	6	1,481	4	3,529	10	103,573	15
65+	6,674	6	852	2	2,929	8	107,477	16
	104,821	99	34,835	100	35,820	100	675,570	100

Source: Central Bureau of Statistics

The Physical Planning Process

The physical planning process in the Netherlands is cyclical (van Zundert, 1977), with national policies and plans designed and established at the state level. The main elements of these policies and plans are executed through the Decision on Physical Planning (Planologische Kernbeslissing), which focuses on major decisions for national physical planning issues.

Each province usually has its own derived planning policies; these are described in the regional plan. If elements of such a plan are not in accordance with national views, it is possible for the minister to force the province to change the content of this plan. However, this is seldom done.

Unlike the municipal master plan, the regional plan does not have the character of law, but does offer a framework for planning at the local level. The "master plan" is the key instrument in the physical planning process and can be established at the local level only. If necessary, the province and the Minister of Housing are able to give instructions concerning the content of the master plan, but this seldom occurs.

Every municipality is obliged to prepare a master plan for areas outside the built environment. Depending on the circumstances, the local government may or may not develop a master plan for part of the built area as well. The contents of such a plan may be general (types of land use) or quite specific (boundaries of buildings, blocks, streets, number and height of buildings per lot, floor space area). Anyone whose interests are negatively affected by a proposed plan can object to the plan, first to the municipality, then to the province, and finally even to the Crown. Due to this extensive protection of citizens' individual interests, the approval procedure may take many years. In general, this system is quite inflexible.

Since a building permit must be issued as long as a project is not in conflict with building codes or the master plan, the lack of a valid master plan leaves a municipality without the proper instrument for regulating the spatial development of an area. Thus, while the building codes only deal with technical matters, the master plan is necessary in order to prevent "undesirable" spatial development. The law, however, allows local governments to anticipate a draft master plan. This anticipation clause has become a very important instrument for local planning purposes, enabling municipalities to regulate development during the period when a proposed master plan is pending approval.

Besides the master plan, a municipality can also prepare a more general town plan, a so-called structure plan. In a structure plan, the long-term development of the municipality (or a group of municipalities) is described. This plan is essentially a letter of intent and has no legal status.

In order to overcome some of the master plan's problems in planning urban renewal areas, the Urban Renewal Act was adopted in 1984. This Act offers the legal basis for reconstructing or improving urban areas without a master plan. An urban area can be given the status of a Renewal Area. This decision requires the approval of the Minister but guarantees financing by the national government. This plan has a status comparable to the master plan, but is more practical in nature. The approval procedure is simplified compared to the master plan, and many decisions can be made at the local level (decentralization).

Programming of Housing Construction

The planning of housing construction and rehabilitation and the allocation of production quotas to municipalities are ad hoc procedures that are nevertheless very important for local housing markets. Every year housing quotas for new construction, reconstruction, and improvement are allocated to each region by the central government. Separate quotas are fixed for Amsterdam and other large cities.

In order to determine the quotas, local governments must first determine their housing needs for the next five years, usually on the basis of a housing plan. From this information, the total number of new houses by type and size, as well as reconstructions and rehabilitations, can be deduced. These local housing needs are reported to a state commission, and an overall plan is prepared for every province. In general, these overall plans satisfy approximately 50 percent of a municipality's needs.

In addition, the provincial plans serve to advise the central government on housing construction. At the central level, this advice is considered along with budgetary constraints and other policy issues. Once determined, the resulting quotas are allocated for the provinces and the four major cities (including Amsterdam). The large cities usually benefit from this allocation procedure. A relatively large share of the quota is first allocated to the large cities, with the remainder going to the provinces and smaller municipalities.

Usually, the relative shares of various housing types are also adjusted by the central government. In 1984, only one-third of the national quota for council houses was actually allocated by the central government, while 123 percent of the quota for subsidized owner-occupied houses was allocated.

PRICING AND FINANCING

The Rental Sector

In 1979, the Housing Rent and Allocation Act (Huurprijzenwet Woonruimte) was introduced. This act prescribes the annual changes of rents in the rental housing stock in the private as well as the subsidized sector. In the subsidized sector, initial rental prices and the annual changes of rents are determined by the so-called "housing quality rating system." The number of points for a dwelling determines its allowable rent and rent increase. In this rating system, points are given for the presence of a central heating system or a bath, for example.

Environmental elements such as schools, parks, shops, and public transport are also valued. These environmental points are set by the municipality for every city quarter and are often used by the local authorities to influence rent levels in certain areas. In the private housing stock, landlords and renters are free in principle to negotiate the initial rent level. However, the common rule is that the norms set by the rating system are followed. When tenants vacate a dwelling, the number of points determined by the rating system are recalculated and a new rent is then set.

Once a rent is fixed, however, annual changes are related to initial housing quality by means of this rating system. It is argued that this system will lead to a "harmonic" rent level in the housing stock: equal quality, equal price. In this system, rent decreases are even possible if the house is too expensive vis-a-vis quality. Similarly, if the rent is too low, one can expect an extra rent increase above the trend. In the event of a disagreement between landlord and renter, the Commission on Housing Rents (Huurcommissie) will arbitrate. In practice, the landlord seldom increases the rent above the trend. Instead, he or she negotiates larger rent increases only when new renters occupy the house.

The annual trend is determined by the Minister and is related to the financing system of the subsidized sector. Since 1973, a system of dynamic cost-pricing (dynamische kostprijsberekening) has been applied. This system is based on graduated payment annuities and results in low initial rent levels, followed by annual rent increases guaranteed by the government. In the system that was used before 1973, the initial rent without object subsidy (supply-side) was 10 percent of the construction cost. After object subsidies, a rent level resulted in approximately 5 percent of costs. Using the dynamic cost-pricing system, initial rents without object subsidies amounted to approximately 6 percent. In the first years of the term, extra financing was needed because the initial rents were lower than the interest payment. In the second half of the term (which was fixed at 50 years), the reverse was true: rents were higher than interest payments (see Priemus, 1983).

Yearly rent increases are an integral part of this mode of financing. If rents were fully harmonized, the whole existing stock would have to follow. From a social housing standpoint, the following disadvantages can be mentioned:

· The increasing construction costs and the increasing annuity system are taken into account for the whole stock. This means large capital gains for landlords.

· The adverse price/quantity ratio of the newly built houses would originally be the norm for the whole stock, but this element has been changed. The basis of the quality rating system is now a "standard dwelling."

Apart from the newly built rental stock and the existing housing stock, there is a third housing category: the "reconstruction sector" (housing improvement in the existing stock). For these dwellings, a separate arrangement applies, the so-called "2 percent arrangement." This means that monthly rents, after housing improvement, can be increased by 2 percent of the costs of improvement, unless a lower rent is determined according to the rating system.

In the long term, the increased financial burden for renters was removed by a system of object and subject subsidies. The object subsidies bridge the gap between the 6 percent initial rents following the dynamic costing principle and the "social housing" price of 5 percent. In addition, specific subsidies were needed for dwellings in urban renewal areas, new towns, and so on, in order to keep them competitive with the normal new construction. The subject subsidies were necessary in order to keep housing affordable for all dwellers. Since its introduction in 1970, this subsidy program has increased explosively (see table 4-1).

Despite the increasing rent level, the gap between actual rent level and the dynamic rent price is increasing (figure 4-15); the annual rent increases have been insufficient to keep up with the increasing annuities. As a result, object subsidies also increased dramatically in the 1970s (see table 4-1). A reversal of this trend is difficult to foresee, given incomes and other housing costs (e.g., heating) (Priemus, 1983, p. 50).

FIGURE 4-15
Dynamic Cost-Pricing in Practice.

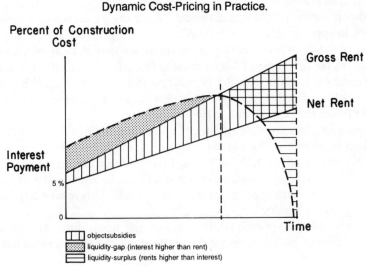

The system of dynamic rent prices was not ideal for institutional investment funds either (Nycolaas, 1974, p. 118). In the first place, the 50-year length of the term was quite long (20 years is the usual maximum length of a term). Additionally, selling the stock before 50 years is difficult because of the dynamic pricing principle. Finally, the investors were dependent on the government for the annual rent increases.

More profitable alternatives for large pension funds and insurance companies were available outside of the public housing sector. First, the real estate market became less important overall in the 1970s. The relative share of investments of pension funds in this sector decreased from 14.3 percent in 1968 to 12.4 percent in 1981 (Jaarverslagen Verzekeringskamers, Annual Reports of the Chamber of Insurance). The life insurance funds, which traditionally have maintained small investments in real estate, showed a decrease in relative share in real estate from 8.7 to 7.2 percent. Even more important was the decrease of the relative share of housing in the real estate market. In 1968, pension funds invested 86.8 percent of their real estate capital in housing. By 1981, this percentage had been reduced to 62 percent. For the life insurance companies, these numbers were 72.3 and 47.1 percent, respectively.

The Owner-Occupied Sector

The government also plays an important price regulating role in owner-occupied housing. Three types of subsidies can be distinguished which depend on house values, premium-A, -B, and - C. In addition, the housing built under control of the municipality or a housing corporation for low-income households is a protected submarket. This subsector lacks the risk of large capital losses or gains for the owner occupant. The size of this submarket is very small, however. Of more importance are direct subsidies, primarily the A and B premium categories, but more recently category C as well.

The premium-A category is the least expensive housing category. In 1985, the maximum allowable price of these houses was 142,000 Dfl., and the subsidy was dependent on housing price and income. Until 1984, the subsidy was in the form of an annually decreasing contribution to interest and principal for a market rate loan. The decrease was based on assumptions about long-term inflation and income improvement. These assumptions no longer hold, and the subsidy arrangement has been changed recently. The government now takes over a share of the total loan, up to a maximum of 48,000 Dfl. (depending upon income), and is reponsible for amortization and interest of this share. The subsidy is considered as income, and is therefore taxable. Households with incomes of higher than 70,000 Dfl. may not enter this submarket.

For premium-B, a maximum house price of 162,000 Dfl. applies. For a maximum of five years, a yearly contribution is given of 5,000 Dfl. This

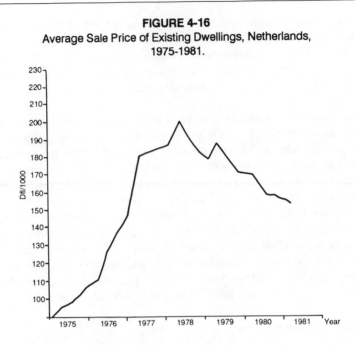

FIGURE 4-16
Average Sale Price of Existing Dwellings, Netherlands,
1975-1981.

contribution is dependent only on housing prices, and is also taxable. An upper income limit of 70,000 Dfl. applies.

The highest-priced housing sector for which subsidies are available is the premium-C sector. Houses built under this arrangement may not exceed 180,000 Dfl. in price, and a one-time only contribution of 6,500 Dfl. is given. No income limits are applicable.

In addition to these subsidy programs, some supplemental owner occupant benefits exist. The subsidy for premium-A is transferrable to the next owner occupier within ten years of construction. If an owner occupier sells the house in this period, an antispeculation condition applies; capital gains on subsidized dwellings are not permitted.

The developments in housing prices have been tempestuous. Until 1978, housing prices rose dramatically. Since then, due to the economic recession and high interest rates, the housing market has collapsed (see figure 4-16). Until 1985, prices remained at a relatively low level, but in 1985 there were signs of an increase.

Taxes

Housing costs not only are affected by government subsidies but also through the taxation system; subsidies are taxable, while interest on mortgages is tax deductible. In 1973, the total amount of money involved in such tax deductions was 1,839 million Dfl. (van Wijk, 1979). This deduction of interest is more profitable for high- rather than low-income groups, due to the progressive income tax system.

Capital gains or losses, through changes in the value of houses, are free from taxation. On the other hand, if an existing house is transferred from one owner to the other, transfer taxes have to be paid (5 percent of the selling price). For many households, this transfer tax is a threshold for buying a new house, and consequently it has been an issue of political debate in the eighties.

THE ALLOCATION OF HOUSEHOLDS TO DWELLINGS

Rehousing Services and Urgency Certificates

Amsterdam has a large municipal service agency charged with housing allocation. More than 350 persons are employed in the Municipal Service of Rehousing (Gemeentelijke Dienst Herhuisvesting, abbreviated as GDH). As described before, this service has a history that dates back to the Second World War. In 1972, it became an independent municipal service, and the name was changed from the Housing Bureau to the Rehousing Service, indicating a major shift in goals. From 1945 onward, the main goal of the Bureau was to allocate scarce dwellings throughout the population with a mandate to care for underprivileged groups. In the 1970s, another major goal was introduced: the relocation of households as a result of urban renewal activities. It appeared that the success of urban renewal plans was very much dependent on the speed of relocation of households.

To pursue these goals three major tasks can be identified:
- registration of house hunters within the distribution sector;
- registration of vacant dwellings in the distribution sector; and
- granting of housing permits and mediation between renters and landlords.

Until 1975, a housing permit was necessary for every residential move, according to the Housing Allocation Act of 1947. After 1975, some parts of the market were freed from this obligation (the more expensive parts of the rental and owner-occupied sectors). In addition to a housing permit, however, a certificate of urgency is necessary to enter the controlled market. Those with urgency certificates may enter a queue for the distribution of dwellings. A household's position in the queue is determined by its degree of urgency. Urgency increases with:
- increasing age;
- decreasing income;
- overcrowding in current housing situation;

FIGURE 4-17
Total Number of Urgencies and Supply in the Distribution Sector, 1972-1984.

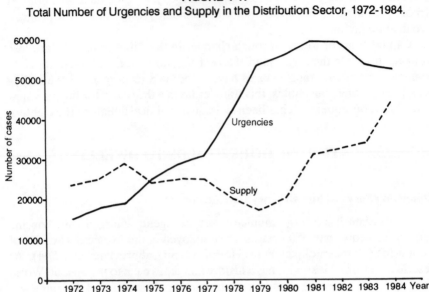

·   social and medical needs;
·   increasing length of stay in Amsterdam; and
·   distance to place of work.

These criteria have changed considerably over time. Singles were not allowed to get an urgency certificate until 1969, and then only if they were over 27 years of age. In 1975, the minimum age was lowered to 25 years, and in 1978 to 18. The relaxation of the age criterion resulted in a dramatic increase in the number of urgencies in the 1970s-- from 11,782 in 1972 to 59,173 in 1982 (figure 4-17). In 1981, more than 60 percent of these households were younger than 30 years, and over 65 percent were single (figures 4-18 and 4-19; see also Annual Report GDH, 1981, pp. 10-11).

Another criterion for obtaining an urgency certificate is the current housing situation. In 1985, an urgency certificate could be issued on the grounds of overcrowding under the following conditions:

·   two persons, living in one room;
·   a household with one child living in one or two rooms;
·   a household with two or three children living in three or fewer rooms; and
·   a household with four or more children living in four or fewer rooms.

In order to prevent house hunters in neighboring municipalities from entering the Amsterdam housing market, a minimum length of two years of residence, work, or study in Amsterdam is prescribed to obtain a certificate.

FIGURE 4-18
Age Composition of Urgencies, 1972-1983.

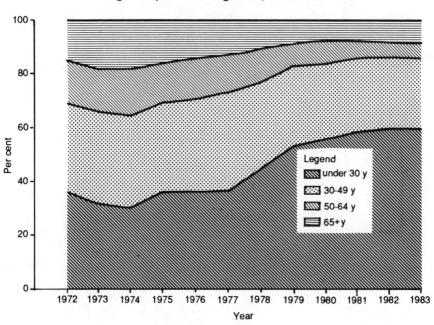

FIGURE 4-19
Household Composition of Urgencies, 1972-1983.

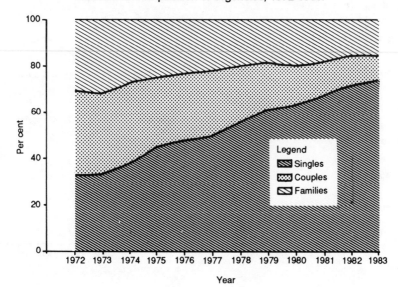

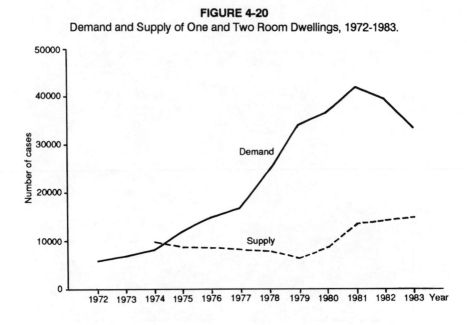

FIGURE 4-20
Demand and Supply of One and Two Room Dwellings, 1972-1983.

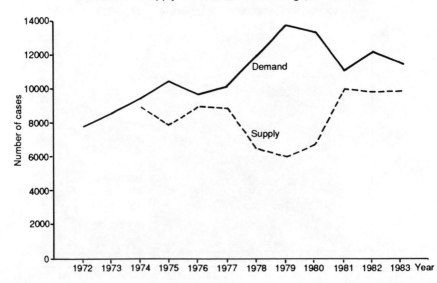

FIGURE 4-21
Demand and Supply of Three Room Dwellings, 1972-1983.

FIGURE 4-22
Demand and Supply of Four Room Dwellings, 1972-1983.

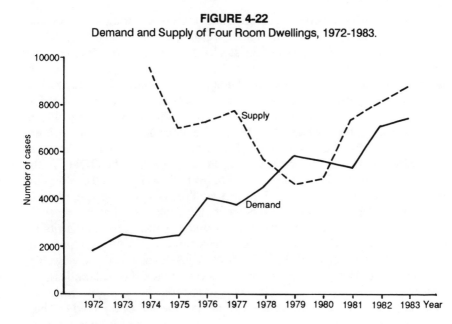

The Distribution Sector

The dwellings allocated through this distribution sector are specified by price: all rental dwellings above a certain minimum rent level and below an upper level are included. In 1985, the limits of these categories were 150 Dfl. and 563 Dfl. per month, respectively. In the 1980s, some specific submarkets were excluded from the distribution sector in order to make them more attractive: for example, the Bijlmermeer category, and one-room dwellings. The number of units allocated through this distribution sector dropped until 1978, and then increased sharply (see figure 4-17). This increase was mainly due to new construction activities in the southeast. Despite this increase, the gap between supply and demand widened. The situation is especially dramatic for one-person households. (Figures 4-20, 4-21, and 4-22 show the imbalance between supply and demand for different sized dwellings.)

A dwelling allocated through the distribution sector can be owned by one of the following three parties:
·   private landlords;
·   housing corporations; or
·   the municipality.
Private landords and corporations have to report vacancies in the distribution sector to the GDH.

Municipally owned houses are fully under GDH control, and every vacancy is allocated by the GDH to a household registered in the queue. Until 1978, vacancies in the remaining part of the stock were allocated on a 50/50 percent basis, alternately by the landlord and by the GDH. However, by manipulating the order of reporting their vacancies, landlords were able to retain the highest quality dwellings under their own control. Cooperative houses built before 1940 were all allocated by the GDH, but the newer houses were controlled by the cooperatives themselves. As a result, the older, lower quality stock was overrepresented in the GDH sector. This system was changed in 1978 so that any vacancy in the distribution sector could be claimed by the GDH. In this arrangement, the GDH has the first choice over all dwellings and can pick out those with the highest demand. For every landlord or corporation, a record is kept by the GDH to preserve a 50 percent allocation per supplier.

As described above, the vacancies controlled by the GDH are distributed according to a queueing system, where placement in the queue depends on urgency as well as length of the wait. Some households need a new dwelling instantly (for example, those displaced by urban renewal or calamities), and these households have first priority. Due to insufficient supply, however, the "normal" urgencies have little chance of being allocated by the GDH. These households must rely on other initiatives (e.g., joining a housing cooperative). The alternative institutions use their own allocation system. Members, ranked by length of membership and the time since the last move, are given a priority for vacancies within the housing stock of the corporation. For an available dwelling, priority depends upon possession of an urgency certificate and a match between household size and the size of the available dwelling.

Other alternatives outside the GDH allocation include the private rental sector, home ownership, or swapping. In order to rent a house in the private rental sector, its size must be "appropriate" to the household, as specified by regulation. In the homeownership market, certain restrictions apply. For houses selling for less than 180,000 Dfl., a housing permit is necessary. Special requirements exist for houses that change from the rental to the owner-occupied sector. For the swapping of dwellings, permission of both landlords is required.

With regulated prices, there exists a huge gap between demand and supply which impedes the functioning of the GDH. Many people do not accept the strict regulations and enter the black market described below. In an attempt to simplify the rules and to formalize existing (illegal) practices by renters and owners, a number of changes were made in 1985. First, the distribution sector is smaller: the lower rent limit went up from 75 Dfl. to 150 Dfl., and the upper limit went down from 650 Dfl. to 563 Dfl. Second, for every dwelling that becomes vacant, a landlord can now propose a renter. If this renter meets certain criteria (i.e., having an urgency certificate for at least two and a half years and other distribution criteria), the GDH cannot claim the dwelling.

Thus, active groups on the housing market have more chances in this arrangement.

THE BLACK MARKET: SQUATTING

A common characteristic of regulated markets is the phenomenon of black markets, and in this respect, the Amsterdam housing market is certainly no exception.

Different forms of "illegal" behavior can be distinguished. The supplier of housing can accept a tenant without a housing permit or the supplier can withdraw a dwelling from the distribution market. He or she can also inflate rents or require key money from the tenant. With or without permission of the landlord, a tenant may occupy a dwelling without a housing permit.

Illegal occupancy of a dwelling with permission of the landlord occurs in many forms:

· The main tenant moves to another dwelling and leaves one or more household members behind. In some cases this is permitted, but often it is not, especially if parents leave the house and a child stays behind.

· An illegal contract is made between a landlord and a high paying tenant without registration at the GDH. This common practice was legalized in 1985. If a landlord registers a vacancy and proposes a tenant who meets certain urgency criteria to the GDH, a housing permit is usually granted.

· A dwelling unit is left vacant in order to speculate on higher prices in the future. However, due to effective controlling mechanisms, the vacancy rate in the distribution sector is very low.

Vacancy control is an important municipal instrument to prevent and eliminate illegal occupancy or withdrawal of housing space by landlords from the market. For example, in 1981, the GDH investigated more than 7,000 cases. The majority of these vacancies were occupied by renters on a semilegal or illegal basis. In principle, almost half of the occupants of these dwellings could have been evicted by the municipality, but only 365 evictions actually took place. Also, more than 500 vacant houses were requisitioned by the GDH. Although the number of requisitions is small, it is nevertheless an effective deterrent against private landlords leaving their property vacant. The same applies to the tenant with respect to the GDH's vacating of houses. The GDH became much more active in this field in the 1970s, but it is still unknown how extensive illegal occupancy is today. The large number of ex post legalizations indicates that a number of actions outside the distribution rules are worth trying for both tenant and landlord.

Occupancy of a dwelling without permission of the landlord is called squatting (kraken). Although figures are very difficult to obtain, in 1981, it was estimated that approximately 9,000 persons in Amsterdam were living as squatters (van der Raad, 1982). With an estimated number of six persons per unit (van den Boon, 1982), this would amount to approximately 1,500 squatter units in 1982. This seems to be a very conservative estimate (0.5 percent of the housing stock). Since 1981, this number has certainly increased, with some older neighborhoods being highly overrepresented (e.g., the so-called Staatslie-denbuurt).

Approximately 50 percent of these squatter units are houses or a house plus commercial property. Of these houses, more than 90 percent had been left vacant for more than six months (Hanemaayer, 1983). About 50 percent of these units are actually owned by the municipality, while the other half are private property. In municipal squats, more than 50 percent of the units are slated to be converted to youth housing, while approximately 26 percent are awaiting demolition for urban renewal.

Initially, the Amsterdam municipality was very skeptical about squatting. Now, despite a number of incidents between local government and groups of squatters, most of the occupied dwellings have been legalized through usage contracts (occupancy until demolition and the guarantee of a suitable dwelling afterwards).

Illegal occupancy of dwellings allocated to the GDH usually results in an immediate ejection order. However, if a house is indeed unoccupied for a long period, squatting is not illegal. The Leegstandswet (Vacancy Act) has been established to protect the private property of landlords, but this Act has met much criticism: it lacks any firm regulation against structural vacancy.

A shortage of cheap housing is the primary reason for squatting. In addition, it is an important means of establishing alternative living styles and modes of cohabitation (Hanemaayer, 1983). The regulated market offers virtually no possibility of this.

CONCLUSIONS

Urban housing market policy in the Netherlands is influenced by both national and local policy choices. The strict regulation of the housing market has to be seen against the background of enormous shortages after World War II. In addition to centrally planned residential building programs, price controls and allocative rules were the dominant instruments in this period. In the period of the rise of the welfare state, housing commodities were considered merit goods, the consumption of which had to be stimulated by means of complicated subsidy and taxation schemes. The qualitative change in the structure of households from the 1970s on has caused another imbalance in the housing market, with Amsterdam as a noticeable example. This has also led to the emergence of black market segments and the squatting phenomenon.

An ex post evaluation of housing policy in Amsterdam is far from easy. Seen from the viewpoint of current trends towards decentralization and deregulation, it is clear that the strict regulatory policy pursued after World War II has by no means been efficient and, because of its rigidity, has been unable to solve the problem of structural sociodemographic changes in household size in the Amsterdam housing market. If the national and local housing market policy had not taken place along these institutional policy directions, it is evident that the current housing market would have exhibited an entirely different pattern, with more market-oriented building programs.

However, it is also fair to note that in such a situation, the equity problem would have led to unacceptable housing situations for low-income groups in the housing market in Amsterdam. Furthermore, the protection of historical districts and of urban monuments would-- in a period of absolute scarcity-- have been impossible without strict building and allocation rules. Thus, from a historical and social viewpoint, the policies undertaken in the past decades are justifiable, although a greater market orientation-- within certain strict boundaries-- would have led to more efficient outcomes.

In the current situation, where the absolute scarcity (in a quantitative sense) is gradually vanishing, more emphasis on market rules and on deregulation promises significant economic benefits, provided distributional equity and the protection of valuable historical quarters are not sacrificed.

REFERENCES

Blankenstein-Bouwmeesters, A.A.M., and P. Lukkes. 1984. Institutionele beleggers op de markt voor onroerend goed. Sociaal-geografische reeks, 29, Geografisch Instituut Groningen.

Boon, A. van den. 1982. *Krakers en Amsterdam; Meningen van krakers en Amsterdammers*. Amsterdam: Baschwitz Instituut.

Conijn, I.B.S. 1984. Vrije sector in begroting 1985 via premie C ingepolderd. *Bouw*, 29.

Hanemaayer, D. 1983. Kraken en volkshuisvesting. Feiten en implikaties. *Stedebouw en Volkshuisvesting* :362-370.

Houben, P.P.J., and H. Priemus. 1981. 80 jaar woningwet, volkshuisvestingbeleid en verzorgingsstaat. *Stedebouw en Volkshuisvesting*.: 437-448.

Jaarverslagen Gemeentelijke Dienst Herhuisvesting. 1972-1985.

Jaarverslagen Gemeentelijke Dienst Volkshuisvesting. 1972-1984.

Jobse, R.J. 1980. Van kelderwoning tot hoogbouwflat, honderd jaar bouwen en wonen in Amsterdam. *In Wonen, werken en verkeer in Amsterdam 1880-1980,* Bijdragen tot de sociale geografie en planologie no. 1, GPNU, Amsterdam.

Lambooy, J.J., P.C.M. Huigsloot, and R.E. van de Lustgraaf. 1982. *Greep op de Stad?* Staatsuitgeverij: Gravenhage.

McGuire, Charles. 1981. *International housing policies, a comparative analysis.* Lexington: D.C. Heath.

Nota Toestand Oude Stad, Amsterdam, 1962.

Nota Volkshuisvesting, Tweede Kamer der Staten-Generaal. Zitting 1971-1972, 11784, no. 1, 's Gravenhage, Staatsuitgeverij.

Nycolaas, J. 1974. Volkshuisvesting, een bijdrage tot de geschiedenis van woningbouw en woningbouwbeleid. Nijmegen, SUN.

Ottens, E. 1975. Ik moet naar een kleinere woning omzien want mijn gezin wordt te groot. *125 Jaar Sociale Woningbouw in Amsterdam,* Stadsdruk-kerij, Amsterdam.

Ottens, E. 1979. Volkshuisvesting op een keerpunt, het volkshuisvestingsbeleid. In Amsterdam in de tweede helft van de jaren zestig en het begin van de jaren zeventig. *Wonen-AT/BK.*

Priemus, H. 1983. *Huurprijsbeheersing: Omstreden instrument van volkshuisvestingsbeleid.* Volkshuisvesting in Theorie en Ppraktijk, 2, Delftse Universitaire Pers, Delft.

Raad, J.W. van der. 1982. *Dit pand is gekraakt.* Amsterdam: Roelof Kellerstichting.

Schaar, J. van der. 1984. Trends in woonlasten. Working paper no. 7. Delft: Delft University Press.

Stahl, K., and R. Struyk. 1984. U.S. and German housing markets and policies: A comparative economic analysis. Working paper 8408. Department of Economics, University of Dortmund.

Tweede Nota Bouwbeleid. Tweede kamer der Staten-Generaal. Zitting 1977-1978, 15118, nos. 1-2, 's Gravenhage, Staatsuitgeverij.

Weesep, J. van. 1982. Production and allocation of housing, the case of the Netherlands. *Geografische en planologische notities,* no. 11, GPIVU, Amsterdam.

Werkgroep Koppeling Vastgoed-Bevolking. 1983. *De huisvesting van de Amsterdammers in 1983*. Amsterdam.

Wijk, F. van. 1979. Belastingen en het beheer van woningen. Een onderzoek naar de rijksbelastingen en de verschillende beheerders van woningen. Research Instituut Gebouwde Omgeving, Amsterdam.

Zundert, J.W. van. 1977. *Het bestemmingsplan*, samson. Alphen aan de Rijn.

5
HOUSING IN SAN FRANCISCO: SHELTER IN THE MARKET ECONOMY
John A. Hird
John M. Quigley
Michael L. Wiseman

INTRODUCTION

Housing policy in the United States relies upon private enterprise to supply shelter for virtually all households in an allocation process realized by free markets. On the demand side, households generally receive housing in amounts and qualities consistent with their own choices, given their preferences, their overall budgets, and market prices. On the supply side, the design, construction, and financing of housing are organized by the private sector, with only limited and often indirect government involvement. Housing production is undertaken by entrepreneurs, many quite small, who construct housing in local and regional markets. This housing is distributed to citizens through markets in which prices are determined by supply and demand. Housing finance is governed not by direct political or parliamentary decisions, but rather by those of private financial intermediaries who offer a variety of long- and short-term financing mechanisms depending upon market conditions.

All of these statements require considerable qualification. Although housing is overwhelmingly the responsibility of the private sector in the United States, all levels of the U.S. government play important roles in the determination of both housing supply and demand. In some cases, local governments build, own, and manage housing using resources provided by the federal (central) government. The financing of new construction and of mortgage obligations has been greatly influenced by the regulations and credit guarantees of the federal government. The availability of land for housing and for other urban development is quite heavily regulated by state and local authorities, and the construction process itself is regulated at the local level. Moreover, the attractiveness of housing and residential construction is greatly influenced by the tax policies adopted by the federal government and by the systems of taxation used by local governments. Thus, it would be a mistake to conclude that because the market plays a dominant role in the housing sector of the United States, the role of government is insignificant.

This chapter provides an overview of the housing market and housing conditions in the San Francisco Bay Area of California and suggests some of the ways in which housing outcomes are related to housing policies. The essay starts by describing the characteristics of the Bay Area, its housing market, and its housing problems. Following this, we present a general discussion of the U.S. federal and state housing assistance policies and their interaction with local housing policies in California. Bay Area regionalism and localism in land use and development are then followed by a summary and some conclusions.

THE SAN FRANCISCO BAY AREA

The state of California has the largest population of any of the 50 U.S. states.[1] It ranks third among the states in area, and is roughly the size of Austria, West Germany, and Hungary combined, but smaller than either Sweden or France. Situated on the long western coast of the United States, California's massive economy includes a diverse array of export products-- agriculture, electronics, entertainment, and tourism, to note merely a few. (Its gross state product of more than $600 billion, around 12 percent of the U.S. GNP, is larger than the combined GNPs of the Scandinavian and Benelux countries.) The state governor, together with the two representative legislative bodies, the State Assembly and Senate, commands a taxation and spending authority commensurate with a large economy. The state's expenditures for fiscal year 1987 totalled more than $60 billion.

The Bay Area is located advantageously on the coast of this most wealthy and populous state. The area is situated about 300 miles north of Los Angeles, the third largest American city. Figure 5-1 shows the geographical position of the Bay Area in California. Figure 5-2 indicates the position of San Francisco, as well as its principal satellite cities, San Jose and Oakland, within the Bay Area.

The Bay Area includes the nine California counties surrounding the San

---

[1] For a more comprehensive review of the Bay Area economy, see Hoerter and Wiseman (1988).

FIGURE 5-1
The San Francisco-Oakland-San Jose Region.

FIGURE 5-2
The Bay Area.

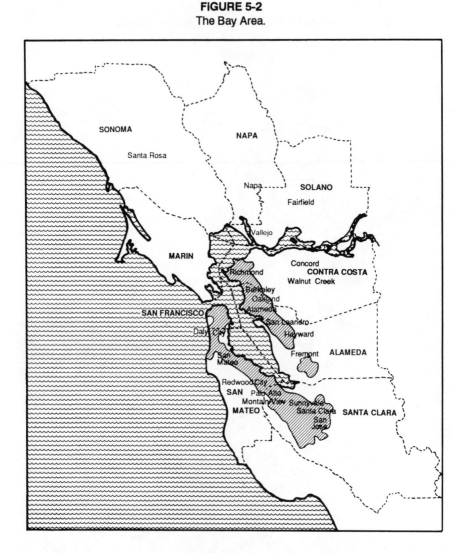

Francisco Bay. Socially, politically, and economically, the Bay Area is dominated by the (combined) City and County of San Francisco, which is located on
the peninsula that forms the southwestern side of the Bay itself. Although the
city was originally settled by Spanish explorers in the early 1800s, the housing,
industry, and infrastructure of San Francisco and the entire region were virtually built anew after a massive earthquake in April 1906. While it is the
earthquake itself that remains prominent in the minds of today's Bay Area
residents, it was the ensuing fire that caused most of the property damage. This

fire burned for three days and two nights and spread over more than 500 city blocks. It destroyed 28,000 houses, claimed the lives of more than 500 persons, and caused property damage in excess of $500 million. However, with the aid of $300 million in fire insurance payments, San Francisco was largely rebuilt in less than five years. The capstone of the reconstruction was the new Civic Center. The Panama-Pacific International Exposition of 1915 left the city with the existing Palace of Fine Arts and a renewed sense of pride (see Cleland, 1947).

Because it was at first the state's only metropolis, San Francisco was long and familiarly known in California as "the City," and the Bay Area was the home of the state's only university campus in Berkeley. By the 1920s, however, Los Angeles had surpassed San Francisco in both population and industry. In part because of its great natural harbor, San Francisco remained a major military, manufacturing, and shipping center during World War II, and many who passed through the area later settled in and around San Francisco (see Hart, 1978). The San Francisco-Oakland Bay Bridge, erected in 1936, connected San Francisco with the "East Bay" (replacing a ferry system), and provided a vital transportation link for those working in San Francisco but living outside. Two years later, the Golden Gate Bridge was completed, connecting San Francisco with Marin County, and San Francisco became accessible to all areas surrounding the Bay. Prior to World War II, land use outside of San Francisco and the older cities between Oakland and Richmond was predominantly agricultural. The Veterans' Administration home loan program for returning veterans helped to finance new development outside the major cities, and the Bay Area's agricultural foundation gave way to a regional economy of some cohesion.

Today, San Francisco is both the smallest (119 square kilometers) and the most densely populated (5,700 persons per square kilometer) county in California. With a population of 679,000, San Francisco ranked 13th in city size in the United States in 1980 (down from 9th in 1900). When compared with other similarly defined conurbations, however, the Bay Area ranks fifth among large American agglomerations in population and sixth in population density. Table 5-1 indicates the position of San Francisco in the U.S. urban hierarchy.

Population and Housing

As table 5-2 indicates, San Francisco's population declined moderately between 1950 and 1980 and increased by only 7 percent between 1940 and 1980. In contrast, the populations of California and the rest of the Bay Area grew dramatically over the same period. California's population increased by almost 250 percent while the population of the Bay Area (excluding San Francisco) quadrupled. While the share of state population located in the Bay Area declined only slightly during this period (from 25 to 22 percent), San Francisco's share of Bay Area population fell much more precipitously. As

TABLE 5-1
Population Rank of U.S. Cities and Metropolitan Agglomerations, 1980.

Rank	City	Population (thousands)	Agglomeration	Contiguous urban pop. (millions)
1	New York City	7,072	New York City-Northeastern New Jersey-Southern Connecticut	18.0
2	Chicago	3,005	Los Angeles-Long Beach-San Bernardino-Riverside	10.0
3	Los Angeles	2,967	Chicago-Northwest Indiana-Aurora-Elgin-Joliet	7.2
4	Philadelphia	1,688	Philadelphia-Wilmington-Trenton	4.8
5	Houston	1,595	*San Francisco-Oakland-San Jose*	4.4
6	Detroit	1,203	Detroit	3.8
7	Dallas	904	Boston-Brockton-Lowell-Lawrence/Haverhill	3.2
8	San Diego	876	Miami-Fort Lauderdale-Hollywood-West Palm Beach	3.1
9	Phoenix	790	Washington, D.C.	2.8
10	Baltimore	787	Houston-Texas City-Lamarque	2.5
11	San Antonio	786	Cleveland-Akron-Lorain-Elyria	2.5
12	Indianapolis	701	Dallas-Ft. Worth	2.4
13	*San Francisco*	679	St. Louis	1.8

Source: Long and De Are (1983).

TABLE 5-2
Bay Area Population by County, 1940-1980
(thousands).

County	1940	1950	1960	1970	1980	Percent change 1940-1980
Alameda	513	740	908	1,073	1,105	+116 %
Contra Costa	100	299	409	558	656	+553
Marin	53	86	147	206	223	+321
Napa	29	47	66	79	99	+248
San Francisco	635	775	740	716	679	+7
San Mateo	112	236	444	556	587	+425
Santa Clara	175	291	642	1,065	1,295	+640
Solano	49	105	135	170	235	+379
Sonoma	69	103	147	205	300	+334
Bay Area total	1,734	2,681	3,639	4,628	5,180	+199
Bay Area excluding San Francisco	1,100	1,906	2,899	3,913	4,501	+309
California	6,907	10,586	15,717	19,958	23,668	+243

Source: U.S. Census.

indicated in figure 5-3, in 1900 the central city/county contained more than half of the region's population; in 1980 San Francisco had only slightly more than 13 percent of area population. Clearly, San Francisco is no longer the only center of population in the Bay Area, and as a result it can no longer dominate regional politics as it did in years past.

The relative importance of natural population increase and net migration in the growth of the Bay Area varies considerably by region. As indicated in table 5-4, about half of all population growth in the decade 1970-1980 resulted from net migration. In the northern counties, three-quarters of the increased population arose from relocations; in the East Bay, it was less than one-quarter.

San Francisco is one of the most ethnically diverse cities in one of the most ethnically diverse states in the United States. While the U.S. population is over 83 percent white, California's is just 77 percent white and San Francisco is less than 60 percent white. Nearly 22 percent of San Francisco's population is Asian, from dozens of countries; over 12 percent of the population is black; and over 12 percent is Hispanic. For the United States as a whole, in 1980 the

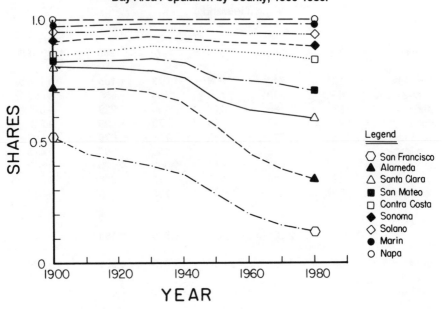

FIGURE 5-3
Bay Area Population by County, 1900-1980.

population was 1.6 percent Asian, 11.7 percent black, and 6.5 percent persons of Spanish origin. In addition, San Francisco has a higher percentage of older residents and persons living below what the federal government designates as the poverty level than does either California as a whole or the United States.[2]

The demographic data for the rest of the Bay Area make a sharp contrast. As noted in table 5-4, the population in the other eight counties of the Bay Area is generally less ethnically diverse, younger, and wealthier. In the eight surrounding counties, almost 80 percent of the population is white, and less than 10 percent of the population is elderly (compared to 15 percent in the central city). The poverty rate is 13.7 percent in the city of San Francisco, yet only 8.4 percent in the rest of the Bay Area.

Table 5-5 provides more information on household size and relative incomes in the Bay Area. The region has somewhat smaller households, on average, than the rest of the state. By any measure, households in the region are prosperous, at least on average. The mixture of household types in the Bay

---

[2] The federal government classed a family of three as poor in 1980 if pretax family income was less than $6,565; the threshold for a family of four was $8,414. The corresponding standards for 1986 were $8,570 and $10,990, respectively.

TABLE 5-3
Natural Increase and Migration as Sources of Bay Area Growth,
1970-1980.

Area/ Year	Population	Change in population	Annual change	Natural increase	Net migration
San Francisco					
1970	715,674				
1980	678,974	-36,700	-0.5%	3,789	-40,489
North Bay[a]					
1970	662,598				
1980	856,654	+194,056	+2.9	42,837	+151,219
East Bay[b]					
1970	1,628,989				
1980	1,761,764	+132,775	+0.8	102,650	+30,125
South Bay[c]					
1970	1,623,022				
1980	1,882,401	+259,379	+1.6	140,507	+118,872

Source: U.S. Census.

[a] "North Bay" includes Marin, Sonoma, Napa, and Solano counties.
[b] "East Bay" includes Alameda and Contra Costa counties.
[c] "South Bay" includes San Mateo and Santa Clara counties.

Area and in San Francisco has changed, particularly since 1970. On the one hand, the number of single-parent, childless married couples and single adult households has increased. By and large, this change amounts to a shift toward household types that have traditionally had lower incomes. On the other hand, the city has become especially attractive to highly educated workers in the business service sector and to homosexuals; in particular, the number of young single males, living alone or in couples, has increased. The economic consequences of this turn largely on the fact that these groups are relatively affluent, have a high labor force participation rate, and have a strong preference for residing in the central city.

Housing in the Bay Area (and in California) has grown dramatically since 1940. As table 5-6 shows, San Francisco's total housing stock grew by only 42 percent since 1940, while the stock of the rest of the region has more than quadrupled. In part as a result of the boom in the semiconductor industry, the

TABLE 5-4
Comparative Bay Area Demographic and Income Characteristics,
1940-1980.

Category	Region	1940	1950	1960	1970	1980
Percent White						
	San Francisco	95.0%	89.5%	90.0%	71.7%	59.2%
	Other counties	96.3	92.6	96.2	89.5	78.6
	California	95.5	93.7	94.4	89.5	77.0
Percent Hispanic						
	San Francisco	--	--	--	14.2	12.4
	Other counties	--	--	--	12.5	12.2
	California	--	--	--	15.5	19.2
Percent Elderly						
	San Francisco	8.2	9.6	12.6	14.0	15.4
	Other counties	8.1	7.6	7.9	7.9	9.5
	California	8.0	8.5	8.8	9.1	10.2
Percent Poor						
	San Francisco	--	--	--	9.9	13.7
	Other counties	--	--	--	6.6	8.4
	California	--	--	--	8.4	11.4
Median Age (years)						
	San Francisco		36.2	37.3	34.5	34.1
	Other counties		31.0	29.4	28.0	30.8
	California		32.1	30.0	28.4	29.9
Median Family Income (thousands of 1980 dollars)						
	San Francisco		$13.4	$18.7	$22.3	$23.7
	Other counties		13.2	20.2	25.4	28.6
	California		12.3	18.7	22.8	24.4

Note: -- Not available.

Due to a change in definition, 1980 "Hispanic" proportions are not strictly comparable to those for earlier years.

Source: U.S. Census.

TABLE 5-5

Selected Income and Poverty Characteristics, 1979.

Region	Average hshld. size	Tot.civ. employed per hshld.	Average. hshld income	Median. hshld income	Per capita income	Poverty rate, persons[1]	Poverty rate, families[2]	Percent high income[3]
United States	2.74	1.21	$20,306	$16,841	$7,400	12.4%	9.6%	1.4%
California	2.67	1.23	22,415	18,243	8,388	11.4	8.7	2.0
Bay Area	2.56	1.28	24,303	--	9,483	--	--	--
Cities								
San Francisco	2.18	1.14	20,551	15,866	9,413	13.7	10.3	1.9
Oakland	2.33	1.00	17,969	13,780	7,720	18.5	16.0	1.1
San Jose	2.96	1.47	24,946	22,886	8,441	8.2	6.3	1.2
Counties								
Alameda[4]	2.52	1.20	21,772	18,700	8,636	11.3	8.7	1.4
Contra Costa	2.69	1.26	26,538	22,870	9,863	7.6	6.1	2.6
Marin	2.43	1.32	30,757	24,554	12,673	7.0	4.9	5.2
Napa	2.54	1.17	22,616	18,887	8,891	8.1	6.0	1.7
San Francisco[5]	2.18	1.14	20,551	15,866	9,413	13.7	10.3	1.9
San Mateo	2.58	1.39	27,640	23,172	10,730	6.1	4.5	3.2
Santa Clara[6]	2.76	1.44	26,588	23,369	9,624	7.1	5.3	2.2
Solano	2.82	1.12	21,104	19,264	7,497	9.4	8.1	0.8
Sonoma	2.55	1.13	20,944	17,732	8,212	9.5	7.1	1.3

Notes: -- Not Available

1 Percent of persons, poverty status determined.
2 Families, 1979 income below poverty level, as a percent of all families.
3 Percentage of households with 1979 income greater than $75,000.

4 Includes Oakland.
5 Coextensive with San Francisco city.
6 Includes San Jose.

Source: U.S. Department of Labor, Employment and Training Administration, unpublished census tabulations, 1980.

housing stock in Santa Clara county, in the South Bay, increased eightfold. Growth in housing in Contra Costa county, in the East Bay, was a close second.

As table 5-7 indicates, the portion of total dwelling units in California occupied by owners peaked around 1960 when the "baby-boom" generation reached home-buying age; despite the ensuing decline in the proportion of owner-occupied units, by 1980 owner occupancy in California was still substantially above the levels of 1940-1950. Though reliable statistics are not available for more recent years, widespread evidence of condominium conversion and the coming of age of the children of the baby-boom generation suggest that owner-occupied units are playing an increasing role in today's housing market.

Housing Conditions

By any comparative standard, Americans are on average well housed, and San Franciscans are no exception. Table 5-8 indicates trends in the level of

TABLE 5-6
Total Year-Round Housing Units, by County, 1940-1980
(thousands).

County	1940	1950	1960	1970	1980	Percent change 1940-1980
Alameda	173.0	247.1	310.3	379.7	444.4	+157 %
Contra Costa	31.3	90.6	124.3	178.3	251.7	+704
Marin	16.5	28.6	49.6	70.6	92.4	+461
Napa	8.8	13.7	21.2	26.8	38.4	+339
San Francisco	222.2	265.7	310.6	310.4	316.4	+42
San Mateo	37.2	76.6	141.8	190.1	232.9	+526
Santa Clara	56.4	91.7	199.9	336.2	473.5	+740
Solano	15.3	33.0	41.9	53.5	84.1	+449
Sonoma	26.8	40.0	59.8	77.2	123.7	+361
Bay Area total	587.5	887.0	1,259.3	1,622.8	2,057.5	+250
Bay Area excluding San Francisco	365.3	621.3	948.7	1,312.4	1,741.1	+377
California	2,340.4	3,590.7	5,465.9	6,976.3	9,220.4	+294

Source: U.S. Census.

TABLE 5-7
Owner-Occupied Housing Units, 1940-1980.

	1940	1950	1960	1970	1980	Percent change 1940-1980
San Francisco						
Owner-occupied units	69,541	97,521	108,696	101,806	106,610	+53.0%
Total dwelling units	222,176	265,726	310,559	310,383	316,351	+42
% Owner occupied	31.3	36.7	35.0	32.8	33.7	+8
Other Bay Area						
Owner-occupied units	186,166	360,685	616,189	786,379	1,041,802	+460
Total dwelling units	365,331	621,324	948,718	1,321,426	1,741,127	+377
% Owner occupied	51.0	58.1	64.9	59.5	59.8	+17
California						
Owner-occupied units	936,149	1,949,728	3,192,068	3,836,944	5,154,215	+451
Total dwelling units	2,340,373	3,590,660	5,465,870	6,976,261	9,220,421	+294
% Owner occupied	40.0	54.3	58.4	55.0	55.9	+40

Source: U.S. Census.

overcrowding of dwellings (defined as units with more than one person per room, kitchen excluded).

During the 40 year period, the level of overcrowding in California has declined by more than 40 percent. In the Bay Area as a whole, less than 5 percent of households live in overcrowded conditions. During this period, the reduction in overcrowding was much less in San Francisco than in any of the other counties. In fact, during the 1960 to 1980 period, the level of overcrowding increased from 6.3 to 7.3 percent in San Francisco. In part, this reflects the living conditions of low-income recent immigrants, especially Southeast Asians. During this same period, utilization of dwellings with substandard sanitary conditions (dwellings lacking toilet, bath, or running water) was virtually eliminated. By 1980, less than 1 percent of Bay Area dwellings outside of San Francisco were substandard on this criterion. In the central city, almost 4 percent of dwellings lack sanitary facilities (or else they are shared), down from 20

TABLE 5-8
Crowded[a] Dwellings, by County, 1940-1980
(in percent).

County	1940	1950	1960	1970	1980	Percent change 1940-1980
Alameda	7.4%	9.3%	8.2%	6.3%	4.7%	-36.1%
Contra Costa	13.1	17.6	9.1	5.5	2.9	-77.9
Marin	4.9	8.9	6.1	3.4	1.7	-65.3
Napa	5.3	8.9	7.4	5.4	3.4	-35.8
San Francisco	7.8	7.7	6.3	6.8	7.3	-6.4
San Mateo	7.3	6.2	6.2	4.9	5.1	-30.1
Santa Clara	11.0	12.3	9.0	6.4	5.3	-51.8
Solano	11.7	11.7	10.6	7.3	4.5	-61.5
Sonoma	8.4	9.9	8.9	6.5	3.3	-60.7
Bay Area total	8.2	9.8	7.7	6.1	4.8	-41.6
Bay Area excluding San Francisco	8.5	10.7	8.2	5.9	4.4	-48.8
California	12.9	12.3	9.5	7.7	7.4	-42.6

[a] "Crowded" is defined as dwellings with 1.01 or more persons per room, excluding kitchen.

Source: U.S. Census.

percent in 1940 (see table 5-9). Table 5-10 reports similar changes in the fraction of dwellings lacking heat. By 1980, virtually all dwellings in the Bay Area had heat, even though the rather mild climatic conditions make a deficiency in heating less significant here than elsewhere.

One further measure of the quality, or at least the character, of the housing stock may be its age. Limited information is available on the year of construction of owner-occupied housing. More than half of the owner-occupied dwellings in San Francisco were built before 1939. For other parts of the region, the stock is much newer, with less than 15 percent dating from before World War II (see table 5-11).

Housing Adequacy

Not surprisingly, given the free market orientation of the U.S. housing market, most of the substandard and low-quality dwellings noted above are also

TABLE 5-9
Occupied Dwellings Lacking Complete Plumbing for Exclusive Use,
by County, 1940-1980
(in percent).

County	1940	1950	1960	1970	1980	Percent change 1940-1980
Alameda	14.5%	7.8%	5.3%	1.9%	1.2%	-91.7%
Contra Costa	17.6	6.7	4.3	0.9	0.5	-97.2
Marin	13.7	4.9	3.7	0.8	0.8	-94.2
Napa	20.9	8.6	7.1	0.8	0.6	-97.1
San Francisco	19.6	8.9	13.2	6.4	3.8	-80.6
San Mateo	10.2	2.5	1.7	0.8	0.9	-91.1
Santa Clara	18.0	10.6	4.4	0.8	0.9	-95.0
Solano	20.8	7.5	6.2	0.8	0.6	-97.1
Sonoma	23.8	10.5	8.0	1.1	0.8	-96.6
Bay Area total	17.3	7.9	6.7	2.2	1.3	-92.3
Bay Area excluding San Francisco	15.9	7.4	4.6	1.1	0.9	-94.4
California	22.0	14.1	6.8	1.5	1.2	-94.5

Source: U.S. Census.

TABLE 5-10
Dwellings Lacking Heat, by County, 1950-1980
(in percent).

County	1950	1960	1970	1980	Percent change 1940-1980
Alameda	1.6%	1.2%	0.4%	0.3%	-81.3%
Contra Costa	1.3	0.6	0.1	0.2	-84.6
Marin	0.9	1.0	0.1	0.2	-77.8
Napa	0.6	1.1	0.3	0.2	-66.7
San Francisco	4.8	5.3	2.4	1.1	-77.1
San Mateo	0.8	0.5	0.2	0.2	-75.0
Santa Clara	1.8	1.0	0.2	0.2	-88.9
Solano	0.8	0.9	0.1	0.2	-75.0
Sonoma	1.0	12.6	0.5	0.4	-60.0
Bay Area Total	2.4	2.1	0.7	0.4	-83.3
Bay Area excluding San Francisco	1.3	1.0	0.2	0.2	-84.6
California	1.7	2.1	0.9	0.9	-47.1

Source: U.S. Census.

the least expensive and occupied by the lowest income households. But as table 5-12 indicates, this does not mean that the incidence of substandard housing is particularly high, even among the poor. A similar impression is gained from data on overcrowding.

Housing Affordability

Housing in the Bay Area is among the most expensive in the United States. Though this is no doubt due in part to quality differences, serious problems of housing affordability have arisen and will continue to affect the welfare of Bay Area residents.

Table 5-13 summarizes median gross rents and housing values for San Francisco and for the remainder of the Bay Area. Table 5-14 reports housing expenditures for renters, as a fraction of income, as reported by the 1980 U.S. census. These rent-to-income figures are high by international standards and are also well above the U.S. average. About 55 percent of San Francisco renters

TABLE 5-11
Vintage of Owner-Occupied Housing Stock, 1980
(in percent).

Area	Before 1939	1940-49	1950-59	1960-69	1970-74	1975-80
San Francisco						
CC	58.2%	22.0%	12.0%	5.2%	1.1%	1.5%
MSA	23.5	16.4	24.8	19.6	7.3	8.3
San Jose						
CC	6.6	4.4	17.1	34.8	19.3	17.8
MSA	7.2	7.4	28.1	30.5	13.0	13.7
Santa Rosa						
CC	9.8	10.2	16.0	26.2	15.7	22.1
MSA	12.9	10.1	16.8	24.3	15.9	20.0
Napa						
CC	11.6	12.5	24.5	23.2	15.6	12.6
MSA	10.1	10.9	21.2	20.0	13.2	24.7

CC = Central City.

MSA = Metropolitan Statistical Area. The San Francisco-Oakland MSA includes
Marin, San Francisco, San Mateo, Alameda,and Contra Costa Counties. The
San Jose MSA includes only Santa Clara County. The Santa Rosa MSA
includes Sonoma County. The Vallejo-Fairfield-Napa MSA includes Napa
and Solano counties.

Source: U.S. Census.

spend more than one-quarter of their incomes on rent; one-third of San Francisco renters pay rents that are above 35 percent of their incomes.

The percentage increase in San Francisco's median gross rent exceeded the increase in median income (both in constant dollars) in every decade since 1950. The same has been true for median housing prices since 1960. Most notably, however, in the 1970s the inflation-adjusted median house value in San Francisco rose by 75 percent while gross rents, population, and median incomes fell (see table 5-15).

TABLE 5-12

Apartments Lacking Complete Plumbing, by Income Class of Residents, 1980
(in percent).

	1979 Household Income ($)									All renting
	<5000	5000-9999	10,000-12,499	12,500-14,999	15,000-19,999	20,000-24,999	25,000-34,999	35,000-49,999	50,000+	households
San Francisco										
CC	12.13%	6.72%	3.52%	2.85%	2.46%	2.17%	1.44%	1.44%	0.96%	5.08%
MSA	6.73	3.61	2.19	1.85	1.52	1.59	1.07	0.97	0.92	2.85
San Jose										
CC	3.27	1.58	2.06	1.57	1.63	1.06	0.82	1.51	0.80	1.70
MSA	3.19	1.71	1.83	1.46	1.55	1.18	0.87	0.70	0.51	1.56
Santa Rosa										
CC	2.18	0.25	0.51	1.73	0.29	0.00	0.00	0.00	0.00	0.71
MSA	3.18	1.10	1.44	1.11	0.63	0.50	0.58	1.08	1.13	1.32
Napa										
CC	2.07	1.50	0.00	1.48	0.97	0.00	0.00	0.00	0.00	0.95
MSA	2.05	1.51	0.91	0.61	0.77	0.13	0.39	0.00	0.00	1.03

CC = Central City.

MSA = Metropolitan Statistical Area. The San Francisco-Oakland MSA includes Marin, San Francisco, San Mateo, Alameda, and Contra Costa Counties. The San Jose MSA includes only Santa Clara County. The Santa Rosa MSA includes Sonoma County. The Vallejo-Fairfield-Napa MSA includes Napa and Solano Counties.

Source: U.S. Census.

TABLE 5-13

Bay Area Rents and Housing Values, by County, 1940-1980
(Median gross monthly rents in 1980 dollars[a]).

County	1940	1950	1960	1970	1980	% change 1940-1980
Alameda	$160	$147	$217	$278	$266	+66
Contra Costa	131	116	214	289	294	+124
Marin	157	161	270	365	373	+138
Napa	123	130	198	253	281	+128
San Francisco	176	144	203	286	285	+62
San Mateo	176	192	298	354	336	+91
Santa Clara	135	147	262	333	334	+147
Solano	153	130	203	259	246	+61
Sonoma	112	140	206	257	289	+159
Bay Area total	163	144	223	300	299	+84
Bay Area excluding San Francisco	151	145	235	305	304	+101
California	159	144	220	267	283	+78

Median Value of Owner-Occupied One-Family Dwellings
(in 1980 dollars[a]).

County	1940	1950	1960	1970	1980	% change 1940-1980
Alameda	$24,500	$37,100	$41,700	$50,300	$ 85,300	+248 %
Contra Costa	20,400	33,100	40,600	54,700	94,600	+364
Marin	25,300	42,300	56,200	71,800	151,000	+497
Napa	18,200	28,100	35,600	45,400	78,200	+329
San Franicsco	29,200	40,800	48,100	59,800	104,600	+258
San Mateo	28,800	42,900	51,200	64,700	124,400	+332
Santa Clara	21,200	36,400	47,600	58,000	109,400	+415
Solano	20,500	29,900	34,500	39,800	67,500	+230
Sonoma	16,900	28,700	37,300	44,800	88,400	+423
Bay Area total	24,800	37,400	45,100	56,000	101,600	+309
Bay Area excluding San Francisco	23,200	36,500	44,500	55,500	101,200	+336
California	19,700	32,700	42,000	49,000	84,700	+329

[a] Consumer Price Index used to convert values to 1980 dollars.
Source: U.S. Census.

TABLE 5-14

Average Ratio of Gross Rent to Income, by Income Class, 1980
(in percent).

	<5000	5000-9999	10,000-12,499	12,500-14,999	15,000-19,999	20,000-24,999	25,000-34,999	35,000-49,999	50,000+	All renting households
					1979 Household Income ($)					
San Francisco										
CC	50.8%	40.9%	31.5%	26.8%	22.5%	18.0%	14.4%	10.8%	7.6%	30.1%
MSA	52.3	42.0	32.0	27.2	22.5	18.3	14.6	11.1	7.8	30.1
San Jose										
CC	54.5	45.2	34.9	29.0	24.5	20.3	15.8	12.5	8.1	31.1
MSA	54.9	46.2	35.1	29.7	24.5	20.2	15.7	12.0	8.0	29.7
Santa Rosa										
CC	54.3	44.6	32.9	28.1	23.4	18.3	15.1	10.0	7.5	33.1
MSA	53.3	43.1	32.0	27.2	22.8	18.1	14.5	10.4	7.7	32.0
Napa										
CC	53.1	42.8	32.7	27.2	22.5	17.6	14.9	11.3	7.5	31.4
MSA	52.8	38.5	28.4	24.1	20.1	15.8	13.0	9.4	7.5	29.4

CC = Central City.

MSA = Metropolitan Statistical Area. The San Francisco-Oakland MSA includes Marin, San Francisco, San Mateo, Alameda, and Contra Costa Counties. The San Jose MSA includes only Santa Clara County. The Santa Rosa MSA includes Sonoma County. The Vallejo-Fairfield-Napa MSA includes Napa and Solano Counties.

Source: U.S. Census.

TABLE 5-15

Population, Housing Value, Rent, and Income in Bay Area,1940-1980
(in 1980 dollars, where applicable).

Region		1940	1950	1960	1970	1980
San Francisco						
(Number)	Population	634,635	775,357	740,316	715,674	678,974
(Median values)	Family income	$29,187	$13,428	$18,689	$22,271	$20,911
	Housing value	--	$40,826	$48,136	$59,769	$104,600
	Gross rent	$176	$144	$203	$286	$285
Other counties						
(Number)	Population	1,099,772	1,905,965	2,898,623	3,912,525	4,500,810
(Median values)	Family income	$23,209	$13,213	$19,961	$25,422	$25,221
	Housing value	--	$36,509	$44,514	$55,471	$101,243
	Gross rent	$151	$145	$235	$305	$304

		1940-1950	1950-1960	1960-1970	1970-1980
San Francisco					
(% change)	Population	22.2%	-4.5%	-3.3%	-5.1%
	Family income	--	39.2	19.2	-6.1
	Housing value	39.9	17.9	24.2	75.0
	Gross rent	-18.2	41.0	40.9	-0.3
Other counties					
(% change)	Population	73.3%	52.1%	35.0%	15.0%
	Family income	--	51.1	27.4	-0.8
	Housing value	57.3	21.9	24.6	82.5
	Gross rent	-4.0	62.1	29.8	-0.3

Note: The change in housing cost is understated since housing prices are included in the Consumer Price Index, which is used to convert values to 1980 dollars. The growth in gross rent for much of the Bay Area is understated after 1960 due to housing rent controls in effect in Berkeley, San Francisco, Oakland, and six other Bay Area localities.

FEDERAL AND STATE HOUSING POLICY

General Overview

The United States does not have a national housing policy in the comprehensive sense in which the term is typically used in Europe. Most federal and state housing policies operate through tax and capital markets to increase the demand for housing or the supply of capital to the housing sector. At the same time, the regulation of public health, safety, and welfare is undertaken by the 50 states and by the many counties, cities, and towns within them. These public health, safety, and welfare regulations may include the establishment of standards for construction and maintenance of dwellings and even the regulation of rents. Local governments are empowered to regulate existing housing and the conditions under which new housing is constructed. Even when new housing construction is funded directly by higher levels of government, it is carried out at the local level. The important aspect is that while many levels and agencies of government participate in the process that leads to the provision of housing, unlike the circumstances in many other countries, no agency in the United States has comprehensive responsibility for the growth of the housing supply. While local governments are nominally created by the states (and are not, in fact, acknowledged in the U.S. Constitution), in most states the rights of local government to housing regulation are entrenched in constitution, custom, and popular sentiment and thus are challenged only at substantial political peril.

The conflict between local government activities and the broader objectives of housing policy is readily illustrated by developments in the Bay Area. In this section, the attempts of federal and state governments to increase the supply of housing are discussed in four general categories. The first includes direct housing assistance and direct government subsidies for housing. The second is the relationship between housing policy and the various systems of taxation at the federal, state, and local levels. The third section discusses mortgage insurance, credit guarantees, and credit institutions, while the final section involves secondary market operations.

Direct Expenditures

Direct Federal Housing Assistance

Direct federal government subsidies for housing in the United States are restricted to low-income households-- generally to households with incomes that are less than half of the median income of a local area. The costs of these programs have been substantial, but the fraction of eligible households served by direct housing assistance is relatively low. Such programs are not "categorical"-- that is, they do not serve all households meeting their eligibility criteria-- but are rather "selective." Households who are eligible under the income guidelines of housing programs may apply for assistance; if there are sufficient units, these households are served by these programs. It is estimated that in the early 1980s, about one out of every eight low-income households who would qualify for assistance on the basis of their incomes actually received direct housing assistance from the federal government. Although there are a variety of direct housing subsidy programs currently in force in the United States, the two principal programs are the Public Housing Program, authorized by the Public Housing Act of 1937,and the Low Income Rental Assistance Program operated under Section 8 of the U.S. Housing Act of 1974.[3]

Public Housing

Subsidies are provided for public housing by a federal government cabinet ministry, the Department of Housing and Urban Development (HUD). Under the Public Housing Act, each community may decide for itself whether public housing is to be built. If public housing is needed in a local community, then the local government forms a Local Housing Authority (LHA), a distinct legal entity. The housing authority takes responsibility for designing, developing, owning, operating, and maintaining the public housing facilities, in addition to determining need, selecting sites, and planning and managing the housing project.

The LHA may apply to the federal government for various kinds of assistance. The most important form of assistance from the federal government comes in the form of an "annual contributions contract." Under this contract, the federal government agrees to pay the interest and the amortization of 40-year bonds issued by the local planning authority for the entire construction of a designated public housing project. While an additional form of assistance, annual federal appropriations for operating and maintenance expenditures, was introduced in the early 1970s, the annual contributions contract remains the principal form of assistance for public housing. In practice, this means that the federal government is willing to bear all the capital costs of construction and only a small fraction of the operating costs. This form of subsidy encourages local authorities to reduce maintenance expenditures through overdesign, a consequence that is often reflected in the physical appearance of projects. In recent years LHAs have been encouraged to lease housing units under long-term contracts from private landlords rather than to construct facilities themselves.

---

[3] It should be noted that a substantial amount of general welfare assistance (income support) is spent by recipients on housing, though it is omitted from this discussion of specific housing programs.

In return for these federal subsidies, the local planning authority must agree to accept residents in low-income public housing under guidelines issued by the federal government. These guidelines specify that at the time of admission, tenant incomes must be quite low. Until recently, they also specified that the local planning authority could not charge more than 25 percent of a household's income for rent. As a consequence of the low rents charged (currently no more than 30 percent of tenants' incomes), public housing provides a substantial subsidy to those eligible households who are fortunate enough to be housed. The equity of this subsidy is questionable, however, since it is currently estimated that only about 10 percent of U.S. households eligible on income terms are actually served by low-rent public housing.

Section 8

The so-called "Section 8" program has higher income limits than the public housing program, but it still serves poor households.[4] In contrast to the public housing program, the dwelling units provided under Section 8 are all owned and managed privately, not by housing authorities. Housing is supplied by private, profit-motivated owners, and by nonprofit or cooperative organizations. Under this program, the owners enter into long-term agreements with the U.S. Department of Housing and Urban Development. HUD agrees to pay the so-called "fair market rent" of the dwelling (certified by local surveys of market rents in the area) over an extended period of time. The owner agrees to accept low-income tenants under federal guidelines. Households participating in the program pay 30 percent of their income towards rent, and the federal government makes up the difference between this contribution and the "fair market rent" for similar dwellings in the local market.

When originally introduced in 1974, the program emphasized construction of new facilities for occupancy by eligible households. Later in the decade, the focus of the program was changed to encourage the "substantial rehabilitation" of dwellings for occupancy by low-income households. This emphasis has continued throughout the 1980s.

Although government payments under the Section 8 program are made to landlords, the legislation incorporates many of the features of housing allowances in other countries. A principal difference remains, however: the Section 8 program is not an entitlement program for all low-income households. It is a program providing valuable housing benefits to a small fraction of eligible households.

---

[4] Although most families participating in the program have incomes which do not exceed 50 percent of the median income of the area, some fraction of the dwelling units provided under the Section 8 program may be rented to households whose incomes are between 50 and 80 percent of the median income.

Direct State Housing Assistance

U.S. states differ substantially in their activism with respect to housing policy and in the distribution of responsibilities between state and local governments. In California, direct expenditures specifically on housing or rent subsidies by the state or local government are quite small. The state does administer over a dozen loan programs that aid various segments of the population. In 1981, 135,000 households were served by state loan programs. Currently, the state has about $3.2 billion in outstanding loans; loans to war veterans account for nearly 80 percent of the total.

Local Housing Authorities

The 100 local housing authorities (LHAs) in California are authorized by the Health and Safety Code to provide housing for "persons or families who lack the amount of income necessary...to enable them to live in decent, safe and sanitary dwellings." Housing authorities receive financial assistance from public or private sources, and they prepare, acquire, lease, and operate housing projects on a nonprofit basis. They provide for the construction or reparation of housing projects and acquire property for constructing low-income housing. They also issue revenue bonds to finance rehabilitation, and operate leased housing, temporary housing, and farmworker housing.

California's LHAs primarily operate Federal programs such as public housing and Section 8 housing assistance programs, discussed above. In addition, state-sponsored programs, such as those for migrants, are operated by local housing authorities as well. In California, a local election is required before a housing authority can develop, construct, or acquire a low-rent housing project.

Local housing authorities in California serve an ethnically diverse population. The largest ethnic group served is white (38 percent), followed by black (32 percent), and Hispanic (24 percent). Thirty-nine percent of the households served are elderly, and about 1 in 12 units were occupied by disabled persons. Most of the units under LHA management are one- or two-bedroom units (70.6 percent), while less than one-fourth are 3 or more bedroom units. The remaining 5 percent are one-room units.

As table 5-16 illustrates, the growth of Section 8 units since the mid-1970s has been substantial, while conventional public housing assistance has grown only modestly. Over time, the share of publicly provided low-income housing in all housing has grown, but such units still amount to less than 2% of the total stock.

Table 5-17 summarizes the distribution of programs under LHA control in the nine Bay Area counties as of 1983. Most county programs reflect the statewide dominance of Section 8 LHA units over conventional public hous-

TABLE 5-16
California Trends in Major Locally Administered Programs, 1969-1983
(thousands of units).

Program	1969	1972	1976	1978	1980	1983
Conventional	30.9	33.4	35.1	35.5	36.8	38.6
Section 23[a]	10.3	28.5	31.6	21.8	9.5	1.1
Section 8	---	---	21.2	70.2	98.6	120.4
Total	41.2	61.8	87.8	127.5	144.8	160.1
Estimated total California dwelling units	7,711.5	8,139.0	8,709.0	8,994.0	9,279.0	9,633.2
LHA housing as % of all units	0.5%	0.8%	1.0%	1.4%	1.6%	1.7%

Notes: --- Not existing.

[a]The Housing and Community Development Act of 1974 created the Section 8 program and began phasing out the Section 23 program.

Sources: *California Housing Authorities: Summary of 1983 Activities*, California Department of Housing and Community Development, Tables 5-4 and 5-7; and California Housing Finance Agency.

ing; however, nearly 75 percent of San Francisco's LHA units are funded by public housing expenditures, while fewer than one-fourth are financed by Section 8 monies. Most striking, however, is that fewer than 44,000 Bay Area units are financed directly through LHAs by federal and state programs, compared with over 2 million year-round units in the Bay Area. Thus, like the rest of the state, less than 2 percent of all Bay Area households receive direct federal or state assistance.

Taxation and Housing Policy

By far the largest subsidies to housing from both the federal and state governments in the United States arise indirectly through the operation of the federal and state income tax systems. These subsidies arise from the tax treatment of owner-occupied housing and the special regulations that cover the expenses associated with investment in rental housing.

TABLE 5-17
Units Under Local Housing Authority Management, by Type of
Government Program, 1983.

County	Section 8	Conventional public housing	Other[a]	Total LHA managed	Total dwellings (1980)
Alameda	9,359	3,751	305	13,415	444,422
Contra Costa	4,703	1,882	105	6,690	251,721
Marin	921	500	49	1,470	92,357
Napa	533	0	11	544	38,405
San Francisco	2,208	6,933	145	9,286	316,351
San Mateo	2,515	230	97	2,842	232,917
Santa Clara	5,808	275	175	6,258	473,523
Solano	1,698	75	205	1,978	84,073
Sonoma	817	0	46	863	123,709
Bay Area total	28,562	13,646	1,138	43,346	2,057,478
California total	120,394	38,636	10,576	169,606	9,220,421

Note: [a]"Other" includes Section 23 (now terminated), FMHA 514/516, State Migrant, Aftercare, and all other programs.

Sources: *California Housing Authorities: Summary of 1983 Activities,* California Department of Housing and Community Development, September 1986, Appendix, pp. 13-17; and U.S. Census.

Federal Tax Expenditures

Under the federal Internal Revenue Code (IRC), an investment in owner-occupied housing is treated differently from an investment in other assets in the calculation of the personal income tax liabilities of individuals. If one owns rental property, the net income earned[5] is taxable at the household's marginal tax rate.[6] If, instead of renting property, the household "rents to itself," the

---

[5] Net rental income is the gross rent earned by the property minus expenditures on maintenance and depreciation, interest payments, and taxes paid on that property.

[6] Until the Tax Reform Act of 1986, the highest federal marginal tax rate was 50 percent; this marginal tax rate will be reduced under the Act to a high of 31 percent .

implicit rent need not be reported as income, but the household can still deduct interest and tax payments as personal expenses. This difference in the treatment of otherwise similar transactions is substantial. The tax subsidy increases with income, since both home values and marginal tax rates increase as households become better off. The regressivity of the subsidy is enhanced by the fact that it is only available to homeowners, since in the United States homeowners are generally wealthier than renters. The cost of this subsidy of homeownership to the federal government is quite large; it increased from about $31 billion in 1981 to $83 billion in 1986 and exceeded $100 billion in 1990 (see Congressional Budget Office, 1981).

In addition to the provisions associated with net rental income, several other aspects of the tax code subsidize owner occupancy. Capital gains on housing can be deferred with the purchase of another dwelling, and at age 55 households qualify for a one-time exclusion of $125,000 in capital gains from owner-occupied housing. This means that, for all practical purposes, capital gains on owner-occupied housing escape taxation. In addition, there are provisions, discussed below, which permit agencies of state and local governments to issue tax-exempt bonds whose revenues are ultimately used to subsidize owner-occupied housing.

While renters receive no direct concessions in the federal tax code, owners of rental properties do. It has long been possible for landlords to depreciate the value of investment in rental properties much more rapidly for tax purposes than the rate at which true economic depreciation occurs. When this is done, properties often show negative profits for tax purposes at the same time cash flow-- that is rents minus expenses other than depreciation-- is positive. These "losses" can then be used to offset taxes that would otherwise be levied on other income. Until the 1986 reform of the federal tax laws, an investor could often deduct for tax purposes losses from investment that exceed the amount the investor actually had "at risk" in an investment activity.

The Tax Reform Act of 1986 changed these regulations, increasing the period for which investments in real property may be depreciated for tax purposes and reducing deductions to the amount which an investor actually has at risk. Nevertheless, it is still true that the depreciation schedules for real property investment are considerably shorter than the expected economic life of the investment. The value of this subsidy is substantial. While it initially accrues to the owners of the investment property, in a competitive market some fraction of the subsidy is passed on to the renters of those properties.

State and Local Tax Expenditures

In California, the state personal income tax accounts for over 40 percent of the total state taxes collected. In 1984, the personal income tax yielded $11.1 billion (from 11.6 million personal income tax returns), while $9.8 billion was raised through retail sales and use taxes; banks and corporations paid $3.8 billion. Local governments in California are financed largely by ad valorem taxes on real property, including owner-occupied and rental housing. Property tax revenues account for 40 percent of the own-source revenue of local governments in the state. The importance of income and property taxes for state and local government means that tax policy and housing policy are inextricably linked.

California follows the federal law in the tax treatment of owner-occupied housing; the net income from owner occupancy is not recorded, but interest payments are deductible from income. In 1984, $20.9 billion was subtracted from personal income tax returns using this deduction alone. Predictably, most of the benefits of the deduction accrue to higher-income households for whom the tax deduction is the most valuable; nearly three-fourths of the deductions were made by households with an adjusted gross income (AGI) of over $30,000, one-third by those with AGIs over $55,000, and 12.5 percent ($2.6 billion) to those with AGIs in excess of $90,000. For those with AGIs over $1 million in 1984, the average deduction was over $37,000, while those making between $29,000 and $30,000 annually (roughly the median state income) received an average mortgage interest deduction of $4,600.

In order to compensate renters who do not qualify for mortgage interest deductions, a renter's tax credit[7] is allowed in California. In 1984, the renter's credit amounted to $474 million for 4.8 million persons, or about $100 per claimant. These benefits accrue directly to middle- and low-income renters.

The state government provides property tax relief to households both through the income tax and by manipulating the operation of the property tax. Senior citizens, the disabled, and low-income homeowners are reimbursed for a fraction of the property taxes they pay on personal residences. The amount reimbursed varies with income and ranges between 4 and 96 percent of total taxes paid. Each renter is assumed to pay $250 per year in property taxes; tax relief is based on income. Totally disabled veterans and totally blind persons are exempted from property tax obligations. The first $7,000 in home value is exempted from property taxation for all homeowners; local governments are compensated directly for this loss by the state. Table 5-18 reports the direct payments made by the state to Bay Area households under this program.

Taken together, these tax adjustments constitute by far the most expensive housing policies of the state. Table 5-19 summarizes the value of housing-related tax expenditures in 1981. In that year, the mortgage interest deduction

---

7 A "credit" is subtracted directly from personal tax liability, while a "deduction" is subtracted from income before computing taxes. Thus, the numbers that follow concerning the renter's credit do not compare directly with those of the mortgage interest deduction since the former is a direct benefit and does not depend on one's income.

TABLE 5-18
California Franchise Tax Board
Homeowner and Renter Property Tax Assistance, 1985.

Homeowners

County	Number of claimants	Amount of assistance	Average assistance
Alameda	3,582	$369,369	$103
Contra Costa	2,075	192,039	93
Marin	393	47,420	121
Napa	290	25,436	88
San Francisco	2,105	220,160	105
San Mateo	1,572	176,120	112
Santa Clara	2,511	261,291	104
Solano	508	40,277	79
Sonoma	1,011	91,238	90
Bay Area total	14,047	1,423,350	101
California total	68,985	6,206,936	90

Renters

County	Number of claimants	Amount of assistance	Average assistance
Alameda	10,272	$1,320,337	$129
Contra Costa	4,652	588,198	126
Marin	753	92,007	122
Napa	814	88,442	109
San Francisco	14,373	1,825,609	127
San Mateo	2,501	299,971	120
Santa Clara	6,353	774,611	122
Solano	1,991	245,314	123
Sonoma	2,525	295,060	117
Bay Area total	44,234	5,529,549	125
California total	224,883	28,274,851	126

Source: California Franchise Tax Board, *1985 Annual Report*, pp. 90, 95.

alone cost the state $825 million; permitting taxpayers to deduct property taxes from income before calculating state tax liability cost $160 million; compensation of local governments through the homeowner assessment exemption cost $334 million, and so on. In sum, housing-related state tax expenditures totaled

$1.86 billion in1981. Estimated total federal tax expenditures in California during the same year were $4.26 billion, more than twice the state cost.

Tax Exemptions: Mortgage Revenue Bonds and the California Housing Finance Agency

Tax subsidies to selected home buyers are available through state mortgage revenue bond (MRB) programs, used by over a half-million U.S. households since 1982. Interest paid to holders of these bonds is exempt from federal and most state (including California) taxes, and thus the bonds can be sold to investors at lower interest rates. The bonds, authorized by the U.S. Revenue and Expenditure Control Act of 1968, may be used for acquiring residential property (and a variety of other private pursuits), and considerable controversy

TABLE 5-19

Summary of California Housing-Related Tax Expenditures,[a] 1981.

Tax expenditures of the federal government in California	Public cost (millions of 1981 dollars)
Mortgage interest deduction	$3,505
Real property tax deduction	680
Energy-related tax credits	53
CHFA mortgage revenue bonds	23
Total	$4,261

Tax expenditures of the California state government	
Mortgage interest deduction	$825
Real property tax deduction	160
Real property tax exemption	334
Renters income tax credit	407
Property tax credit for elderly, disabled owners	19
Tax credit for elderly, disabled renters	48
Property tax postponement for elderly owners	2
Property tax exemption for disabled veterans	1
Energy-related tax credits	58
CHFA mortgage revenue bonds	5
Total	$1,859

Note: [a] Foregone government revenues.

Source: Furry (1983).

has surrounded the unrestricted use of private-purpose bonds by state and local governments (see Durning, 1986).

In California, state MRBs are issued by the California Housing Finance Agency (CHFA), created in 1975 to assist in providing affordable housing to low- and moderate-income persons and families. The agency passes the savings from below-market interest rates on to home buyers and rental tenants.

The CHFA is a self-supporting state agency, relying on the spread between CHFA loan interest rates and the tax-free bond interest rates to cover its administrative expenses. Direct tax dollars are not used, and the subsidy arises from income taxes foregone. The value of MRB loans to prospective home buyers, however, can be substantial.[8]

Figure 5-4 shows the growth of lending activity sponsored by the CHFA since 1976. The Agency has financed nearly 35,000 units and has assets in excess of $2.8 billion. In 1981, the total cost of California's CHFA Mortgage Revenue Bonds was $22.6 million to the federal government and $4.8 million to the state. The difference reflects higher federal marginal tax rates (see table 5-19).[9]

To ensure that mortgage money is channeled to low-income residents, the State of California has required that any multi-family project financed with tax-exempt bond proceeds set aside 10 percent of the units for very low-income tenants (those with incomes less than 50 percent of the county median income) and another 10 percent for households which are slightly better off (less than 80 percent of the median county income).[10] Many of the low-income tenants in these projects pay part of their rent with the aid of the federal Section 8 program, discussed above. Almost 80 percent of units in completed projects (currently 9,661 rent-assisted or regulated units in 158 developments) for which permanent financing has been approved by CHFA are occupied by elderly persons or families with very low incomes.

CHFA's single-family programs operate under less restrictive distribu-

---

[8] The average mortgage amount of a CHFA loan is roughly $75,000. When market interest rates were 10.5 percent, the monthly payment for a 30-year mortgage was $686. At this time, a CHFA bond issue made mortgages available at an interest rate of about 8.5 percent or monthly payments of $577, a savings of $109 per month to the recipient.

[9] It should be noted that local mortgage revenue bond activity has far out-stripped that of the state. Between 1976 and 1983, local governments issued $7.4 billion in tax-exempt bonds, over 80 percent of all such sales during that time. The legislation permitting local governments (which includes local housing authorities and redevelopment agencies) to issue mortgage revenue bonds imposes a ceiling on the total amount of bonds that can be sold in any one year (Wong, 1986).

[10] Federal law had required only a 20 percent set aside for low- income tenants. In any case, the remaining 80 percent of the units may be rented to tenants at market rates (California Housing Finance Agency, 1986a, p. 15).

FIGURE 5-4

CHFA Cumulative Lending Data, 1975-1986.

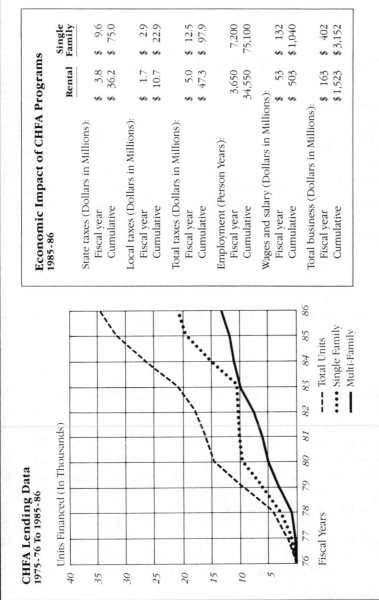

CHFA Lending Data
1975-76 To 1985-86

Units Financed (In Thousands)

Fiscal Years

- - - Total Units
••••• Single Family
——— Multi-Family

Economic Impact of CHFA Programs
1985-86

	Rental	Single Family
State taxes (Dollars in Millions):		
Fiscal year	$ 3.8	$ 9.6
Cumulative	$ 36.2	$ 75.0
Local taxes (Dollars in Millions):		
Fiscal year	$ 1.7	$ 2.9
Cumulative	$ 10.7	$ 22.9
Total taxes (Dollars in Millions):		
Fiscal year	$ 5.0	$ 12.5
Cumulative	$ 47.3	$ 97.9
Employment (Person Years):		
Fiscal year	3,650	7,200
Cumulative	34,550	75,100
Wages and salary (Dollars in Millions):		
Fiscal year	$ 53	$ 132
Cumulative	$ 503	$1,040
Total business (Dollars in Millions):		
Fiscal year	$ 163	$ 402
Cumulative	$1,523	$3,152

TABLE 5-20
California Housing Finance Agency Lending Activity;
Cumulative Loans by Type: June 30, 1986.

Loan amount (thousands of 1986 dollars)

County	Multifamily rental	Single-family	Total
Alameda	$45,241	$67,742	$112,982
Contra Costa	21,173	77,839	99,012
Marin	0	3,209	3,209
Napa	4,802	2,793	7,595
San Francisco	38,919	18,197	57,116
San Mateo	9,867	11,536	21,403
Santa Clara	16,797	74,957	91,753
Solano	17,894	25,260	43,154
Sonoma	9,399	37,249	46,648
Bay Area total	164,092	318,782	482,872
California	555,078	1,205,596	1,760,674

Note: Figures may not sum to total due to rounding.

Source: California Housing Finance Agency, *1985-86 Annual Report Supplement*,
         Table II, pp. 3-4.

tional rules. Of the more than 10,000 units financed by CHFA's Home Mortgage and Ownership Program, 82 percent of the mortgages were made to households earning $25,000 annually or more, and nearly one-fourth to those earning in excess of $35,000. In contrast, less than 1 percent of CHFA single-family mortgages were channeled to persons earning $15,000 or less. The sales price of most houses (64 percent) was between $60,000 and $90,000, but about 6 percent of CHFA-financed houses cost more than $110,000 (California Housing Finance Agency,1986b, p. 27).[11]

Table 5-20 shows the CHFA's cumulative lending activity for each Bay Area county for multifamily rental housing and single-family housing. More than one-fourth (27.4 percent) of all CHFA loans go to Bay Area residents.

Though the magnitude of the effect is as yet unclear, the U.S. Tax Reform

[11] Since figures reported are summaries for a number of years and are not adjusted for inflation, housing prices are actually more expensive (in current dollars) than indicated, and state-financed mortgages are channelled to households with higher incomes than shown. The extent of the bias is unknown.

Act of 1986 has most surely curtailed the use of mortgage revenue bonds, particularly for multifamily dwellings. The tax revision includes several provisions related to MRBs, for example, a limitation on the volume of bonds issued by each state. This limitation will substantially reduce MRB activity in California.

Proposition 13

The rapid increase in property values during the 1970s (see table 5-13) interacted with the system of property taxes and the efficient tax collection mechanisms in the state to produce a crisis. As real capital values rose substantially, tax bills increased dramatically even though tax rates remained relatively constant. Citizens came to resent the taxation of unrealized capital gains; the result was Proposition 13.

The California state constitution allows citizens to pass laws directly and to amend the constitution through a process of petition gathering and popular vote. Proposition 13 was one of a series of citizen-initiated measures intended to reduce tax bills. The initiative received an overwhelming majority of votes in the 1978 general election amidst a tide of resentment over big government, inflated property values, and correspondingly high property taxes. Proposition 13 restricted both property tax rates and the growth of the property tax base in the state. Property taxes were limited by the initiative to 1 percent of assessed value. Growth of the base was restricted by a shift from annual assessment of all properties, based on estimated market value, to a system in which assessments are restored to market value only on transfer of ownership. Until transfer occurs, assessments may increase by at most 2 percent per year regardless of actual increases in property values. Since property taxes are the preeminent source of local government revenues, the ability of localities to generate revenues was greatly impaired.

One effect of Proposition 13 was that many communities were forced either to restrict their community services sharply or else to find other sources of revenue to make up for reduced property tax revenues. Not surprisingly, both occurred. Many towns, including those in the Bay Area, have stepped up efforts to attract new businesses in order to broaden their tax bases.

The commensurate need for new residential single-family housing, however, has not been met. After Proposition 13, localities have been reluctant to zone for such housing because the new development would not pay, in terms of additional property taxes generated, for the cost of public services required for their occupants. As a result, affordable housing near employment centers has become scarce, and communities try to import their labor force from neighboring jurisdictions. Since some development inevitably must occur, local officials have been more likely to permit the construction of apartment complexes with small units; this tends to discourage young families with children, whose demand for expensive public schooling is high.

A second and related effect of Proposition 13 has been a shift by communities to alternative methods of service finance. Communities unable to finance infrastructure development and service costs through general tax levies have attempted to impose such costs directly upon developers. These impositions have been levied through forced provision of infrastructure and through increases in charges. For example, in the East Bay city of Concord, new developers have financed the extension of sewer lines in order to gain building permits; other cities have required provision of park land or roads. The charge approach is apparent in the city of Fremont, where a one-time school impact fee is levied on all new development. In addition, housing permit charges and application fees have risen dramatically since 1978. It is now commonplace for communities to conduct cost-revenue assessments, estimating whether the tax revenue generated will pay for the increased public services required by new residents. Concern has shifted from development that would enhance the physical character of the community to that which could pay its own way. Not surprisingly, the added scrutiny has also lengthened the time required to gain acceptance of a new development project and has increased construction costs. (See Dowall, 1984, for more detail.)

Simultaneously, Proposition 13 has become a weapon for slow-growth advocates who wish to curtail the spread of "suburban sprawl" and to preserve environmentally sensitive areas. Groups such as the Bay Area's People for Open Space and the Sierra Club consistently oppose measures that expand the amount of developable land, and instead support more clustered development at higher densities.

Mortgage Insurance, Credit Guarantees, and Credit Institutions

The federal government undertakes a number of programs designed to help purchasers borrow funds for home mortgages on favorable terms. The largest and most important are the programs of mortgage insurance of the Federal Housing Administration (FHA) and the system of loan guarantees administered by the Veterans' Administration (VA). Both of these programs protect private lenders against losses from default by borrowers. The basic FHA mortgage insurance program is designed to be financially self-supporting; that is, it operates principally to pool risks, and on average, fees paid by homeowners cover default risk.[12] In contrast, the VA guarantee program provides modest subsidies to eligible veterans. Both programs transfer loss risk from the lender to the government.

One consequence of these federal programs has been a broader and more

---

[12] The guidelines for the FHA program include a maximum mortgage amount and maximum interest rate. The maximum amount means that upper middle-income households buying more expensive dwellings generally do not qualify for FHA insurance.

liberal set of terms throughout the mortgage market. Terms for a typical home mortgage have changed radically since the FHA began insuring default risk, with higher loan-to-value ratios and lengthier repayment periods than previously. It has been argued that the principal effect of the FHA has been to cause banks to understand that it is in their self-interest to offer more liberal terms for all residential mortgages, including those that are not covered by FHA insurance.

Since the 1970s, the importance of private mortgage insurance companies has increased substantially. By 1981, they accounted for some 36 percent of the market.

The sources of finance for housing include savings banks, commercial banks, and savings and loan associations (S&Ls). Historically, about 40 percent of mortgages originated in any year have been provided by savings and loan associations, another 30 percent by mortgage banks, 20 percent by commercial banks, and the remainder by savings banks and other agencies. Savings and loan associations are similar in many respects to the building associations of Britain and the Commonwealth. Until the 1970s, housing finance was rather straightforward: loans were made for a fixed term at a fixed rate of interest by S&Ls, savings banks, or commercial banks. The interest rate charges varied with monetary conditions, but long-term rates generally were low. The sources of loanable funds were individual savers, in the case of savings and loan associations and savings banks, or corporate investors, in the case of commercial banks.

Until as late as 1980, S&Ls were subject to a variety of legal restrictions.[13] In return for an advantage in attracting the deposits of small savers, S&Ls were legally required to invest a fixed percentage of their assets in home mortgages. This notion, which was a part of the original Federal Home Loan Bank Act of 1932, was to channel money into the housing market at favorable interest rates to promote home ownership.

The period of rapidly rising interest rates in the late 1970s and early 1980s caused a real crisis among S&Ls, who found themselves caught in a position of borrowing short (issuing passbooks) and lending long (issuing 30-year mortgages). When market interest rates exceeded the regulated interest rate on deposits, S&Ls quickly lost deposits at the same time that the real value of their mortgage holdings declined. The Monetary Reform and Decontrol Act of 1980 was intended to remedy some of these problems and to permit S&Ls to compete more fully for funds. The Act permitted S&Ls to issue longer maturity

---

[13] They were allowed to issue only certain types of deposits, essentially passbook time deposits, at interest rates which were controlled by the federal government. These interest rates were set slightly higher than the interest rate paid by commercial banks on time deposits.

savings certificates, removed regulated deposit rate ceilings for savers, and permitted S&Ls to diversify their investments.

As the asset side of the balance sheet of the S&L industry was deregulated in the early 1980s, the liabilities of these institutions continued to be guaranteed by the federal government. The "moral hazard" thus created encouraged S&Ls to invest in riskier assets than they otherwise would have in the pursuit of higher returns-- with dire consequences for general taxpayers who insured the losses. Current estimates of the taxpayer cost of bailing out the failed S&Ls run in the hundreds of billions of dollars.

Higher and more volatile interest rates in the early 1980s also led to the introduction of new mortgage instruments in the United States. Adjustable interest rate mortgages (ARMs), under which the mortgage interest rate varies with market conditions, were one such innovation. Often variable interest rate mortgages call for level monthly payments and make up the difference by adjusting the amortization period of the mortgage itself. This protects the lending institution from some of the interest rate risk and presumably lowers costs to borrowers. In addition to these ARMs, other financing instruments, such as shared equity arrangements, began to flourish. Under shared equity arrangements, a third party agrees to pay some part of the monthly mortgage payments, and perhaps part of the down payment, in return for a fraction of the capital gain at the time of the sale of the house. Use of these alternative mortgage instruments was widespread in the early 1980s, but with the return of rather stable interest rates by 1984, the fraction of the market devoted to alternative mortgages declined substantially.

Secondary Market Operations

The distinguishing feature of the housing finance system of the United States is the existence of a thriving secondary market for mortgages. A large fraction of the mortgages originated by S&Ls, commercial banks, and mortgage bankers is sold to investors on a secondary market. This secondary market developed initially for FHA and VA loans, since the guarantee by the federal government made the mortgages highly liquid. A logical next step was the formation of mortgage pools which could be sold in shares. The Federal National Mortgage Association[14] (FNMA, or "Fanny Mae") has been the largest purchaser of mortgages in this secondary market.

Fannie Mae borrows money in the capital markets by issuing bonds which are then used to purchase mortgages from lending institutions. Profitability depends upon the spread between the interest income on its mortgage portfo-

---

[14] Fanny Mae is a rather unusual corporation. It was initially wholly owned by the federal government but, in the late 1960s, shares were sold and it became a privately-owned corporation.

lio and the cost of borrowing. Initially, Fannie Mae purchased only FHA and VA mortgage loans, but since the early 1970s it has purchased "conventional" (that is, privately insured and uninsured) mortgage loans. These now account for an increasingly large fraction of its activity. Fanny Mae also sells mortgage-backed securities, that is, securities backed by its own portfolio of loans.

The Federal Home Loan Mortgage Corporation (FHLMC or "Freddie Mac"), created by Congress in 1970, was charged with developing and maintaining a nationwide secondary market for conventional mortgages. This corporation purchases loans, both traditional fixed rate loans and also the more recent ARMs, from S&Ls and other institutions. It then resells these loans in a variety of securities.[15]

These government-sponsored institutions have changed substantially the circumstances of mortgage finance in the United States. In the 1930s, S&Ls collected the savings of local residents and pooled them to provide mortgage money for other local consumers in the manner of traditional building societies. By the 1980s, financial institutions were permitting sophisticated investors to invest in shares backed by large mortgage pools, including mortgage contracts made by residents thousands of miles away, in many different local markets -- individuals whose identities were unknown to the investors themselves. The increase in the liquidity of the residential mortgage market has been remarkable, especially in the last decade.

REGIONALISM AND LOCALISM IN BAY AREA LAND USE AND DEVELOPMENT

Local and Regional Regulation

The San Francisco Bay Area is an identifiably regional economy that developed and spread from the older cities near the Bay (such as San Francisco and Oakland) out to the once-rural areas where new cities now stand. Nonetheless, planning and land-use policies largely are a result of local governance, not comprehensive regional or state planning. With nine counties, over 100 municipalities, and several hundred school districts and special districts, governance in the Bay Area is an extremely complicated process involving both public and private actors. To be sure, federal and state policies play a large role

---

[15] For example, Freddie Mac sells mortgage participation certificates (PCs), representing an undivided interest in a specific pool of mortgages. As the secondary mortgage market has increased in importance in the last few years, the Freddie Mac corporation has grown substantially. Freddie Mac has been able to structure PCs to minimize interest rate risks, buying and selling loans with a positive spread rather than holding them in its own portfolio.

in determining the location of the new development projects which they sponsor. However, as we have seen, the bulk of new development does not utilize direct state or federal support, and local jurisdictions have the final word. This reflects both a federalist attitude-- that localities should make land-use decisions for themselves-- and a long-standing Bay Area tradition of "home rule." Local governments control development through a variety of land-use planning, zoning, building standards, and rent control policies.

In order to increase local cooperation in land-use practices, the Association of Bay Area Governments (ABAG) was established in 1961 as a voluntary association of local governments. ABAG was originally an advisory organization that studied problems and recommended solutions, but it did not institute programs. ABAG was not created to dictate policy, but rather to prevent the imposition of a strong regional authority that could usurp traditional local political power.[16] However, the 1960s saw increasing interest and emphasis upon regional planning. Despite the original intention, in 1964 ABAG began preparing a comprehensive regional development plan. In addition, a federal program enabled ABAG to become a regional clearinghouse with the right to review and comment upon local government applications for federal funds for development projects. At that time, however, ABAG received only modest federal grant monies earmarked for planning activities. With the assistance of state legislators, ABAG continued to press for regional control, but in 1968 the agency was beset by an embezzlement scandal that weakened its efforts to secure authority and power from the state legislature.

Despite its inability to obtain state statutory authority, ABAG enjoyed increasing Federal support for regional planning. By 1977, ABAG had a budget of $3.4 million and a staff of over 100 who reviewed applications for federal aid and were completing a large-scale regional Environmental Management Plan. It was supported by the dues of its voluntary local government members and had won support as an association of local governments helping to achieve regional goals, not a regional government trying to usurp authority from its member jurisdictions.

ABAG's prosperity came to an abrupt end when, two weeks after the passage of Proposition 13, member governments cut their ABAG dues by 70 percent. It was quite apparent that ABAG was not seen as a high priority when money was tight. In addition, ABAG's role as a regional clearinghouse ended when federal resources for planning assistance were eliminated in 1982. By 1984, ABAG's budget was only $1.8 million, a decline of 47 percent over seven years; the staff decreased commensurately, from 109 in 1977 to only 33 by 1984.

---

[16] Several single-purpose regional agencies with real authority were also established during this period, most notably the Metropolitan Transportation Commission (MTC) and the Bay Conservation and Development Commission (BCDC).

The rapid decline in funding and staff illuminated ABAG's inherent difficulties: because it has no statutory authority, it must rely on voluntary local government member contributions for financial and political support. Consequently, ABAG's present role is, just as it was 20 years ago, merely to advise local governments in planning decisions and to provide information such as land-use projections to localities, often on a fee-for-service basis.

The Metropolitan Transportation Commission (MTC), on the other hand, maintains broad responsibility for regional transportation planning, and must approve all applications for state and federal funding for highway construction and for transit agencies. Unlike ABAG, the commission can rely on revenues from Bay Area bridge tolls for financial support. Its chief influence on local planning and land use is through the siting of new highways and in approving additions to the Bay Area Rapid Transit (BART) system. In addition, the MTC has the powerful role of allocating funds from a portion of the sales tax reserved expressly for support of local and regional transit.

In addition to these and smaller regional authorities, the state of California monitors land-use development through "housing elements," which are five-year development plans created by, and required of, all jurisdictions. Each jurisdiction must show how it intends to provide for anticipated population increases, and for low-income and elderly residents; zoning and other subdivisions must also conform to the local housing element. Each plan must be approved by the state Department of Housing and Community Development. However, the state has no enforcement mechanism to compel localities to comply with their own plans. For jurisdictions grossly out of compliance, the state must rely on individuals to sue the locality in court in order to force the adoption of a legally-adequate general plan for development. Typically, larger jurisdictions, which are often monitored closely by citizen groups, must conform to state guidelines and regulations, but smaller jurisdictions may be able to sidestep them.

As noted above, localities have asserted their autonomy in implementing growth controls, partly as a backlash against growth in the Bay Area and partly for environmental or fiscal reasons. In the wake of encroachment upon vineyards by developers, in 1977 the city of Petaluma (in Sonoma county) implemented the first growth management plan in the state by limiting new building permits to 500 per year. This was a radical departure from traditional land-use planning, not only because it did not accommodate orderly growth but also because it was so overt. The "Petaluma Plan" was the subject of considerable regional and national controversy and spawned a variety of growth management plans in other Bay Area cities and towns. The competition between jurisdictions changed from one of attracting residential development in the 1960s to one of widespread resistance to development.

In apparent contrast to Petaluma and its imitators, in 1980 voters in San

Francisco passed by referendum a declaration that it should be city policy to encourage the development of 20,000 new housing units by 1985. However, through a combination of high land costs, a lengthy permitting procedure, and restrictive development controls, the actual growth of housing was at most 15 percent of this goal. The city has attempted since 1981 to link the booming growth of its downtown business area to housing construction by taxing new office developments. The city's "Downtown Plan," adopted in 1984, requires developers of office space to construct 386 low-income housing units or contribute $5.34 million for every million square feet of office space constructed to a city program offering assistance to first-time home buyers. It is difficult to assess the impact of these programs, though their consequence clearly depends upon continued construction in the downtown area. Critics claim that the imposition of such charges weakens the city in competition for office location with suburban communities.

Both Petaluma's and San Francisco's policies illustrate the competitive nature of interjurisdictional relationships and also the power localities have in making essentially regional decisions for themselves. This competition has many perverse consequences. Residential growth of any kind is restrained, and communities universally discourage housing for poor families with children, since such housing typically adds substantially to service costs and little to tax rolls. Communities generally encourage economic development, especially when such development involves retail trade and the sales tax proceeds that accompany it. But obviously all jurisdictions in the Bay Area cannot enjoy expanding employment without additional housing. Eventually the shortage of housing is certain to retard growth of employment. While this is obvious to many people, individual communities are caught in a "prisoner's dilemma." If they adopt a permissive stance toward housing construction, their neighbors may choose not to do so. Indeed if one community allows housing construction, the pressures upon its neighbors to do so are reduced.

Communities in the Bay Area are likely to continue to pursue independent land-use policies unless the state legislature imposes a regional agency with the authority to bring about significant change. Given the strong Californian predisposition toward decentralized government, this change seems unlikely in the near future. Nonetheless, it is important to emphasize that the overwhelming importance of local decision-making as a determinant of regional housing policy is not the necessary result of the constitutional structure of American government. Rather, it is the consequence of an unwillingness of the state to exercise authority.

In addition to controls on land use and building design, communities in California have the authority to impose rent control. Currently a total of 15 local jurisdictions in the state (out of 428 municipalities statewide) impose some form of rent control or price regulation. While this number is small, the communities account for a sizable proportion (22 percent) of the state's population. Nine of these jurisdictions are found within the San Francisco Bay Area, including the central cities of San Francisco, Oakland, and San Jose, the city of Berkeley, and the suburbs of Hayward, East Palo Alto, Los Gatos, Cotati, and Campbell. These rent regulations vary widely in content and intensity. On one extreme, Berkeley's rent control board has never permitted general annual rent increases as large as the increase in consumer prices, does not allow rent adjustment on vacancy, and exempts only buildings with one or two rental units. One the other hand, San Jose's ordinance limits rent increases to 8 percent per year, allows general rent adjustments when apartments become vacant, and allows most increases in operating costs to be passed through to tenants.

Assessing the consequences of these controls for housing costs and supply is difficult due to their variety . Evidence exists, however, that controls have reduced housing supply, particularly in cities such as Berkeley where programs appear exceptionally stringent. As with other types of local regulation, rent control has effects that spread beyond the boundaries of the controlling jurisdiction; Berkeley's law affects the demand for and supply of housing in all surrounding jurisdictions. Here again, the state has authority to regulate the design and application of rent control systems in ways that recognize the regional consequences of such policies. To date, however, the state government has been unwilling to do so.

Effects on Local Housing Development

There are many reasons for the housing affordability/availability problems described at the beginning of this essay. Both demand and supply factors are involved. Demand-side influences include changes in population and demography, high levels of employment, and personal investment behavior. Supply-side factors include the shortage of developable land, reduced support of general infrastructure, laws protecting the environment, and the local building limitations discussed in the previous section. Since changes in these factors will determine the future course of housing costs and affordability, it is important to review them all. Our conclusion is, however, that the most significant factor in the future outlook is government regulation.

Housing Demand

Population increase alone has assured a surge in the demand for housing. Between 1960 and 1980, the population in the nine-county Bay Area grew by 42 percent. However, the effect of this change on housing demand involves more than just total numbers. As a result of the post-World War II "baby boom," in the 1970s a sizable cohort reached the age at which people typically purchase housing. Between 1960 and 1980, the number of persons in the Bay Area over

20 years old nearly doubled, rising from roughly 2.2 million to over 4 million, while over the same time period average household size shrunk from 3.1 to 2.6 persons per household. The population is expected to continue to grow, but the decline in household size has ceased, and households likely to purchase homes should decline as a proportion of total population, even with the arrival in the housing market of the second generation of the baby boom.

The Bay Area also witnessed unusually strong employment growth between 1975 and 1980, when more than 560,000 new jobs were added to the economy. Almost half of these new jobs were located in and about the Silicon Valley. This drew residents to the Bay Area, increased the adult population, and also reoriented much new demand toward the south. The outlook for future Bay Area employment growth is uncertain, in part because at least in the south, it will depend significantly upon the availability of housing.

To understand the origins of the demand influences on Bay Area housing costs, it is necessary to look beyond demographic factors to motivation for housing investment. Over the 1970s, the interaction of general inflation, rising real income, and the tax treatment of owner-occupied housing (described above) strengthened the attractiveness of housing as an investment. Broadly speaking, the user cost of owner-occupied housing has three components: 1.) the cost of the capital required for the investment, 2.) depreciation, and 3.) gains from value appreciation. During the late 1970s and early 1980s, both inflation and interest rates were high. In the absence of special tax treatment of housing investment, the two factors might cancel out-- interest rates would raise user costs, but the loss would be offset by the inflation-driven appreciation in housing value. However, mortgage interest payments are deducted from income before computation of tax liability, while capital gains on housing are untaxed. This means that in an inflationary environment, the user cost of owner-occupied housing can fall even when interest rates increase by the expected inflation rates and housing prices go up only at the general rate of inflation. Thus, demand for housing during this era gained impetus from the consequences of inflation for the perceived user cost of housing. Ironically, the high interest rates of the early 1980s made owner-occupied housing less "affordable" (since monthly payments at higher interest rates were greater) at the same time that the true economic costs of owner occupancy were lower. This suggests that the "affordability crisis" in owner-occupied housing arose in part from the liquidity constraints of households and the capital constraints imposed by lenders, rather than increases in the price of housing services themselves.

Both declining rates of inflation and reductions in tax rates have reduced the attractiveness of housing as an investment. Thus, while continued (and interdependent) economic and population growth will expand housing demand, nothing as unusual as the recent housing cost inflation is likely to be repeated. This does not mean that the Bay Area has solved the affordability problem. Rather, it indicates that the source of the problem lies not with demand, but with supply.

Housing Supply

The first point to be made about housing supply in the San Francisco Bay Area is that construction costs are not a source of exceptional inflationary pressure. Figure 5-5 compares the course of consumer prices in the Bay Area with the estimated costs of constructing a standard, three-bedroom home. These construction costs do not include the cost of the site upon which it is constructed. As the figure indicates, construction costs increased more rapidly than general inflation in the late 1970s and less rapidly in the early 1980s. Over the decade as a whole, construction costs increased at about the same rate as

FIGURE 5-5

Consumer Prices and Construction Costs in the San Francisco Bay Area
1975 - 1986.

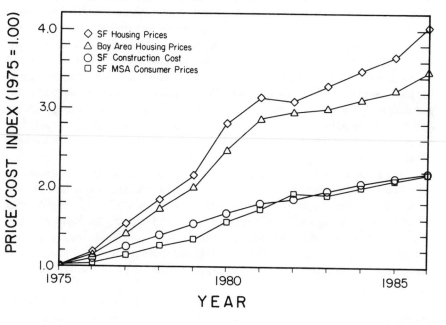

other prices. However, the increase in housing prices, particularly in San Francisco but also in the entire Bay Area, far outstripped construction costs and consumer prices. Thus, the extraordinary rate of change in new home prices must be traced to other influences.

The first of these is the physical configuration of the Bay Area itself, with a significant portion of the land in both the East and West Bay physically unsuited for development because of irregular terrain, unstable soil, or other factors. Development in other areas is constrained by environmental concerns. Much of the coastline adjoining San Francisco is protected by the California Coastal Act of 1975, which all but prohibits any new development within 1,000 meters of the coastline. This eliminates thousands of hectares of highly desirable land near San Francisco for housing development, but it preserves the unique Pacific coastline for the enjoyment of local residents and for the booming tourist industry. Increasing awareness of environmental degradation in the 1970s led to the passage of the California Environmental Quality Act and other laws which, through systematic scrutiny of new development plans, also slowed the pace of new development and added to housing costs.

As already discussed, reduced local government support in the wake of Proposition 13 and the federal cutbacks in grants for local services have made the expansion of the infrastructure and public services necessary for housing development difficult to finance. Because communities could not increase property taxes enough to pay for local services needed by new residents (schools, sewers, etc.), fees were imposed on new housing development, increasing housing prices. As a result, much of the new development excluded housing that could serve low-income persons. New construction approved at the local level tended to be small units that would cater to older couples (who use relatively few local services) and discouraged housing for young families (who use many public services, particularly schools.) The problems created by Proposition 13 are unresolved; in consequence, local governments are likely to continue to resist rapid development of housing.

In addition to these direct causes of high housing prices, there are a number of indirect market effects that influence the local market. Important among these are bottlenecks and monopoly power (see Dowall, 1984). Bottlenecks occur when housing demand exceeds supply and either prices do not rise sufficiently to clear the market (e.g., rent controls) or local land-use controls do not permit expanding supply. The result is the low vacancy rates that exist in many Bay Area communities. In others, high housing prices have forced out low-income residents.

Monopoly power can be exercised by developers through the use of restrictive land-use regulation, which limits the amount of land available for development and makes controlling local land markets easier. The use of complex administrative procedures, lengthy application periods, and other measures that typify Bay Area local development policies can induce monopolistic control of local land markets. One study of developers in San Jose found that their excess profits were largely attributable to constrained housing supply and the lack of competition. In other areas, such as Marin and Napa counties, the lack of developable land and high development fees have given dominant control of the housing market to a few large developers (see Dowall, 1984).These indirect effects may exert a powerful influence over local land use and development. Any policies to improve the present housing conditions in the Bay Area must recognize these important, though subtle, consequences. Environmentalism and local land regulations preventing rapid growth are supported by many Bay Area residents, and attempts to change this pattern are not likely to be initiated by local governments.

SUMMARY AND CONCLUSIONS

As we have seen, the Bay Area housing market is characterized by a complex weave of the public and private sectors. Public activity in the market comes in the form of direct subsidies (e.g., the construction of low-income housing units) and indirect subsidies (e.g., tax exemptions and mortgage guarantees) from federal, state, and local governments. In the Bay Area, and indeed throughout the United States, housing assistance is predominantly indirect. While direct housing assistance is aimed primarily at low-income or otherwise disadvantaged groups, indirect subsidies are often decidedly regressive, serving wealthy homeowners more than poorer homeowners or renters. One major study of California housing policies concluded that the consequence of this combination was that the poor and the wealthy received the bulk of the assistance, while middle-class residents received the least (Furry, 1983). Due to the size and scope of indirect benefits to homeowners, it is unlikely that attempts to redress the balance will be met with much success.[17] The predominance of indirect benefits also eliminates much of the federal and state control over local development that follows with direct benefits. Individuals and localities essentially determine growth patterns regardless of the potentially negative regional impacts.

With the low levels of direct housing assistance in the United States, it is not surprising that mortgage revenue bonds and other market-based credit instruments have increasingly dominated housing policy. Politically, it is much easier to "spend" an untaxed dollar through tax expenditures than to transfer directly money through "tax-and-spend" policies.

---

[17] For example, attempts made during the major revisions of the U.S. Tax Code in 1986 to eliminate the mortgage interest deduction were met with substantial resistance and were abandoned.

By far the largest provision of housing in the United States, however, is simply through the decentralized market mechanism and, as a result, housing quality and price differences are larger than in most European countries where the provision of housing is more highly centralized. The average standard of housing consumption is quite high, and the variety of housing available is broad. Nevertheless, with the exceptions noted above, housing is allocated on the basis of willingness and ability to pay, and housing consumption represents a larger fraction of households' budgets than in many other societies.

REFERENCES

Association of Bay Area Governments. 1983. *Housing needs determination: San Francisco bay region*. San Francisco, CA: Association of Bay Area Governments.

Bay Area Council. 1986. Bay area housing: The state of the market today; an overview of trends, 1980-85. San Francisco, CA: Bay Area Council.

Bay Area Council. 1985. Rental housing in the bay area: Opportunity knocks again. San Francisco, CA: Bay Area Council.

California Department of Housing and Community Development. California affordable housing legislation: A study of local implementation. Vol. 1.

California Department of Housing and Community Development. California affordable housing legislation: Case studies; a study of local implementation. Vol. II.

California Department of Housing and Community Development. California housing authorities: Summary of 1983 activities. 1986.

California Franchise Tax Board. 1985 annual report.

California Housing Finance Agency. 1986a. 1985-86 annual report. Sacramento, CA: California Housing Finance Agency.

California Housing Finance Agency. 1986b. 1985-86 annual report supplement. Sacramento, CA: California Housing Finance Agency.

Cleland, Robert Glass. 1947. *California in our time, 1900-1940*. New York, NY: Alfred A. Knopf.

Dowall, David E. 1984. *The suburban squeeze: Land conversion and regulation in the San Francisco Bay Area*. Berkeley, CA: University of California Press.

Durning, Danny Wayne. 1986. Essays on home ownership subsidy policies.

Ph.D. dissertation, University of California, Berkeley.

Furry, William S. 1983. *Housing assistance in California: A program analysis.* Santa Monica, CA: The Rand Corporation.

Hart, James D. 1978. *A companion to California.* New York: Oxford University Press.

Hoerter, Darrell, and Michael Wiseman. 1988. Metropolitan development in the San Francisco Bay Area. *Annals of Regional Science,* 22(3): 11-33.

Jones, Victor. 1974. Bay Area regionalism. In *The regionalist papers,* pp.122-145. Detroit, MI: The Metropolitan Fund.

LeGrant, Matthew Lawrence. 1984. ABAG's changing role and the local government response: Lessons for the design of a metropolitan planning system. Master's thesis, Department of City and Regional Planning, University of California, Berkeley.

Long, Larry, and Diana De Are. 1983. The slowing of urbanization in the U.S. *Scientific American,* 249: 33-41.

National Association of Home Builders. 1986. *Home building after tax reform: A buyer's guide.* Washington: NAHB.

Orman, Larry Allan. 1976. Planning the metropolis: Regional planning in the San Francisco Bay Area, 1945-1975. Master's thesis, Department of City and Regional Planning, University of California, Berkeley.

People for Open Space. 1983. Room enough: Housing and open space in the Bay Area.

U.S. Census. *City and county data book.* Washington, DC: Government Printing Office, various editions.

U.S. Congressional Budget Office. 1981. *The tax treatment of homeownership: Issues and options.* Washington, DC: U.S. Government Printing Office.

Wong, Susan M. 1986. Tax-exempt bond financing: Who are the beneficiaries in the San Francisco Bay Area? University of California, Graduate School of Public Policy, Berkeley. Mimeo.

6
ANALYSIS OF THE HOUSING SECTOR, THE HOUSING MARKET, AND HOUSING POLICY IN THE BUDAPEST METROPOLITAN AREA

Sàndor Kàdas

INTRODUCTION

The housing sector is a crucial component in the functioning of a metropolitan area. In the context of Budapest, there are several different aspects relevant to evaluating the housing sector, especially:

- the relation of the housing sector to the economic structure and industrial development of the area (see Dienes, 1973);

- the sociological aspects of the development of the housing sector (see Szelenyi, 1972; Szelènyi and Konrad, 1969; Hoffmann, 1981);

- the distributional issues implicit in housing policy (see Daniel, 1985); and

- the role of housing as an ingredient in social class segregation and as an element of significant political concern (see Hegedùs and Tosics, 1983).

This chapter combines several of these aspects. We concentrate on explaining and tracing back the most important structural characteristics, problems, and contradictions of present housing conditions in Budapest. We also present and analyze the most important data on recent housing development. To a certain degree, we aim also to integrate the findings discussed recently in English language articles on the subject of housing in the Hungarian economy (Dienes, 1973; Compton, 1979; Hegedus and Tosics, 1983; Daniel, 1985; Sillince, 1985).

THE BUDAPEST METROPOLITAN AREA IN THE SETTLEMENT SYSTEM OF HUNGARY AND CENTRAL EUROPE

Budapest, the capital of Hungary, was established by integrating three towns, Buda, Obuda, and Pest, on both sides of the Danube River in 1870. Buda had become the principal residence of Hungarian kings by the 14th century and had the largest and most magnificent Renaissance castle of Central Europe in the golden age of King Matthias. In the second half of the 15th century, Hungary had the same population and economic power as England. Thereafter, its position was significantly weakened by the occupation of the Turks from 1526 until 1689. After 150 years, Turkish rule over a third of the country had substantially reduced economic development. Industrial growth accelerated only in the beginning of the 19th century. After the war of independence against the Habsburg monarchy (1848 to 1849), and after a compromise treaty in 1867 with the Habsburgs, rapid industrial growth began in Hungary, concentrated in the modernizing capital of Budapest.

The population of Budapest grew rapidly, from 300,000 in 1870 to 400,000; 560,000 and 860,000 in 1880, 1890, and 1900, respectively. At the outbreak of the First World War, the population of Budapest was about 1.2 million or about 6 percent of the country's population. As a consequence of the Treaty of Versailles in 1920, Hungary lost more than half of its population and about two-thirds of its territory; Budapest came to represent about 16 percent of the country's population. Between the two world wars, the population in Budapest grew. The capital reached 1.7 million inhabitants by 1941, while the total population of the country was fairly stagnant.

The Second World War was followed by rapid reconstruction in Budapest between 1945 and 1948, and a massive industrialization program was undertaken in the years 1950 to 1954 after the consolidation of power in the Communist Party. As a result, the centralization of population and economic, cultural, and administrative power in Budapest was complete, despite the establishment of a few new "socialist" industrial towns in outlying areas. This period of rapid economic growth slowed down in the sixties and came to a halt in the seventies. The Budapest metropolitan area now contains 29 percent of the country's population. Budapest and its environs account for over 40 percent of the country's total industrial employment and produce about half of the value of its manufactured goods. The city is also the center of scientific and cultural life in Hungary. In 1970, 106 of the country's 130 research institutes were in Budapest (Dienes,1973), and they employed 87 percent of all research personnel. The establishment of new research institutes and high-tech plants outside Budapest in the 1970s and 1980s, such as the large research institute of biology in Szeged, the computer and electronics concentration in Szekesfehervar, and modern factories in Györ, has reduced the city's central role in Hungary's scientific and cultural life.

From an international perspective, the Budapest Metropolitan Area is the largest one in Central Europe apart from Berlin. The only other European capitals with a comparable high share of the country's total population are Vienna, Copenhagen, and Athens. In these cities, however, industrial production is less concentrated and scientific and cultural potential are less concentrated than in Budapest.

Figure 6-1 indicates the geographical position of Budapest in Hungary and in Central Europe. Figure 6-2 displays the division of Budapest into 22 districts

FIGURE 6-1
Geographical Situation of Budapest in Central Europe.

FIGURE 6-2
Districts of Budapest and Settlements of the First Agglomeration Ring.

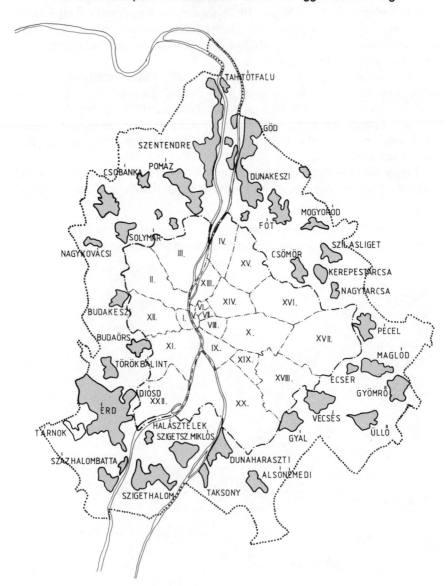

TABLE 6-1

Population of Budapest and its Suburban Rings, 1960 and 1980.

District		Population (in thousands)		Percent change in population
		1960	1980	1960-1980
Inner city				
	1	44.1	40.6	-7.9%
	5	65.5	51.7	-21.1
	6	90.4	72.5	-19.8
	7	118.8	93.8	-21.0
	8	134.6	108.8	-19.2
	9	88.7	85.2	-3.9
Other central city				
	2	94.0	103.5	+10.1
	3	72.7	119.6	+64.5
	4	76.8	81.3	+5.9
	10	64.7	97.4	+50.5
	11	114.5	167.8	+46.6
	12	66.0	78.4	+18.8
	13	138.8	128.9	-7.1
	14	117.7	159.7	+35.7
	15	60.9	113.8	+86.9
	16	53.5	71.1	+32.9
	17	41.6	54.7	+31.5
	18	69.1	89.1	+28.9
	19	64.9	59.0	-9.1
	20	100.8	100.6	-0.2
	21	57.1	73.4	+28.5
	22	37.6	48.2	+28.2
	Total	1783	1999	+15.5
Inner ring		246	410	+66.7
Outer ring		327	378	+15.6
Suburban Area		573	788	+37.5

Source: *Statistical Yearbook of Budapest 1970-1984,* Central Statistical Office, Budapest.

and the most important suburban settlements around Budapest.

Table 6-1 indicates the distribution of population in the metropolitan area in 1960 and in 1980. As the table notes, the population of inner-city districts has decreased in most cases, but there has been a substantial increase in population in districts outside the town center and in the inner ring around Budapest (see figure 6-2).

Figures 6-3 and 6-4 indicate the principal regional transportation systems. Figure 6-3 shows the existing and proposed suburban rail and subway lines, and figure 6-4 indicates major roads and motorways.

FIGURE 6-3
Network of Metropolitan Railways in Budapest.

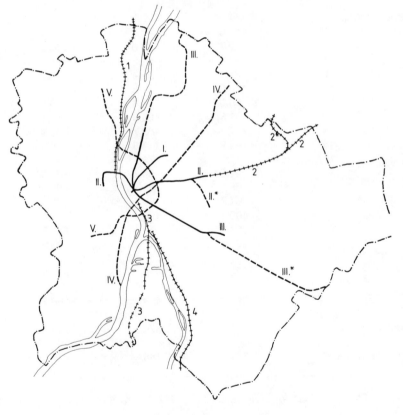

————	existing, resp. planned underground line
+++++++	existing, resp. planned suburban railway

FIGURE 6-4
Network of Principal Roads in Budapest.

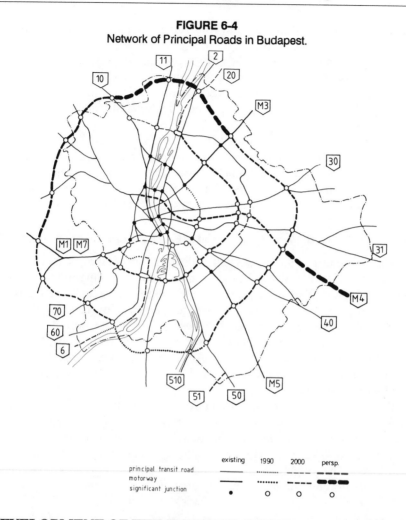

	existing	1990	2000	persp.
principal transit road	——	··········	– – – –	▬ ▬ ▬
motorway	——	········	– – – –	●●●●
significant junction	●	○	○	○

DEVELOPMENT OF THE HOUSING SECTOR IN BUDAPEST

This section presents the main characteristics of the housing sector in Budapest in a dynamic-historical perspective. Due to limited data, information for the surrounding metropolitan agglomeration is not presented in detail, except in connection with the development of Budapest itself.

The Emerging Modern Metropolis, 1870-1920

As noted above, the population of Budapest tripled within 30 years of its incorporation, reaching almost 900,000 by 1900. This growth slowed down during and after the First World War. The metropolis took its present shape in this age. The period marked the construction of most of the government, cultural, and office buildings.

During this period many of the city's architectural monuments were built- the large neogothic complex of Parliament, the magnificent State Opera House, and St. Stephen's Basilica. Also completed were ministerial buildings, the city park with its large neoclassical museum buildings, and the Milleneum Memorial.[1]

Urban infrastructure was established and rapidly extended in the first 50 years of metropolitan development, including electrical, sewage, water, and gas networks, bridges over the Danube, railways and railway stations, tram lines and the main urban roads. The first underground line on the continent (preceded only by London's) was also opened here in 1896.

Budapest Between the Wars: The Period of Further Concentration, 1920-1945

The annexation of more than half of the territory of Hungary by neighboring countries after World War I gave a controversial new impetus for immigration to Budapest. This was especially true among intellectuals and industrial workers employed in manufacturing, who left their homes (ceded by then to a foreign country) and moved to Budapest. This is the period when the agglomeration ring began to emerge, with many of its settlements becoming "bedroom" satellites of the capital. After the great economic depression, industrial growth in Budapest accelerated again from 1933 onward, reinforced by military production.

Figure 6-5 shows the development of population up to 1985. The 50 year period before World War II was a time of rapid population growth as well as rapid housing construction. In the densely populated inner-city districts (districts 1, 5, 6, 7, 8), about 90 percent of the current existing housing stock was constructed. The roughly 400,000 dwellings built in this 50-year period-- about half in the aforementioned inner-city districts and half outside-- represent more than half of the present housing stock.

The Period of Reconstruction and Rapid Socialist Industrialization, 1945-1960

The housing situation in the Hungarian capital improved rapidly, in relative terms, between 1945 and 1949. Reconstruction following the war was faster than expected, and almost all dwellings destroyed during the war had been reconstructed by the end of the first three-year plan (1947 to 1949). In addition, during the course of the three-year plan, which aimed mainly at restoring the productive capacity of industry, 3,500 new dwellings were built in

---

[1] Hungary celebrated the 1,000 year anniversary of the settling of the seven Hungarian tribes inside the Carpathian Range in 1896.

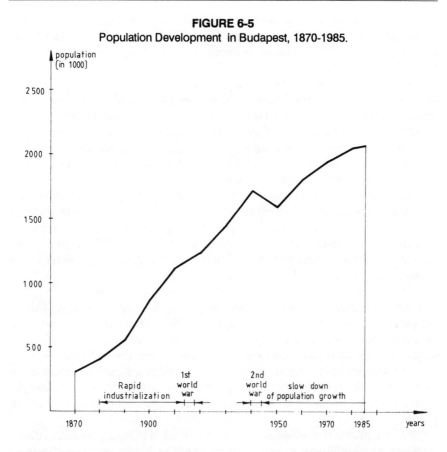

FIGURE 6-5
Population Development in Budapest, 1870-1985.

Budapest (more than in the next three-year period). In addition to the new construction, there was also some subdivision of large dwellings. By 1948, there were more dwellings in the capital than in 1941, while population had decreased. The number of inhabitants per 100 dwellings was 383 in 1930, 368 in 1941, and 335 in 1949, indicating continuous reduction in overcrowded living conditions. The rate of new housing construction, considered satisfactory in the first years of the postwar reconstruction period, seemed rather modest from the broader perspective of the 1950s. The program of enforced industrial investments in the first five-year plan, started in 1950, made it clear that a "restrained" housing construction policy would continue. The raising of target figures of the plan (in 1951) for industrial output reinforced these restraints. The growing emphasis on heavy industry led to a general drop in consumption and living standards and an absolute decrease in housing construction.

From a broader historical perspective, roughly half of the national investment funds in Hungary were allocated to infrastructure (housing, transport network, education, etc.) in the first half of the twentieth century, but in the 1950s this ratio dropped to approximately one-third. This ratio compared with a ratio of about two-thirds for many developed European economies after the Second World War.

Several factors explain the rapid growth of population in Budapest in the late 1940s and early 1950s. First, there was an unexpected wave of migration into the capital (30,000 to 50,000 people per year), caused partly by the substantial rise in the number of industrial workplaces, but also by the enforced collectivization policy in the agricultural sectors. Second, there was the introduction of a law in 1951 prohibiting abortion, which contributed to a rise in birth rate in Budapest from about 8,000 to 18,000 per year.

The political events of June 1953 effected changes in economic orientation and in housing policy. Development of heavy industry and of new socialist towns was de-emphasized, facilitating investments and allowing for a temporary increase in housing investment allocated for Budapest. The result was an increase in housing construction in Budapest accompanied by a decrease in immigration to the capital.

The pressure on the housing market eased considerably in the wake of the October 1956 events as about 100,000 people left the capital. (Most of these people left the country as well.) A completely new era started after the political events in Hungary in October 1956. A political and economic liberalization began; the first years passed in a spirit of strengthening consolidation. In these years a tolerant way of collectivization had achieved considerable success in the agricultural sector, though the resulting immigration from the countryside put pressure on the Budapest housing market, causing growing anxiety for urban planners.

At first, planners attempted to limit immigration to Budapest and to direct migrants into satellite cities around the capital. The development of infrastructure in these satellite settlements, however, was very much neglected. In response, an alternative policy was adopted to advance the development of "growth pole cities." The next largest cities after Budapest were Miskolc, Debrecen, Szeged, Pecs, and Gyor. In fact, though, not one of them exceeded 150,000 inhabitants, and these five biggest country towns together represented only about 30 percent of Hungary's population. None of these cities had much more population than an average-sized municipal district (among the 22 districts) in Budapest.

In an attempt to reduce pressure on the capital's housing market, a decree was passed by the municipal council of Budapest in 1958. The decree stated that only those who had been living or working in the capital for at least five years could obtain or buy a Budapest flat or building site. Figure 6-6 shows the pattern of natural population increase and immigration in Budapest during this period.

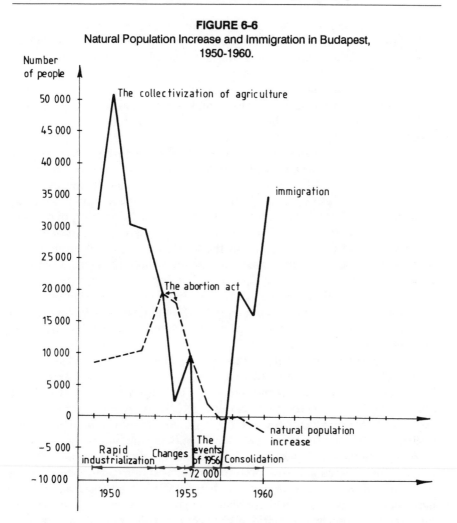

FIGURE 6-6
Natural Population Increase and Immigration in Budapest,
1950-1960.

The Period of Dynamic Economic Growth: The New Economic Mechanism and the First 15-Year Housing Plan, 1960-1975

In the beginning of the 1960s, some Budapest industrial enterprises were forced to leave the capital, but they tried to reestablish their plants nearby. Consequently, the rate of migration into the suburban ring surrounding Budapest increased from an average of 3,000 persons per year in the 1950s to 6,000 persons per year during the 1960s. This migration rate was about twice as high as the migration rate to the capital. The first 15-year Housing Development Plan (covering the period 1960 to 1975) approved by the government earmarked a 25 percent share of total national housing construction for

Budapest. By the middle of the decade, however, this share was reduced to about 16 percent-- partly because of the enforcement of the "growth pole" city concept. But the decline in housing construction did not cause or coincide with a similar decline in immigration, resulting in an aggravation of housing tensions in the capital. When the planners recognized the aggravated housing tensions in 1965, they reviewed earlier development strategies and gave a high priority to housing development in Budapest. (Of course, the effects of this policy reversal were not felt for several years.)

The 1960 to 1973 years were characterized by relatively fast and stable economic growth in Hungary. However, by the end of the 1960s, the underemployed labor force in the agricultural sector -- which had fueled extensive industrialization -- was eroding. Redirecting the labor force from the agricultural sector to industry became more and more difficult for a variety of reasons. For example, the number of workers commuting weekly to industrial centers and returning to the countryside on the weekends could not be increased substantially. The long-term changes in agricultural policy had created circumstances whereby the advantages of an urban job in comparison with the improved job facilities at home in the agricultural sector no longer compensated for the disadvantages of commuting. Simultaneously, the low rate of housing construction limited the capacity for year-round population growth in these industrial centers.

A reform of economic regulations was launched in 1968, aimed at increasing the role of material incentives in improving the intensity of work effort and in strengthening the market mechanism. The reform also sought to bring prices and real costs of production closer together, thus reducing subsidies and taxes. In the housing sector, these reforms promoted private initiatives and the formation of a better functioning market for building sites and privately owned dwellings. At the same time, these reforms increased state assistance, mainly in the form of state loans with preferential interest rates (2 to 3 percent per year) for private construction of dwellings. Due to an increase in rural industrial investment and further policy changes for the benefit of the agricultural sector, there was a considerable decline in the rate of migration to Budapest during the 1970s. At the same time, there was a rapid increase in the rate of housing construction and in the share of capital directed to housing. These two trends ameliorated the tensions encountered in the housing sector in the 1960s.

The pattern of natural population increase and immigration is demonstrated in figure 6-7. Partly because of the emerging economic regulatory reform, the New Economic Mechanism of 1968, and partly because of a radical rise in the world market prices of oil and raw materials, the inflation rate rose in the 1970s to about 5 to 6 percent per year, in contrast to 2 to 4 percent previously. The price levels of dwellings, construction costs, and building sites

FIGURE 6-7
Natural Population Increase and Immigration in Budapest,
1960-1985.

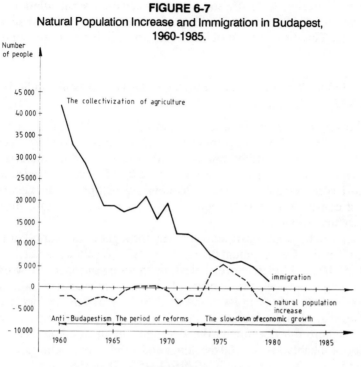

FIGURE 6-8
Development of Price Levels in Hungary, 1960-1975.

rose steadily during the 1970s, and a gap between the overall inflation rate and the inflation rate of prices for dwellings, construction, and building sites began to emerge. This development of increasing prices is demonstrated in figure 6-8.

The Period of Slow Economic Growth and De-emphasis of Public Housing, 1975-1985

The unprecedented drastic increases in the world market price of oil between 1973 and 1976-- altogether about 500 percent-- also induced a substantial price increase in other raw materials and in building materials. An unanticipated worsening in the terms of trade for Hungary in foreign markets also had serious consequences. Economic development in general, and housing construction development in particular, became more difficult in Hungary than expected.

Intensive housing construction activity throughout the period of the first 15-year Housing Development Plan (1960 to 1975) resulted in a net increase of about 150,000 dwellings. Nevertheless, the housing shortage had worsened-- the difference between the number of families and available dwellings was 170,000 in 1950, 176,000 in 1960, and 185,000 in 1975. The net increase of the dwelling stock has diminished in the 1975 to 1985 period, especially in the 1980s. Figure 6-9 documents the development of dwelling use-- average number of inhabitants per 100 dwellings and number of dwellings.

For recent five-year periods, 1970 to 1975, 1975 to 1980, and 1980 to 1985, the net increase in the dwelling stock has been 57,000, 54,000, and 41,000, respectively. New construction averaged about 16,000 to 17,000 dwellings per year in the years 1976 to 1983, decreasing to 12,000 and 10,000 in the years 1984 and 1985, respectively. Table 6-2 shows recent trends in new construction and demolition in the Budapest housing stock.

Table 6-2 indicates a radical change in the distribution of new construction between the state and the private sector. The state-financed fraction of newly constructed dwellings, 60 to 70 percent in the years 1971 to 1981, dropped to 47 percent and 25 percent in 1983 and 1984, respectively. A similar relationship is expected for the next five years or more. Several different factors are at work.

The majority of state-financed dwellings have been built in newly established large housing complexes using mainly prefabricated elements. Costs in this type of housing construction have risen more than the average. During the last decade, planners and architects, as well as those moving into these dwellings, began to realize the disadvantages of living in such large housing complexes. This resulted in a significant reduction in construction plans for large high-rise housing complexes, mainly on the urban fringe of Budapest.

State construction activity has also been curtailed by the overall rise of costs of housing construction. The inflation rate in this sector is approximately

FIGURE 6-9
Housing Stock and Occupancy Rates in Budapest,
1950-1984.

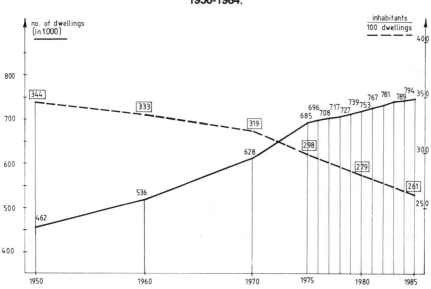

double the average inflation rate in the Hungarian economy (the latter has been roughly 6 to 8 percent in the period from 1975 to 1985), and state-financed housing construction has direct impacts on the government budget. In addition, young families trying to undertake a dwelling construction activity-- usually by establishing a cooperative-like venture of four to ten families to organize the construction of housing-- require financial assistance because of high inflation rates in the housing sector and of the overall stagnation of the standard of living. Thus, more money for long-term loans with preferential interest rates is sought from the National Bank for private housing construction ventures. These pressures are manifested in the recent trend of policy changes: a reduction of state-financed new construction and an attempt to offset the above-average increase in the price level of housing construction.

Another component of the reduction in the rate of new construction of state-financed dwellings is the increase in reconstruction and urban renewal activity in the inner city of Budapest, especially in districts 5 through 8. Both reconstruction (this may mean the virtual demolition of old houses and the creation of new buildings in their place) and new construction reached their 15-year peak in 1979 (see table 6-2). Since that time, there has been a decrease in

TABLE 6-2
New Construction and Demolition in the Budapest Housing Stock,
1971-1984 (dwellings in thousands).

	1971-1975 Total	1976	1977	1978	1979	1980	1981	1982	1983	1984
New construction	77.3	16.6	17.8	16.4	18.0	16.9	16.9	16.8	15.6	11.8
State-financed	48.4	10.4	12.2	10.8	12.9	11.7	10.2	8.4	7.4	3.0
Privately financed	28.9	6.1	5.6	5.6	5.1	5.2	6.7	8.4	8.2	8.8
Demolitions	16.2	2.8	3.6	4.2	5.8	4.1	3.4	2.5	1.2	1.6
Net increase in units	61.1	13.7	14.2	12.2	12.2	12.8	13.5	14.3	14.4	10.2
State property	34.7	8.1	9.3	7.5	9.8	9.7	9.1	6.6	6.7	2.0
State-financed percentage of new construction	63	63	69	66	72	69	60	50	47	25
Percentage of net increase	57	60	65	61	80	76	67	46	46	20

Source: *Statistical Yearbook of Budapest 1970-1984*, Central Statistical Office, Budapest.

the number of dwellings constructed, but a continual rise in quality standards, as the average area and the average number of rooms per dwelling have risen. Reconstruction of parts of the inner city means restoration and modernization rather than demolition. The increase in construction costs is partly explained by improvements in the quality of new construction: for example, the prescribed minimum standards for insulation of brickwork and windows have been raised significantly in recent years. Roughly 30 percent of the rise in construction costs reflects improvements in quality, and the remainder can be explained by the rise of factor prices.

In addition to the high inflation rate in housing prices, a rapid polarization of prices has been observed in Budapest in the last five to seven years. Around 1978, the largest variation of property prices for dwellings of about the same quality and age but located in different parts of the town was about 20 to 30 percent. Now this variation approaches 100 to 150 percent. The most preferred area of the town is the green-belt of Buda, situated on the right side of the Danube. A number of small hills and valleys (the highest being the "Janos" peak, standing 527 meters high) characterized by woods and parks and a beautiful view of the Danube and the inner city make this area especially attractive. Understandably, parts of this green-belt represent the most expensive locations within easy reach of the town center and also supplied with all public services (electricity, water, sewage, and gas) and good public transit. As building sites in these most preferred areas have become more scarce, the land prices have risen significantly, in some areas 30 to 50 percent annually. The average increase in site prices in the Buda green-belt is at a rate of 15 to 20 percent annually. Speculation is limited by the Property Act-- one family can possess only one dwelling as property, one building site in a residential area, or a single-family house plus a weekend house or site. In addition, capital gains from selling previously acquired dwellings or building sites is heavily taxed, unless the net gains are invested in the purchase or construction of a new dwelling.

An important explanatory factor in the polarization of housing prices is the apparent polarization in income levels for different groups of the population. The increased variation in income levels is mainly a consequence of the New Economic Mechanism, gradually established in Hungary since 1968, which has increased personal material rewards for economic efficiency, strengthened the role of market forces, and stimulated small-scale private economic ventures to enhance competition.

HOUSING QUALITY AND THE EVOLUTION OF FINANCING

The Quality of the Dwelling Stock

The quality of a dwelling is dependent on a number of different factors, some of them of a subjective nature. A major quality characteristic is represented by the size of a dwelling (e.g., the number of rooms) and the availability of running water and sanitary services.

In Hungary, three measures of this latter quality are available, distinguishing among "full comfort" dwellings (containing bathroom and toilet), dwellings with "partial comfort" (containing either a separate bathroom or toilet), and dwellings "without comfort" (containing neither bathroom nor toilet).The number of higher quality dwellings, dwellings with at least two rooms, has risen since 1949. This rise is more substantial in country towns and villages than in the capital. Table 6-3 reports size of dwelling data in 1960 and 1970 for towns, villages, and Budapest, and in 1980 for Budapest only.

TABLE 6-3
Distribution of Hungarian Dwellings by Number of Rooms, 1960-1980
(percent of total dwellings).

	1960			1970			1980
	Budapest	Towns	Villages	Budapest	Towns	Villages	Budapest
One-room dwelling	61 %	62 %	63 %	49 %	45 %	46 %	35 %
Two-room dwelling	31	32	34	35	43	46	47
Three or more rooms	8	6	3	16	12	8	18

Source: *Statistical Yearbooks of Budapest 1970-1984,* Central Statistical Office, Budapest.

The share of "full comfort" and "partial comfort" dwellings is growing in comparison with the share of dwellings "without comfort." Table 6-4 shows the distribution of dwellings in these categories over time. The capital understandably shows the most favorable distribution, and the villages the least modern dwellings. As shown in table 6-4 over three-fourths of the Budapest dwelling stock had achieved the standard of "full comfort" by 1980.

The age of the dwelling stock is also an important quality characteristic. In Budapest in 1980, about 56 percent of the dwellings were built before 1945. Table 6-5 shows distribution of dwellings according to age.

Table 6-6 reports the level of plumbing adequacy in Budapest by the age of dwellings. Substandard dwellings are primarily older units, built before 1925.

As to the ownership of the dwelling stock in Budapest, municipally owned rental dwellings are still the majority. Since the nationalization at the end of the 1940s, there have been virtually no privately owned apartment house complexes. The share of private property dwellings (single-family houses and privately owned apartments) is growing, and this growth has accelerated since the second half of the 1970s. This trend reflects the trends noted above, such as the increased share of privately financed dwellings in new construction (see table 6-2). In addition, however, the state sold some previously state-financed new dwellings to private persons, while providing loans at preferential terms for the buyers. Moreover, some state-owned older houses were sold to their renter occupants at subsidized prices. This "privatization" has become more common but is still not an important factor overall.

The share of owner-occupied private dwellings was 27.9 percent in 1970, increasing to 37.5 percent in 1980. There are also co-tenancies, whereby several (usually two) families share a larger dwelling as joint owners. These tenancies are vestiges of the years of acute housing shortage in the 1950s, and their share is gradually decreasing, from 2.2 percent in 1970 to 1.4 percent in 1980.

TABLE 6-4

Distribution of Hungarian Dwellings by the Degree of Comfort, 1950-1980 (percentage of total dwellings).

Degree of Comfort	1950			1960			1970			1980
	Budapest	Towns	Villages	Budapest	Towns	Villages	Budapest	Towns	Villages	Budapest
Dwellings with "full comfort"	38 %	10 %	2 %	42 %	23 %	3 %	56 %	38 %	28 %	78 %
Dwellings with "partial comfort"	6	4	1	12	4	4	10	9	9	7
Dwellings with "no comfort"	56	86	97	46	73	93	34	53	63	18

Source: *Statistical Yearbooks of Budapest 1970-1984*, Central Statistical Office, Budapest.

Although the number of dwellings and the quality of dwelling stock significantly improved throughout Hungary and especially in Budapest during the period from 1960 to 1985, the housing market still suffers a chronic shortage of supply. This insufficiency is mainly structural. There is a shortage in middle-sized and larger dwellings, but not one-room units. There is a high rate of unsatisfied demand for municipally owned rental dwellings-- despite the fact that only families with low incomes, no real property, and at least three children can apply for this kind of dwelling. This "shortage" is easily understandable, however, because municipally subsidized rents are much lower than the real cost of providing housing.

Acquiring and Financing a New Dwelling: Controversies Concerning the Role of the Municipal Rental Sector

Households interested in purchasing a dwelling can be divided into two groups: those who already possess a dwelling but want a larger or more suitable

TABLE 6-5
Age Distribution of Dwellings in Budapest, 1980.

	Age in years					
	80	60-80	35-60	20-35	10-20	0-10
Percentage of total dwellings	17.3%	14.9%	24.3%	7.7%	14.1%	21.7%

Source: *Statistical Yearbooks of Budapest 1970-1984*, Central Statistical Office, Budapest.

TABLE 6-6
Distribution of Dwellings by Degree of Comfort and Age of Dwelling in Budapest, 1980 (in percent).

Degree of Comfort	Age in years					
	80	60-80	35-60	20-35	10-20	0-10
"Full Comfort"	51 %	58 %	66 %	83 %	94 %	98 %
"Partial Comfort"	10	12	12	7	2	1
"No Comfort"	39	30	21	10	4	1

Source: *Statistical Yearbooks of Budapest 1970-1984*, Central Statistical Office, Budapest.

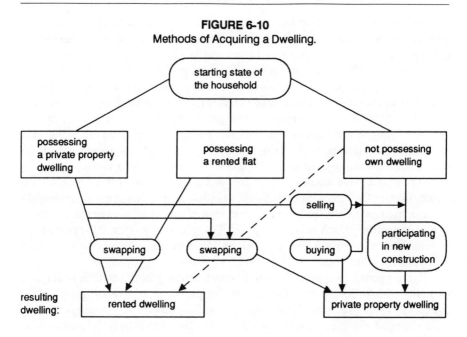

FIGURE 6-10
Methods of Acquiring a Dwelling.

one, and those who have not yet owned an independent dwelling (primarily newly formed households). The position of members of the former group is much more advantageous than that of members of the latter one, as the former possess "starting capital": a dwelling to offer in a complex swapping process. A dwelling, even one rented from the municipal authorities, can be exchanged for another rented dwelling or for a private property dwelling.

There is clearly a capital value associated with rental dwellings, even those rented from the municipality, of roughly 40 to 50 percent of the value of a private property dwelling of comparable size and quality. It is perfectly legal to swap a municipally owned rental unit for a privately owned flat, paying any difference in market price. It is, however, illegal to exchange two municipally rented flats of different sizes and pay the difference in cash. Nevertheless, such illegal swaps are routinely done.

Figure 6-10 indicates the most important methods of acquiring a dwelling. The dotted line indicates a relatively rare transaction: acquiring a rented dwelling through a successful application to the appropriate municipal authority or by the inheritance of a municipal dwelling from close relatives. A third possible way to acquire a dwelling is to agree to support an old person possessing a rented dwelling as long as he lives, in return for the right to inherit the dwelling. Such an agreement is often formulated in a contract approved by the municipal authority.

For the majority of families who do not own their own dwellings, the only way to acquire a flat is to purchase a private dwelling, either by buying an existing unit or by financing new construction. In both cases, savings from income can usually supply only a small fraction of the purchase price, making loans especially important. The supply price or construction cost (including land) per square meter of an average quality dwelling in Budapest in 1986 was 15,000 to 25,000 feet. depending on the geographical situation.[2] This means that an average-sized three-room flat of 65 square meters costs about 980,000 to 1,600,000 Ft. If 30 percent of this money has to be supplied in cash, a married couple with an average income of 150,000 Ft per year and a saving rate of 25 percent would have to save about ten years to acquire this amount. The situation is, in fact, even more difficult, as inflation in housing prices is roughly twice as high as average inflation. The period of saving needed in this example would, therefore, reach beyond 15 years. Therefore, it is normal for parents to provide the "starting capital" for their children for the purchase of their first independent dwelling.

It is not possible to detail fully the many financing schemes (different types of loans with different conditions) for the purchase of private property in Hungary. The ingredients, limits, and relevant conditions of financing schemes have changed continually in the last 20 years. We sketch only the situation in 1986, referring in some cases to relevant past development.

A characteristic feature of the Hungarian system of financing the purchase of a dwelling is that new construction is much more heavily assisted than the purchase of an existing flat or single-family house. For example, the most important component of the financial system, a long-term loan with a preferential interest rate, is supplied only in the case of new construction. The principal components in financing the construction of a privately owned dwelling include eight sources, described below.

1. *Owner's share.* This is the cash down payment financed from savings or by gifts from relatives or parents.

2. *Social aid.* This is a state grant to assist with the down payment or construction costs for families with children. 1986 levels of social aid are 40,000 Ft. for married couples with one child, 105,000 Ft. for married couples with two children, 230,000 Ft. for couples with three children, and for all additional children are granted 40,000 Ft. each. However, social aid may not exceed 45 percent of full construction costs.

---

[2] 62.5 Ft. = $1 U.S. in 1990.

3. *Long-term state mortgage loan at preferential rates.* This first mortgage is usually amortized over 35 years at a 3 percent interest rate. Eligibility for this mortgage varies with family size and housing type, as follows:

Family size	Single-family house	Dwelling in multifamily building
1-2	260,000 Ft.	320,000 Ft.
3-4	320,000 Ft.	380,000 Ft.
5-6	380,000 Ft.	440,000 Ft.
7+	440,000 Ft.	500,000 Ft.

4. *Young peoples' savings premium loan.* After five years of regular monthly savings (starting at an age under 35), the purchaser can obtain an extra loan equal to the face value of the savings up to a maximum of 210,000 Ft. under the same conditions as the long-term preferential loan.

5. *Preferential loan provided by the employer.* The size of this loan varies greatly among employers, from 50,000 to 200,000 Ft., and is typically granted under similar conditions as loans 3 and 4 described above.

6. *Bank loan.* Bank loans are made at more or less market interest rates, secured by property ownership, for terms of less than 15 years. Interest rates vary with the amount borrowed; for example:

Loan amount (in Ft.)	Interest rate (in percent)
0 - 100,000 Ft.	8 %
100,000 - 200,000	10
200,000 - 300,000	12

7. *Municipality's additional preferential loan or aid.* Additional assistance can be provided for families in extremely difficult financial circumstances through no fault of their own.

8. *Bridge loans.* The bridge loan program, with similar conditions as the bank loan noted above, is intended to surmount a temporary shortage in cash (as when, for example, a flat is purchased and the old flat is offered for sale but not yet sold).

From this array of financing instruments, the long-term preferential loan is provided by the National Savings Bank ("OTP") or by the employer only in

TABLE 6-7
Typical Financing of Newly Constructed Housing, Budapest, 1985.

Example 1. Moderate quality, 60 square meter dwelling costing 1,070,000 Ft.
Household earns 8,000 to 14,000 Ft. per month

	Cost	Cost distribution	Monthly payments
Social aid (3 children)	230,000 Ft.	21 %	0 Ft.
Preferential loan Long-term mortgage (35 years, 3%)	440,000	41	1,696
Loan from employer	100,000	9	400
Down payment (cash)	300,000	28	0
Total	1,070,000	100	2,096

Example 2. High quality, 85 square meter dwelling costing 1,600,000 Ft.
Household earns 12,000 to 16,000 Ft. per month

	Cost	Cost distribution	Monthly payments
Social aid (2 children)	105,000 Ft.	7 %	0 Ft.
Long-term mortgage (35 years, 3%)	380,000	24	1,464
Loan from employer	100,000	6	400
Young people's loan	300,000	19	1,100
Bank loan (15 years, 12%)	300,000	19	3,600
Down payment (cash)	415,000	26	0
Total	1,600,000	100	6,464

Note: Percentages may not sum due to rounding.
Source: *Statistical Yearbooks of Budapest 1970-1984*, Central Statistical Office, Budapest.

TABLE 6-8

Typical Costs of Municipally Owned Rental Units, Budapest, 1985.

Rooms	Size (square meters)	Monthly rent (in Ft.)	Key payment (in Ft.)
1	40	207	29,000
2	55	323	53,000
3	75	453	74,000
4	100	615	98,000

Source: *Statistical Yearbooks of Budapest, 1970-1984, Central Statistical Office*, Budapest.

the case of new construction. As is clear from the above discussion, this subsidy is quite considerable (the difference between the nominal interest rate of about 10 to 12 percent in 1986 and the preferential interest rate of 3 percent is subsidized). In the case of employer loans, a significant share of a firm's profits are spent on the support of dwelling purchases by their employees.

When a dwelling is resold, the new owner can usually keep the outstanding part of the long-term preferential loan associated with the construction of the dwelling, but under somewhat less advantageous conditions (e.g., higher monthly repayment obligation). Some part of the subsidy provided by the preferential loan may thus be capitalized upon resale of the dwelling.

Social aid and the preferential loan provided by the employer cannot be transferred when a dwelling is sold, but in certain cases the young people's savings premium loan and the bank loan can be taken over by the new owner with little difficulty.

These financing instruments are illustrated in the two typical examples presented in table 6-7.

In contrast, consider the structure of financing in the municipally owned rental sector. The rent levels are set very low, covering none of the capital costs and only 40 percent of actual repair and maintenance costs of dwellings. (Although rents have been raised repeatedly, they are still relatively low.) Rents are set according to the quality and location of the dwelling, and an official down payment ("key payment") is required when assuming a lease. Table 6-8 reports typical costs for Budapest.

These rent levels reflect historical accident rather than scarcity. If we now compare the case of a rented two-room flat in table 6-8 with example 1 in table 6-7, the sharp disparity is obvious. In the case of the rented flat, the down payment needed is 53,000 Ft.,and monthly rent is 323 Ft. In the case of the privately owned flat, the down payment needed is 300,000 Ft., and monthly repayment is 2,096 Ft.

Municipal housing offices (the Hungarian abbreviation is IKV) of the individual town-districts are responsible for the rented flats-- repair, maintenance, and other matters. Only about 55 percent of their income in 1984 originated from rents paid for dwellings, with the rest originating from rents paid by commercial users (shops, offices, etc). The maintenance and repair costs in 1984 amounted to 4,642 million Ft. in Budapest; 4l percent of this was covered by the income from rents paid for dwellings, 24 percent paid by commercial users, and the rest came from other sources.

If we take into account the capital costs (the opportunity costs or the amortization to create funds for renewal of the housing stock), the subsidy level of municipal rents is far higher. This high subsidy rate is an especially unhealthy economic phenomenon in the Hungarian economy because the subsidy level shows little correlation with the financial position of families. According to an analysis based on household statistics in Hungary, the fraction of households subsidized through low municipal rents varies little by household type. Twenty-three percent of households with children were subsidized by living in municipal housing, while 28 percent of households without children and 24 percent of retired households were subsidized. The subsidy level varies, but not systematically, by household type and income.

The possession of a flat rented from municipal authorities is a valuable capital asset yielding extra income for fortunate households for a long time. This is one of the principal factors that led to the formation of "housing classes" (see Hegedùs and Tosics, 1983) -- groups of people having similar housing conditions over a long period, almost independent of their income levels, their social circumstances, or their employment and productivity in the economy.

CONCLUSION

Although the housing shortage has been reduced and the quality of the dwelling stock raised in the Budapest Metropolitan Area during the last two decades, there is still much to be done. There has been a substantial rise in construction costs, and an increased disparity between rents for community-owned dwellings and the financial burdens of private construction. But there are also positive signs; the pace of inflation in construction costs has slowed down in recent years as a consequence of increased construction capacity. It seems probable that within a few years a new system of financing the maintenance of rental flats will be created, reducing the disparity between rents and real costs. Another positive tendency is the exploration of different ways of reducing construction costs: cooperative-like organizations, the introduction of new low-cost construction technologies, and so forth. Structural improvements in the housing of Hungarians, especially the residents of Budapest, have been observed to the benefit of all society.

REFERENCES

Compton, P.A. 1979. Planning and spatial change in Budapest. *In The socialist city, spatial structure and urban policy*, edited by R.A. French and F.E. Hamilton, 461-492. New York: Wiley.

Daniel, Zs. 1985. Housing as a distributional issue. In *Housing policy in urban areas, principles, planning and policy,* edited by Å.E. Andersson and B. Hårsman, 101-124. Stockholm: Swedish Council for Building Research.

Daniel, Zs., and A. Semjen. 1985. Lakbèrek, bèrlakàshiany, lakasmobilitas (Rents, insufficiency of rented dwellings, housing mobility). Working Paper no. 2575, XVIII, Institute for Economic Planning, Budapest.

Dienes, L. 1973. The Budapest agglomeration and Hungarian industry: A spatial dilemma. *Geographical Review*, 356-377.

Hegedùs, F., and I. Tosics. 1983. Housing classes and housing policy: Some changes in the Budapest housing market. unpublished paper.

Hoffmann, I. 1981. *Lakàskörùlmenyek* (Housing circumstances). Budapest: Kossuth Könyvkiadò.

Hörcher, N., and S. Kàdas. 1984. Past processes, present state and future prospects of the Budapest, metropolitan area. Background Paper for the Metropolitan Project of the IIASA, Laxenburg.

Hörcher, N., S. Kàdas, and J. Temesi. 1985. On the Hungarian/ Budapest housing market, preliminary draft. Paper prepared for the IIASA Seminar on Metropolitan Housing Markets under Different Policy Regimes, 13-14 June 1985, Stockholm.

International Journal of Urban and Regional Research, 7:467-494.

Korcelli, P. 1984. Metropolitan population dynamics: A cross-cutting review. Paper prepared for the IIASA Workshop on Metropolitan Areas, 4-8 June 1984, Rotterdam.

K.S.H. 1970-1984. *Budapest statisztikai èvkönyvei* (Statistical Yearbooks of Budapest). Budapest: K.S.H.

K.S.H. 1980. *Eevi nepszamlalas* (Census). Budapest adatai I-II (Data for Budapest I-II). Budapest: K.S.H.

Leuschacke, C., and M. Wegener. 1985. Metropolitan housing subsystems: A cross-cutting review. Paper prepared for the IIASA Seminar on Metropolitan Housing Markets under Different Policy Regions, 13-14 June 1985, Stockholm.

Sillince, J.A.A. 1985. The housing market of the Budapest urban region 1949-1983. *Urban Studies*, 22: 141-149.

Szelenyi, I. 1972. Tarsadalmi struktura es lakasrendszer (Social structure and housing system). Dissertation, Kandidatusi ertekezes, Budapest.

Szelenyi, I., and G. Konrad. 1969. *Az uj lakotelepek szociologiai problemai* (Sociological problems of the new housing estates). Budapest: Akademiai Kiado.

7

THE VIENNA HOUSING MARKET: STRUCTURE, PROBLEMS, AND POLICIES

E. Aufhauser
M.M. Fischer
H. Schönhofer

INTRODUCTION

The housing sector in Austria is quite different from that in a purely free market society. Government involvement in housing production and consumption has a strong tradition in Austria. Rent control and tenant security legislation, in varying forms, have been continuing features of government housing policy since the First World War, as have government incentives for new housing construction.

The purpose of this chapter is to provide a relatively comprehensive view of Austrian housing policy with a focus on the metropolitan housing market in the agglomeration of Vienna. The chapter is organized as follows: first we characterize the dynamics and present structure of the housing market. In particular, patterns of housing stock variability in time and space are analyzed and the finance system for new housing construction is characterized. The next section is devoted to the role of the state in the housing market. The periods chosen to describe the evolution of housing policy in Austria are the early period (1908-1945), the reconstruction period (1946-1984), and the new era which started quite recently. Finally, the major impacts of assistance and control policies on the housing market are discussed in some detail.

THE STRUCTURE OF THE HOUSING MARKET IN METROPOLITAN VIENNA

Legal and Organizational Background for Austrian Housing Policy

Austria is a federal state consisting of nine autonomous provinces (so-called Länder), each electing its own government and parliament. There is a fixed distribution of legislative and executive power between the federal authority, the regional authority of the Länder, and local authorities (see table 7-1). The federal parliament is responsible for state-wide legislation in the areas of social housing and residential improvement. The federal authority is responsible for rent control and security of tenure legislation. It also sets up the legal framework for housing subsidies, as well as other housing laws, such as those regulating the practice of nonprofit housing associations and real estate agencies, housing assistance for young families, and urban renewal and land acquisition. Furthermore, the federal authority is responsible for federal taxation and fiscal policy. Thus, it specifies the forms of taxation and assigns federal funds (e.g., housing and improvement funds) to the nine Länder.

The nine Länder have executive power in the fields of social housing and residential improvement. Therefore, they set up the regulations for the allocation of the federally legislated housing subsidies and, in fact, allocate these subsidies to the individual developers. Moreover, most of the Länder establish their own housing funds and carry out their own special housing programs. In addition to these special tasks in housing policy, the Länder also have legislative and executive power in other relevant fields like regional planning, building codes, land transactions, and the preservation of the special architectural and aesthetic character of settlements.

The country is subdivided into 99 administrative counties and approximately 2,300 communities with their own elected assemblies. These local (communal or municipal) authorities form the third level of governmental authority. They are responsible for local planning such as setting up local development plans and drawing up land-use and building plans. They also exercise local building control, construct the local infrastructure, and develop land for building purposes.

Besides the exercise of governmental authority, the federal and provincial governments, as well as the local authorities, may become active as private entities in all spheres of planning. The most important example in this context is the council housing activity of the communities.

Due to this division of responsibilities concerning housing and planning matters, there is no Ministry of Housing or Physical Planning in Austria. The federal concerns regarding housing are mainly dealt with by the Ministry of Construction and Engineering. The executive organs for housing and planning

TABLE 7-1
The Main Legal and Organizational Bases for Regulations in the
Housing Sector in Austria.

Exercise of governmental authority	Major tasks	Relevant acts	Administrative authorities
Federal Authority			
Federal taxation and fiscal policy	Regulating the forms of taxation (e.g., deduction of income tax due to housing expenditures; level of rent subsidies)	Income Tax Act; Financial Constitution Act	Ministry of Finance
	Assignment of funds to the federal, Länder and local authorities	Revenue Sharing Act	
	Assignment of housing and improvement funds to the Länder	Housing Promotion Act 1984	
Legislative power in the field of social housing and residential improvement	Rent control and security of tenure	Rent Act 1981; parts in other acts regulating the rents for sub-sidized housing (Housing Promo-tion Act 1984; Nonprofit Housing Association Act 1979)	Ministry of Justice
	Legal and financial framework for housing and improvements subsidies	Housing Promotion Act 1984; Dwelling Improvement Act 1969; Housing Improvement Act 1984; "Althausmilliarde"	Ministry of Construction and Engineering
	Housing construction	Nonprofit Housing Associations Act 1979; Condominiums Act 1975	
	Provision of housing for special social groups	Law for Assisted Housing for Young Families 1982	Ministry of Social Affairs
	Brokerage for housing and real estate agencies	Real Estate Agencies Act 1978	Ministry of Commerce

TABLE 7-1 (continued)
The Main Legal and Organizational Bases for Regulations in the
Housing Sector in Austria.

Exercise of governmental authority	Major tasks	Relevant acts	Administrative authorities
Federal Authority			
	Urban renewal and land acquisition	Urban Renewal Act 1974; Land Acquisition 1974	Minstry of Construction and Engineering
Legislative and executive power for the protection of ancient monuments	Regulating the protection of ancient monuments	Protection of Monuments Act 1973	
Länder Authority			
Indirect federal administration	Allocation of the Federal Revenue Shares to the communities	Revenue Sharing Act	Land Office Director
Autonomous sphere of activities of the land government	Regulating the exclusive land (community) levies	Financial Constitution Act	
	Provision of Länder-funds for housing subsidies		
	Specific housing programs		
Executive power in the field of social housing and residential improvement	Implementing the major part of the Housing Promotion Act		Housing (Construction) Departments in the Land Government Office
	Drawing up of special five-year housing programs		
	Allocation of housing subsidies to the individual developers		

TABLE 7-1 (continued)
The Main Legal and Organizational Bases for Regulations in the
Housing Sector in Austria

Exercise of governmental authority	Major tasks	Relevant acts	Administrative authorities
Länder Authority			
Legislative and executive power in the fields of			
Regional planning	Principles and objectives for regional planning	Regional planning laws (Lower Austria 1976[1])	Regional Planning Departments
	Establishment of supra-local development programs		
	Support given to local authorities in the implementation of local planning		
	Approval of communal land-use and building plans		
Building laws	Regulating building permissions and design standards in general	Building Code of Vienna 1929 (amended version 1976); Building Code of Lower Austria 1969 (amended version 1976)	Land Government Office
Land transactions	General rules regulating land transactions		
	The preservation of the special architectural and aesthetic character of settlements	Regulations concerning the preservation of the Old Town in Vienna 1972	

TABLE 7-1 (continued)
The Main Legal and Organizational Bases for Regulations in the
Housing Sector in Austria.

Exercise of governmental authority	Major tasks	Relevant acts	Administrative authorities
Local (Communal or Municipal) Authority			
Tasks of local planning	Provision of local development plans[2]		Municipal office, town councils with facilities depending on the size of the community; Mayor
	Drawing up land-use plans		
	Drawing up of building plans		
Local building control	Authorization of building activities		
Local infra-structure	Streets, schools, and other facilities		
	Development of building land		
Communal activity as private entity	Council Housing		

---

[1] In Vienna this function is fulfilled by the Building Code.

[2] The Development Plan for the City of Vienna settled by the Viennese Assembly in 1984 has no legal basis because the Land of Vienna possesses no Regional Planning Law.

concerns entrusted to the Länder are the Housing and Regional Planning Departments in the Länder Government Offices. The tasks of the communities are carried out by municipal offices or town councils, with the chosen agency depending largely on the size of the communities. In Vienna, several housing and town planning departments are responsible for specific tasks connected with housing and planning.

Spatial Framework

The delineation of the metropolitan area of Vienna parallels the Viennese labor market and is basically defined as the daily commuting basin. The city of Vienna forms the core of the agglomeration (see figure 7-1). As a political unit, Vienna is not only the largest municipality (community) in Austria but is simultaneously one of the nine autonomous Länder. Thus, the exercise of provincial and municipal governmental authority coincides. For the purpose of this study, the 23 administrative districts of Vienna are aggregated into four residential areas: the Inner City, Vienna West, Vienna South, and Vienna Northeast (see figure 7-1). The communities, counties, and subcounties constituting the four outer regions of the agglomeration belong to another of the Länder, Lower Austria. This political division of the agglomeration into two separate Länder and several communities thwarts a clear-cut and comprehensive policy for the development of the metropolitan area. Since the Länder largely influence the concrete form of housing policy, it is also important to note their different political backgrounds. The Socialist Party is traditionally powerful in Vienna, and the Popular Democratic (conservative) Party dominates Lower Austria.

Housing Conditions

This section characterizes current housing conditions and trends in metropolitan Vienna. First, a short description of the historical building record indicates the cumulative legacy of housing inherited from the past. Second, aggregate measures describe the most important features of current housing within the metropolitan area. Radically increasing housing costs are one of the main problems confronting housing policy today. As will be outlined, the structure of housing costs in different dwelling types depends mainly on institutional settings in Austria. Finally, some remarks concerning the forced migration from the city to the outer regions and the boom of second homes illustrate one of the current housing trends in the agglomeration.

The Development of the Housing Stock

During the last century, Austria's position in Europe, as well as its political and economic relations with other countries, changed several times. Each

FIGURE 7-1
The Agglomeration of Vienna:
Zones Used to Analyze the Housing Market Stucture.

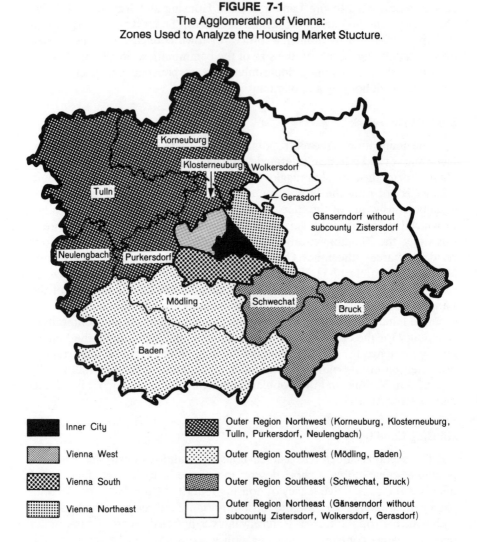

▉ Inner City		▓ Outer Region Northwest (Korneuburg, Klosterneuburg, Tulln, Purkersdorf, Neulengbach)
░ Vienna West		░ Outer Region Southwest (Mödling, Baden)
▓ Vienna South		▓ Outer Region Southeast (Schwechat, Bruck)
▦ Vienna Northeast		☐ Outer Region Northeast (Gänserndorf without subcounty Zistersdorf, Wolkersdorf, Gerasdorf)

Note: The following abbreviations are used in the tables: Zone A for Inner City, Zone B for Vienna West, Zone C for Vienna South, Zone D for Vienna Northeast, Zone E for the outer region Northwest, Zone F for the outer region Southwest, Zone G for the outer region Southeast, and Zone H for the outer region Northeast.

change affected regional development and domestic relations in important ways. This evolution also had a strong impact upon Vienna. As a city with 2.1 million inhabitants before World War I, it was the dynamically growing capital in the center of the Austro-Hungarian monarchy. At the time, Austria-Hungary was a state with a population of more than 50 million and a strong orientation towards economic activity in Eastern and Southeastern Europe. Now, Vienna is the "overdimensioned"capital of Austria, a small country with 7.5 million inhabitants. The country is situated between the important political and economic blocks of the West and East. Although Vienna remains the political and economic center of Austria, its location at the eastern periphery of the country next to the "iron curtain" has decreased its importance.

The specific historical and political development of Vienna during the past hundred years is also evident in the city's Historical Building Record (see figure 7-2). The biggest building boom in Vienna took place in the decades before the First World War (the so-called Founders' Period, 1880-1910). During this time, huge public investment in large infrastructure projects was accompanied by immense private investment in housing construction. Although about 80 percent of the previous housing stock was demolished in the Founders' Period, the number of dwelling units rose from about 146,000 in 1880 to 498,000 in 1910 (see table 7-2). In the center of the city, palaces and rental houses with large flats were built for the upper class, while the main extension of the city took place in a ring from the northwest to the south outside the old fortification line (the so-called Gürtel) in the form of large private tenement houses with high building and population densities. These dwellings were typically small, dark, without plumbing facilities, relatively expensive, and highly overcrowded due to the enormous population increase (see table 7-2 for some aggregate indices of the housing conditions during that period). Today these areas present major problems for urban renewal.

Because of the social and political changes caused by World War I, the dynamic development of the city stopped, as did all private building activities. Figure 7-2 clearly illustrates that from 1914 to 1923 housing production rapidly declined. Although population growth had stagnated, the housing shortage remained an urgent problem. In order to overcome the apparent inability of the private sector to provide housing for the poor in sufficient quantity and adequate quality, the municipality of Vienna interceded directly in 1922 by constructing council housing. Between the wars, the municipality financed, built, owned, and managed about 63,000 dwelling units, located mainly in large-scale tenement blocks with big inner courtyards and equipped with social and service facilities.

Between 1934 and the end of World War II, there was an enormous decline in housing production accompanied by extensive wartime housing damage in 1944 (see figure 7-2). Council housing construction started immediately after

TABLE 7-2

The Development of Housing Conditions in the City of Vienna, 1869-1981.

Year of census	Number of houses (buildings)	Number of dwellings	Average number of rooms per dwelling	Number of resident population	Number of households	Average number of persons per private households	Average number of occupants per dwelling	Average number of occupants per room
1869	10,250	125,182	3.00	632,127	125,182	5.05	5.05	1.68
1880	12,162	145,897	3.40	725,658	141,152	5.14	4.97	1.46
1890	29,259	308,185	3.02	1,363,548	286,345	4.77	4.43	1.47
1900	33,130	392,572	2.96	1,674,957	379,285	4.42	4.27	1.44
1910	40,609	497,549	2.87	2,031,498	479,339	4.24	4.08	1.42
WWI								
1923	44,873	535,067	--	1,865,780	--	--	3.49	--
1934	59,785	613,436	--	1,874,130	633,493	2.96	3.06	--
WWII								
1951	67,292	614,078	1.81	1,616,125	672,237	2.40	2.63	1.45
1961	74,481	686,497[b] 655,104[c]	2.17	1,627,566	693,241	2.35	2.48	1.15
1971	83,681[a]	781,518[b] 712,470[c]	2.19	1,587,429	732,693	2.17	2.27	1.04
1981	134,321[a]	821,175[b] 712,925[c]	2.30	1,493,245	724,993	2.06	2.09	--

Note: All data refer to contemporaneous boundaries of Vienna. From 1961 onwards, boundaries conform to current Vienna.

-- Not available. [a] Definitional change. [b] Total number of dwellings. [c] Number of permanently occupied dwellings.

Sources: Kainrath, 1985; *Hauser- und Wohnungszahlungen*, 1981.

the war. However, the strong social emphasis characteristic of the Viennese housing policy during the prewar period diminished in view of the urgent housing shortage. Moreover, the federal government introduced major incentives (see section 3) to stimulate private construction. With 614,000 dwelling units, the city of Vienna reached the prewar housing stock by 1951 (see table 7-2).The reconstruction phase was more or less finished at the end of the 1950s and a phase of suburbanization started in the sixties. Construction of huge housing estates ("dormitory colonies"), built at the southern and northeastern outskirts of the city, was one of the driving forces of the suburbanization process. They were built by the municipality, housing cooperatives, and non-profit associations. An extension of the city to the west was not possible because there the settlement had reached the slopes of the Vienna Woods which have been protected against building activities since 1906. Strong regulations in the Viennese Building Code impeded high-rise construction in the center of the city. With the enormous building activity in the northeastern part of the city, on the left banks of the Danube, intense settlement crossed the Danube for the first time. The number of dwelling units in this part of the city doubled in the past 30 years (from more than 44,000 in 1951 to almost 99,000 in 1981 -- see table 7-3, zone D). In absolute terms, the biggest development took place at the southern outskirts of Vienna with an increase of 90,000 units between 1951 and 1981 (see table 7-3, zone C).

The intense development in the outskirts of the city diminished with the decrease in building activity since the beginning of the seventies (see figure 7-2). The council housing program was cut to an annual rate of roughly 2,000 to 3,000 newly built dwellings, reflecting a shift in the communal investment budget toward infrastructure projects. Housing associations now carry out half of the building activity.

Post-World War II development of the housing stock in the outer regions occurred significantly later than in Vienna. Until 1955, Soviet occupation impeded economic development in the outer regions. Intensive housing construction started at the end of the fifties and reached a peak in the late seventies. In some parts of the region this development has slowed down recently (see table 7-3). The most dynamic housing construction took place in the southern region (zone F) where the number of dwelling units increased by 56 percent between 1951 and 1981 (see tables 7-3 through 7-6). Recently, development activity has increased in some of the western parts of the outer regions (especially in the attractive communities of the Vienna Woods), along the Danube, and along the main public traffic arterials to the north. Housing development in the outer regions is mainly carried out by private persons. In the southern region (zone F), housing built by associations and cooperatives has some importance. In comparison with Vienna, council housing construction is quite low in the southern region.

FIGURE 7-2
Historical Building Record:
The Development of Housing Construction and Housing
Demolition in Vienna, 1885-1983.

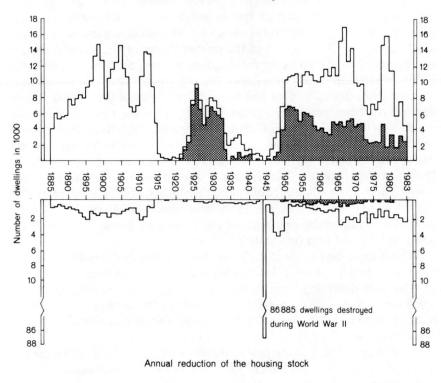

Annual addition to the housing stock

86 885 dwellings destroyed
during World War II

Annual reduction of the housing stock

  Public housing

Note: Because there are no adequate data available for the outer regions before 1971,
the graph traces only the path of new housing construction and housing damage
for the municipality of Vienna. The general shape of the figure is correct. Due to
inaccuracies in the official construction statistics, however, strict annual data
may be misleading. In particular, the building booms in 1970 and 1980 are
exaggerated by including data missing from previous years.

Source: Institutute for Urban Research,1974 - Kurzinformation Wien; *Statistisches Jahrbuch
Der Stadt Wien 1976*, et seq.

TABLE 7-3

Spatial Development of the Housing Stock in the Vienna Metropolitan Area, 1951-1981.

Zone	Total stock of dwellings				Absolute change 1951-1981	Percentage change			
	1951	1961	1971	1981		1951-1961	1961-1971	1971-1981	1951-1981
A	241,764	262,412	280,758	274,664	32,900	8.5%	7.0%	-2.2%	13.6%
B	203,967	212,376	230,416	234,341	30,374	4.1	8.5	1.7	14.9
C	123,864	162,563	192,344	213,546	89,682	31.2	18.3	11.0	72.4
D	44,483	52,884	77,993	98,624	54,141	18.9	47.5	26.5	121.7
Vienna	614,078	675,774	781,518	821,175	207,097	10.0	15.6	5.1	33.7
E	54,040	52,243	66,337	79,386	25,346	-3.3	27.0	19.7	46.9
F	59,096	61,916	77,121	92,105	33,009	4.8	24.6	19.4	55.9
G	24,314	25,062	29,457	34,280	9,966	3.1	17.5	16.4	41.0
H	24,549	23,435	28,212	35,527	10,978	-4.5	20.4	25.9	44.7
Outer regions	162,000	163,035	201,157	241,298	79,298	0.6	23.4	20.0	48.9
Total	776,078	838,809	982,668	1,062,437	286,359	8.1	17.2	8.1	36.9

Sources: *Häuser- und Wohnungszählung*, 1951, et seq.

TABLE 7-4

Permanent Dwellings Completed in the Vienna Metropolitan Area,
1945-1980.

Zone	Total number of dwellings completed in the period		
	1945-1960	1961-1970	1971-1980
A	28,714	26,643	16,894
B	27,926	27,803	21,958
C	39,760	48,606	34,068
D	14,796	27,299	22,001
Vienna	118,030	133,047	94,921
E	11,604	14,593	14,779
F	13,212	18,416	18,195
G	5,810	6,914	7,342
H	4,463	5,405	7,007
Outer regions	35,089	45,328	47,323
Total	153,119	178,375	142,244

Source: Austrian Statistical Office, various publications on housing construction.

Note: Due to under-registration in the Austrian construction statistics, the data for the
outer regions have been estimated. For Vienna the data are accurate, but are
missing for the individual districts 1945-1970. Data from the housing census of
1981 about the age of dwellings were used to estimate the zonal measures 1945-
1960 and 1961-1970. Thus, the total for Vienna differs slightly for these periods.
For the outer regions, data have been estimated from the housing census of
1961, 1971, and 1981.

Housing Conditions and Trends

Because of the intense private building activity in the late nineteenth
century and a relatively moderate demolition rate since World War II, Vienna
has an extremely overaged housing stock. Forty percent of the total stock of
dwellings in the city was built before World War I. Private rental tenure is
typical within this old housing stock. Roughly 350,000 dwelling units in about
27,000 buildings belong to this private rental sector. Private rental housing is
one of the principal alternatives for the Viennese population. After World
War I, private rental housing construction totally disappeared; the level of such
housing construction today is negligible as a result of restrictions on financial
subsidies for private developers. Apart from public or council housing, only

TABLE 7-5
New Housing Construction by Type of Developer.

Zone	Time period	Housing units total	Local authority	Housing associations and co-operatives	Other legal entities	Private (physical) persons
				Percent built by		
Vienna	1956-60	54,253	51	17	13	19
	1961-65	56,875	38	29	10	23
	1966-70	71,170	36	34	13	17
	1971-80	94,921	33	47	10	10
	1981-83	17,479	40	38	14	8
Outer* regions	1970-83	48,809	5	29	3	63
E	1970-83	16,838	1	23	2	74
F	1970-83	19,763	6	43	6	45
G	1970-83	5,274	9	20	4	67
H	1970-83	6,934	7	11	1	82

* No data available for previous periods.

Source: Austrian Statistical Office, various publications on housing construction.

housing associations and cooperatives are adding new tenements to the housing stock.

The public housing sector in the agglomeration is dominated by council housing in Vienna. The municipality owns 210,000 dwelling units (26 percent of the total housing stock). In the outer regions, some housing construction by local authorities occurred in the sixties but has nearly disappeared by now.

Although decreasing, the private rental housing sector is still dominant in Vienna. In 1981, rent controlled housing comprised 93 percent of the rental sector in the municipality, but is found least in the outer regions where a higher proportion of apartments is rented at free market prices. "Subletting" strategies, quite common in the private rental housing sector, avoid the intent of the Rent Control Act, which, in general, incorporates strong security of tenure and sets rent per square meter according to the sanitation standard of the dwelling. "Subletting" allows a tenant with a regulated rent contract to let the dwelling or parts of it by means of a second non regulated contract to another person.

Cooperative housing, with 57,000 dwelling units, forms 8 percent of the total housing stock in Vienna.

The owner-occupied sector is of minor importance in Vienna. However, this sector is increasing due to condominium construction by building associations and condominium conversion in older rent-controlled housing stock. Local authorities do not offer council housing for sale. Owner occupancy of single-family dwellings is the main housing form in the outer regions. Compensatory housing, that is dwellings provided by firms, offices, or other employers to their staff free of charge, as well as dwellings in tenement houses that are occupied by building superintendents or concierges, comprises 4 percent of the housing stock.

Due to the high proportion of old buildings in Vienna, a clear distinction in quality can be made among dwellings according to the standard of sanitation. One can distinguish between dwellings with all facilities (bath, WC, and central heating), dwellings of good standard (with WC and bath), dwellings of middle standard lacking one facility (WC or bath), and substandard dwellings (some without running water). These standards, of course, do not include the inherent quality of the building itself. The number of substandard dwellings has decreased rapidly, especially in the last decade, due to immense private improvement activities by the tenants and some demolition of the old rental housing stock. Nevertheless, there are still 130,000 dwellings (18 percent of the total housing stock) without any sanitation. In 1951, there were 360,000 such dwellings. Usually these substandard dwelling units are smaller than 60 square meters. Sixty thousand of them are even smaller than 35 square meters (see table 7-6).

TABLE 7-6
Housing Conditions in Metropolitan Vienna, 1981.

Zone	Total area (km²)	Population	Population per km² area	Percent Population change 1951-81	Percent Population change 1971-81	Persons per household
A	45.6	487,759	10,708	-28 %	-14 %	1.97
B	88.9	407,056	4,578	+29	-9	2.31
C	132.9	420,697	3,166	-19	0	2.12
D	146.4	215,834	1,474	+78	+16	2.42
Vienna	414.8	1,531,340	3,692	-5	-5	2.05
E	1,736.0	167,880	97	+5	+3	2.64
F	1,030.1	200,556	195	+22	+5	2.45
G	702.3	75,794	108	+3	+8	2.57
H	1,195.4	75,544	63	+2	+1	2.66
Outer regions	4,663.8	519,774	111	+10	+5	2.56
Total	5,078.6	2,051,120	404	-2	-3	2.22

TABLE 7-6 (continued)
Measures of Housing Conditions in Metropolitan Vienna, 1981.

Zone	Total stock of dwellings	Percent change in stock of dwellings 1951-81	Percent change in stock of dwellings 1971-81	Vacancy rate percent dwellings not perm occupied	Percent buildings Total stock of buildings	Owned by private persons	Built before 1919
A	274,664	13.6 %	-2.2 %	13 %	21,965	55 %	59 %
B	213,546	14.9	+1.7	15	37,443	72	33
C	234,34	72.4	+11.0	12	43,901	63	19
D	98,624	121.7	+26.5	11	31,012	70	10
Vienna	821,175	33.7	+5.1	13	134,321	66	27
E	35,517	46.9	+19.7	22	65,243	93	23
F	79,386	55.9	+19.4	14	52,038	88	26
G	52,405	41.0	+16.4	15	22,795	89	20
H	34,280	44.7	+25.9	20	30,754	84	25
Outer regions	241,298	48.9	+20.0	18	170,830	91	24
Total	1,062,437	36.9	+8.1	14	305,151	80	25

Zone	Percentage of Dwellings					
	Percent rental dwellings (1971)	Without sanitation facilities (WC and bath)	With all facilities (bath, WC, central heating)	With 1 or 2 rooms	In multiple dwelling houses	Average size of dwellings (sq meters)
A	83 %	19 %	26 %	62 %	45 %	68
B	80	26	29	67	55	60
C	76	15	42	60	64	62
D	70	8	55	49	63	67
Vienna	79	18	35	61	55	64
E	27	15	49	35	19	81
F	41	14	49	44	41	79
G	33	16	39	46	32	83
H	13	17	46	33	10	90
Outer regions	31	15	47	40	28	83
Total	61	18	37	57	9	69

Sources: *Häuser- und Wohnungszählung* ,1971, et seq.

Although the lowest quality dwellings are concentrated in the private tenement blocks built in the Founders' Period and nearly all dwellings built after World War II are of modern sanitation standard, the correlation between quality, age of dwellings, and sanitation standard is rather weak. A stronger relationship exists between the size of dwellings and their sanitation standards. Two trends characterize changes in the size of dwellings (measured by the number of rooms): First, the number of small dwellings decreased absolutely and relatively; and second, a substantial gap in size of dwellings developed between the city and the outer regions. While the proportion of one-room dwellings in the municipality dropped from 45 percent to 25 percent between 1951 and 1981, the proportion of dwellings in Vienna with more than two rooms is significantly lower than in the outer regions. Thirty-nine percent of all dwellings in Vienna and 60 percent of the dwellings in the outer region currently consist of more than two rooms (see tables 7-6 and 7-8).

TABLE 7-7
Age Structure of the Housing Stock in Metropolitan Vienna, 1981.

Zone	Bldgs (dwellings)*	Percent of buildings (dwellings)* built				
		Before 1919	1919-1944	1945-1960	1961-1970	After 1970
A	21,965	59 %	8 %	11 %	9 %	6 %
	(274,664)	(60)	(8)	(11)	(10)	(6)
B	37,443	33	22	15	13	12
	(234,341)	(50)	(12)	(12)	(12)	(10)
C	43,901	19	23	21	18	14
	(213,546)	(16)	(14)	(19)	(23)	(15)
D	31,012	10	27	20	19	20
	(98,624)	(13)	(16)	(15)	(28)	(27)
Vienna	134,321	27	21	17	15	14
	(821,175)	(43)	(12)	(14)	(16)	(12)
E	65,243	23	15	12	17	29
F	52,038	26	13	12	20	26
G	22,795	20	16	14	18	28
H	30,754	25	15	13	15	30
Outer regions	170,830	24	14	12	18	28
Total	305,151	25	17	15	17	22

* For the outer regions no data on dwellings are available.
Source: *Häuser - und Wohnungszählung* ,1981.

TABLE 7-8
Size of Dwellings in Metropolitan Vienna, 1951-1981.

Year	Zone	Total stock of permanently occupied dwellings	Percent dwellings with				Avg size of dwell. (sq. m)
			One room	Two rooms	Three rooms	Four or more	
1951	Vienna	614,061	45 %	38 %	11 %	6 %	--
	Outer regions	162,000	42	41	13	4	--
	Total	776,078	45	38	11	6	--
1961	Vienna	655,104	34	37	17	12	53
	Outer regions	151,451	24	36	22	18	--
	Total	806,555	32	37	18	13	--
1971	Vienna	712,470	32	37	20	11	56
	Outer regions	171,010	18	33	27	22	69
	Total	884,480	30	36	21	13	--
1981	A	238,463	23	39	25	13	68
	B	199,160	31	36	22	11	60
	C	187,905	25	35	28	12	62
	D	87,397	18	31	35	16	67
	Vienna	712,925	25	36	26	13	64
	E	62,255	10	25	29	36	81
	F	78,927	15	29	29	27	79
	G	29,256	15	31	29	25	83
	H	28,207	8	25	31	36	90
	Outer regions	198,648	12	28	29	31	83
	Total	911,573	22	35	27	16	69

Note: Room count excludes kitchen.
  -- Not available.

Sources: *Häuser - und Wohnungszählung* ,1951, et seq.

As indicated in table 7-6, differences in the average size of net dwelling area exist between the central city (64 square meters) and the outer regions (83 square meters). However, the average net dwelling area per resident is nearly the same in all zones because of larger average household size in the outer regions. Though the size of dwellings increased generally since World War II, no regional shift in the distribution of different dwelling sizes occurred. The largest dwellings are still located in the center of the city, the western outskirts next to the slopes of the Vienna Woods, and the district of Hietzing in the south.

Since World War II, housing supply in the agglomeration increased substantially in quantity as well as in quality. While the population decreased by 2 percent since 1951, the number of dwelling units increased by 37 percent (for detailed information concerning the slightly varied development within the different zones see table 7-3 and table 7-6). However, the ratio of households to available dwelling units changed only slightly (1961: 1.06, 1981: 1.01) because of transitions in the household structure and the fact that an increasing number of dwellings is not used for primary housing supply.

TABLE 7-9

Quality of the Housing Stock in Metropolitan Vienna, 1951-1981.

			Percent of dwellings		
Year	Zone	Total stock of permanently occupied dwellings	With all facilities (bath, WC)	Lacking one facility	Without all facilities (without bath, WC)
1951	Vienna	614,078	14 %	27 %	59 %
1961	Vienna	655,104	27	28	45
1971	Vienna	712,470	48	19	33
1981	A	238,463	68	13	19
	B	199,160	64	10	26
	C	187,905	76	9	15
	D	87,397	83	9	8
	Vienna	712,925	71	11	18
	E	62,258	78	7	15
	F	78,927	79	7	14
	G	29,256	77	7	16
	H	28,207	77	6	17
	Outer regions	198,648	78	7	15
	Total	911,573	72	10	18

Source: *Häuser - und Wohnungszählung* ,1951, et seq.

TABLE 7-10
Rental Housing in Metropolitan Vienna, 1951-1981.

Year	Zone	Total stock of dwellings	Percent rental housing	Rent controlled rental housing
1951	Vienna	614,061	92 %	74 %
	Outer regions	161,910	50	39
	Total	775,971	83	70
1971	Vienna	712,470	79	95
	Outer regions	171,890	31	--
	Total	884,360	61	--
1981	A	238,463	78	93
	B	199,160	69	93
	C	187,905	58	95
	D	87,397	60	95
	Vienna	712,925	68	93

Note: --   Not available.
Sources:*Häuser - und Wohnungszählung* ,1951, et seq.

TABLE 7-11
Tenure Categories in the City of Vienna, 1981.

Tenure form	Number of dwellings	Percent
Owner occupation	40,463	6 %
Condominium	78,874	11
Cooperative	57,313	8
Rental housing	483,861	68
Rent controlled	451,976	63
Rented on free market	31,885	5
Official residence	27,755	4
Unknown (others)	24,659	3
Total	712,925	100

Sources:*Häuser - und Wohnungszählung* ,1951, et seq.

Generally, the occupancy conditions are quite good with an average of 0.9 persons per room and an average of 31 square meters of net dwelling area per occupant. However, inequalities occur with respect to the social status of the occupants, the age of the dwellings (the occupancy conditions are better in the oldest and youngest housing stock), size of dwellings, and size of the households. Overcrowding declined from 40 percent in 1971 to 27 percent in 1981, but is still evident, especially within the small substandard dwellings in the old housing stock.

Due to rent control, security of tenure rules, and the effects of public housing subsidies, spatial segregation of different social groups is not the most pervasive characteristic of the Vienna housing market. Nevertheless, certain interrelations between different housing types and household characteristics occur. A higher proportion of working-class households is found in council housing and substandard private rental housing. Households of retired persons, as well as guest workers, are also concentrated in the worst private rental housing. Cooperative housing is mainly occupied by employees and officials, while the self-employed tend to prefer owner-occupied or single-family dwellings as well as old rental housing of high quality. Young families with children are concentrated in the new council housing, while new cooperative housing and condominiums show a smaller proportion of families with children. Table 7-11 shows the distribution of housing in Vienna by tenure category.

Spatial Distribution of Dwelling Types

Eight percent of the present housing stock dates to the time before 1880. These ancient buildings are concentrated in the center of the city, and are mainly under the protection of historical preservation regulation. Often they are restored for mixed residential and commercial use. In general, the flats in these buildings are quite large and of good quality.

Around the city center is the ring of private tenement houses built in the Founders' Period. The size (and quality) of the dwellings decreases from the palaces along the Ringstraße to the Gürtel (forming the boundary between the inner city and the western and southern districts). The parts of these districts that are close to the center are the preferred housing areas of the self-employed (e.g., physicians, lawyers, merchants).

Beyond the Gürtel lies the ring of the worst residential areas. These areas were constructed before World War I, are of the poorest quality, and are in need of renewal. Numerous factors coincide to impede and complicate the renewal of these areas:

- The typical apartment has a peculiar layout -- a small kitchen with window and entrance to the corridor and just one other room. In most cases, toilet and water facilities are commonly shared. This complicates the construction of a single standard dwelling from several of the unrestored units.

- The tenants are often socially and economically weak, including the elderly, low-income families, and guest workers. These households are not able to invest in improvement or to pay higher rents for improved dwellings. Due to financial conditions, many units are over-crowded.
- The turnover of tenants is relatively high and the population is decreasing constantly.
- Strong rent control and notice regulations impede investment by private owners in the housing stock, even though the costs of improvement can ultimately be passed on to tenants.
- A relatively high proportion of owners occupies a flat and often uses one or more units for their own commercial or industrial purposes. Although they may be interested in improvement, they may be unable to invest using their own funds. The small production units and commercial enterprises which the owners typically operate present liquidity constraints.
- The variegated ownership structure and the high rate of foreclosure cause a great deal of difficulty and delay with regard to a comprehensive renewal.
- Poor infrastructures and a lack of open space coexist with extremely high building and population densities in the area. Comprehensive renewal activity would require remodeling to produce larger dwellings and a reduction in net residential densities.

On the edges of these rings of buildings, which date to the Founders' Period, and also in the districts between the Canal of the Danube and the river itself, one finds large blocks of housing built by the community between the wars. These blocks of housing contain small dwellings of medium quality, now typically occupied by retired workers and large families. In the southwest, there are areas with single-family and terrace houses built by the community during the same period. Such dwellings are also located along the western and southern city boundaries as well as in the zone between the Canal of the Danube and the river.

The northwestern and southwestern outskirts of Vienna, next to the slopes of the Vienna Woods, are the preferred housing areas of the upper class. These areas contain a ring of old villas as well as an area of new construction of condominiums built by housing associations financed on the free market. The northeastern and southern outskirts of the city are mainly characterized by large-scale housing estates constructed in the sixties and seventies by the community and by housing associations and cooperatives. Half of the housing stock in the northeastern part is owned by the community of Vienna, as is one-third in the southern region. Along the city boundary in the northeast, there is an area of single-family houses around old villages.

In the outer regions, 90 percent of the buildings are privately owned. The dominant housing form in the outer regions is the single-family owner-occupied dwelling. Due to the building activity of the sixties and seventies, the age structure is substantially younger than in the city, and hence, the quality of the housing stock is generally better. A higher portion of multiple dwellings can be found in the centers of the southern outer region and in the cities of Neuburg and Korneuburg in the north. The centers of these cities are also characterized by a housing stock dating back to the time before World War I. Public housing reaches a higher proportion only in the southeastern region next to the airport and the refinery of Vienna.

The Structure of Housing Costs

The general structure of housing costs for Austrians depends principally on institutional settings: laws that regulate consumers' housing costs and their components differ for specific dwelling types, and the changing system of state subsidies heavily influences methods of financing housing construction and improvement. Therefore, the financial burden of housing costs for a house-hold depends on more than the qualitative characteristics of the occupied dwelling and the household income situation and financing scheme. The burden also depends on the legal form of the dwelling, its age (year of construction), and the relevant subsidy system in effect. Costs may also depend heavily upon the year a household moved into a specific dwelling since changes in rent are usually only possible when a new household moves into a dwelling.

Table 7-12 presents a general outline of the components of housing costs in different dwelling types in the Vienna metropolitan area. A distinction is made between costs that depend upon investment and autonomous housing costs. The latter may accrue either: once, at the time households move into a dwelling, or currently while living there.

In nearly all sectors of the housing market in the agglomeration, one has to pay a certain amount of money (legally or illegally) before moving into a dwelling. In general, these initial payments are not subsidized. If the initial payments are amortized to a monthly amount, they comprise about 40 percent of total monthly housing costs (see Kaufmann, Knoth, and Hartmann, 1979). In the new housing sector and in new council housing, a new tenant must contribute a certain share to the construction costs (5 percent for rental housing, 10 percent for condominiums) before moving into the dwelling. Low-income and young families may get non-interest bearing loans to cover these down payments. Except for council housing, the applicant has to pay the relevant share of condominium land costs before moving into a dwelling. In the cooperative housing rental sectors, these costs are usually shifted to current payment flows. In public housing, land costs are borne by the communal

TABLE 7-12
The Structure of Housing Costs in Different Dwelling Types.

Dwelling type	Investment dependent		Autonomous (non-investment dependent)	
	Nonrecurring costs	Current costs	Nonrecurring costs	Current costs
I. Private old rental housing	· Costs of improvements	· Annuities for improvement loans · Rental costs due to improvements by the landlord · Maintenance costs	· (Illegal) Key money · Caution money · Contract fees · Commissions to housing agencies.	· Operating costs · Management costs · Utilization costs, e.g., for furniture, etc. · Shares in the rent which are net profits to the landlords · Turnover tax
II. New rental housing sector (nonprofit housing Assns. law 1979)	· Share in land costs · Share in construction costs	· Depreciation (100 years) · Interest costs for the invested own capital · Maintenance costs	· Contract fees · Management and planning costs for construction work	· Management costs · Operating costs · Turnover tax
III. Private subsidized new rental housing (Housing Promotion Act 1968/1984)	· Share in construction costs	· Annuities for loans · 7.1% annuity for privately invested capital · Shares in land costs (6% per year) · Maintenance costs	· Contract fees	· Management cost · Operating costs · Turnover tax
VI. Public (council) housing	· Share in construction costs	· Depreciation · Maintenance costs		· Operating costs

TABLE 7-12 (continued)
The Structure of Housing Costs in Different Dwelling Types.

| Dwelling type | Investment dependent | | Autonomous (non-investment dependent) | |
	Nonrecurring costs	Current costs	Nonrecurring costs	Current costs
V. Condominiums				
New	· Share in land costs · Share in construction costs	· Annuity for redeemable loans	· Management and planning cost for construction · Contract fees · Tax on the purchase of land	· Operating costs · Management costs
Old	· Costs of improvements · Purchase price	· Annuity for loans	· Contract fees	· Operating costs
VI. Single-family houses				
New	· Land costs · Share in construction costs · Land development costs	· Annuity for loans	· Tax on the purchase of land	· Operating costs
Old	· Purchase price · Costs of improvements	· Annuity for loans	· Tax on the purchase of land	· Operating costs

budget. In 1982, on average, a household had to pay roughly 3,000 AS per square meter (130 $U.S.) before moving into a subsidized new dwelling. In the case of removal in the rental and cooperative sectors, these down payments are refundable, reduced by 2 percent per year for depreciation and increased by the inflation rate.

To enter the old private rent controlled housing sector one typically pays illegal key money, in addition to contract fees, commissions to housing agencies, and real costs of improvements (possibly financed by the previous tenant). These payments are received by the landlords or property managements, and in some cases, by the previous tenants. Although no official and exact measure exists to estimate the amount of these illegal payments, on average one needs 30,000 to 100,000 AS (1,300 to 4,300 $U.S.) to obtain the tenancy agreement for a dwelling of substandard quality and up to 300,000 AS (12,000 $U.S.) for a dwelling of good quality (see Korzendörfer and Kaufmann, 1981). Because of rent regulations, housing costs do not officially vary with the quality of the neighborhood, but one may observe differences in the amount of key money paid for dwellings in good and bad neighborhoods. In the free market private housing sector, one normally needs no key money, but these rents are substantially higher.

Generally, housing costs increased radically in metropolitan Vienna during the last decade because of rising construction costs in the new housing sector and new regulations concerning rents in the old housing sector. The current monthly expenditures on housing (including rent payment, operating and management costs, annuity shares, or loans, and energy costs for central heating) doubled in the sixties and exploded in the seventies by 370 percent. In 1985, the average current housing costs amounted to approximately 26 AS per square meter. In nearly all housing types, current expenditures for a household decline with the length of occupancy in a specific dwelling. Age, size, and quality of a dwelling are of relatively limited importance. The spatial differences in housing costs are closely connected to the distribution of specific dwelling types in the agglomeration.

Second Homes and the Migration from the City to the Outer Regions

The desire to own a house with a garden (caused, or at least influenced by, the difficult living conditions in the old housing stock of the city) led to a boom in second homes built in the outer regions of Vienna. The first wave of second homes in the sixties and seventies brought not only weekend houses scattered over the outer regions, but also squatter (cottage) settlements along the Danube in the northeast section of the city and along the southern city boundary. Since the seventies, one may observe a tendency in the population to migrate from the city to the surroundings. In some parts of the outer regions, mainly Viennese carry out the actual building activity. This foreign infiltration in the housing construction in communities of Lower Austria is extremely high along the Danube, the arterials to the west in the Vienna Woods, in the south, and also in the northern parts of the surroundings near the city.

The migration from the city to the suburbs caused special problems between the local authorities of Vienna and those of the surrounding communities. When migrating to a newly built dwelling in the outskirts of the city or to new houses in the outer regions, many Viennese households keep their old flats in the center of Vienna as a "housing reserve" for their children. Rents in these flats are often low because rent contracts date back to periods of low rent levels, and children are allowed to take over an existing rent contract. This phenomenon seems to be one of the main causes for the enormous increase of dwellings in Vienna classified as not permanently used during the last decade. Twelve percent (about 100,000 dwelling units) of the current housing stock in Vienna was registered in 1981 as unoccupied or as not used for primary housing supply. Roughly 55,000 units may be counted as "second domiciles" sprawled over the aged housing stock in the center of the city. At the same time, 15 percent of the housing stock in the outer regions is used for additional residential purposes by a household having a principal dwelling somewhere else. Since the distribution of federal remittances to the communities depends on the number of inhabitants having a primary domicile there, a pitched battle between Vienna and the surrounding communities is underway for the population using and owning domiciles in both areas.

Financing of New Construction

The provision of capital to finance the construction of housing is a very complex subject. Three levels can be distinguished: First, the national level, at which capital is allocated to the housing sector as a governmental decision; second, the firm level, at which capital is allocated to the developers financing housing; and third, the level at which capital is provided to housing consumers (see Bourne, 1981, p. 117).

Joint federal taxes form the backbone of the Federal Housing Funds which are allocated to the Länder according to the Revenue Sharing Act. Two types of agents involved in the actual construction of housing may be distinguished at the firm level: First, the developers, including private and nonprofit housing associations and local authorities; and second, the builders. The builders actually construct housing while the developers assemble the land, finance construction, obtain planning permits, and arrange the sale of the product. In Vienna, most of the developers in both the rental and the owner-occupied (multifamily) housing sector operate on a nonprofit basis. There is a complex interrelationship between developers and builders, as well as between developers and political parties. Private individuals play a major role as developers in the single-family housing market only in the outer regions of the agglomeration.

Since the construction of housing implies a large capital outlay, the developers are dependent on external sources to finance their activities. In Austria, two major sources are available:
    ·   public funds provided by the federal government under the Housing Promotion Act of 1968 (since 1985 under the New Promotion Act of

1984) and distributed by the individual Länder in the form of state loans; and

- funds provided by general financial institutions in the form of market mortgage loans.

In principle, developers are free to finance their housing activities with market rate loans only, but banks typically charge 2.5 points over the rate of interest on other long-term investments. Thus, such a system is only profitable when financing luxury housing in extraordinarily good neighborhoods. About 95 percent of the newly built housing units in the agglomeration are constructed with the help of state loans. In order to qualify for a state loan, a housing association has to fulfill certain requirements. It has to operate on a nonprofit basis, and its construction costs must be approved by the state. The purchase of land by the housing association must also be approved in order to prevent "excessive" land costs, even though land costs cannot be covered by the state loan. Although subsidization of private housing associations is legally possible, the allocation rules and priorities set up by the individual Lander are highly biased towards nonprofit and cooperative associations.

For rental dwellings built by nonprofit associations, privately owned multi-family rental housing, and dwellings in cooperative multifamily buildings, state loans covered 45 percent of the approved construction costs in Vienna in 1975 and 65 percent in 1983. Comparable percentages were of similar magnitude in the outer regions of the agglomeration. With the New Housing Promotion Act of 1984, these shares increased to 70 percent in Vienna and 90 percent in the outer regions. For owner-occupied multifamily housing activities, the state loans covered from 45 percent in 1975 to 60 percent in 1983 of approved construction costs in Vienna and from 60 percent in 1975 to 75 percent in 1983 in the outer regions. In Vienna, loans for single-family, semidetached and row houses are fixed at an amount of 265,000 AS (500,000 AS since 1985) with an addition of 20,000 AS (25,000 AS since 1985) for each child. In the outer regions such loans are 200,000 AS (220,000 AS since 1985) plus 70,000 AS for the first child and 30,000 AS for each additional child (50,000 AS since 1985). For all state loans, a low interest rate of 0.5 percent was charged over a period of 47.5 years until 1984. The annuities were structured to be about 1 percent of the loan per year for the first 20 years and later increased to 3.5 percent per year. From 1985 onward the individual Länder have the responsibility of specifying the terms of the state loans, with a length between 25 and 50 years and an interest rate of up to 6 percent.

Loans from general financial institutions finance the land costs, the remaining portions of capital costs, and any excess of the approved construction costs. This housing finance market is relatively complicated. The complexity derives from the fact that there are no specialized housing finance institutions. The developers usually obtain their financing from more than one institution.

The savings banks are most important in financing the developers' housing activities. They are the major lenders of market mortgage funds. Housing loans are made available at variable rates of interest (2.5 percentage points over the interest rate for long-term investment) and are repaid by the annuity system over 20 or 25 years. With variable rates of interest, the banks are passing interest rate risk from themselves to their borrowers. Dwellings completed by individuals - mostly single-family housing - are financed to a significant extent by personal savings through the so-called Bausparkassen system. The essence of this system is that the individual makes regular payments to a savings account up to a maximum of 8,000 AS per year, over a period of years. A state bonus of 13 percent per year makes this saving scheme generally quite attractive. After 40 percent of the contract sum has been saved, the Bausparkassen provide a long-term loan for the remaining sum. The loan is repayable at a fixed rate of interest below the market level (see Boleat 1985). Approximately 17 percent of all housing investments are financed by these Bausparkassen loans.

Now consider the level at which capital is provided to consumers. Purchasers of owner-occupied dwellings must provide at least 10 percent of the total construction costs from their own resources ("down payments") often through a "savings-for-housing" scheme. Members granted a right in a cooperative dwelling have to pay a down payment, equivalent to 5 percent of the total construction costs, in exchange for which they have the right to occupy the dwelling for an indefinite time. Cooperative housing has elements of both tenancy and owner occupation. It is an Austrian peculiarity that applicants for a newly built rental dwelling have to provide a down payment amounting to five percent of the total construction costs. In the case of moving, these down payments are refunded to the tenants (reduced by 2 percent per year for depreciation and increased by the inflation rate).

Purchasers of dwellings qualifying for state loans can take over both public and private loans from the developers. Until 1984, purchasers have been subsidized in three ways:

- On the long-term state loans, purchasers pay a rate of interest much below the market level.
- On market rate mortgage loans, dwelling purchasers receive a substantial annuity subsidy (50 percent for the first five years reduced by ten percent each year for the next nine years).
- Furthermore, the state aids low-income households in general and young low-income households in particular with interest-free loans for down payments in the new construction sector.

It should be noted that second homes cannot be purchased with state assistance.

Housing Supply and Housing Access

During the last ten years, roughly 7,000 newly built dwellings per year have been added to the housing stock in Vienna. Approximately 6 to 7 percent of these dwellings are single-family dwellings, built by households for their own purposes. Roughly 4,000 subsidized units per year are offered by nonprofit housing associations and cooperatives. Access to this subsidized sector is restricted to Austrian low- to middle-income households. The dwellings are offered either directly by the associations or cooperatives, on lists provided by some of the finance institutions, by announcement in newspapers, or by the official housing office of the municipality. Furthermore, information is passed quickly through personal contacts. Most of the cooperatives are connected with specific labor unions. The only part of the new housing stock without any legal access restrictions is the owner-occupied housing sector financed by the free market. Roughly 1,000 such units are provided annually; they are offered in private announcements in newspapers and housing association magazines by the finance institutions.

About 200,000 dwellings, or 26 percent of the total housing stock, are owned and managed by the municipality. A household that applies for a dwelling in the public sector enters the public queue. In general, only lower-income Austrian households have access to this sector. A point system based upon socioeconomic criteria as well as the date of application regulates the waiting time. Besides the official criteria, personal relations and connections are used quite often to gain access to the public sector. During the recent past, the number of applicants remained more or less constant at about 15,000. In 1981, for example, roughly 14,000 households applied at the municipal office. Six thousand of these households were permitted to enter the public queue. In 1984, there were roughly 13,000 applicants on the waiting list (see Czasny and Kaufmann, 1985). With the allocation of about 6,000 dwellings per year (2,000 newly built units and 4,000 old units), a household is usually forced to wait two to three years to obtain a dwelling. Although demand is substantially higher than supply, some of the newly built units have remained vacant since the early eighties. Due to rising construction costs, the rents in these dwellings are too high for low-income households. Quite recently, the municipal office lifted the income restrictions for newly built publically owned units. Note again that children may take over a lease, and thus the dwelling unit, from their parents.

In general, dwellings belonging to the old private housing stock are offered on the market through announcement in newspapers, either directly by the owner or through the management body, or else indirectly by housing agencies. Recent studies (see Czasny and Kaufmann, 1985) estimate a turnover of about 25,000 units annually within this sector. Although households do not face any legal access restrictions in this sector, social restrictions limit the choices of specific groups; for example, guest workers, students, or families with children are not accepted by all landlords. These households are often forced to move into relatively expensive dwellings offered as "sublets." Furthermore, note that many dwellings within the old sector are passed on through informal contacts. Again, in the rent-controlled units, children are allowed to take over the leases of their parents. One of the most preferred housing alternatives for low-income households (especially guest workers from Yugoslavia) are so-called Hausbesorgerwohnungen dwellings in tenement houses provided at low rents to the superintendent.

As this discussion makes clear, "information," especially that provided by informal personal contacts, is one of the key factors of housing search in the Vienna metropolitan area.

THE GOVERNMENTAL ROLE IN THE HOUSING MARKET

As noted previously, government involvement in housing production and consumption has a strong tradition in Austria. The present pattern of intervention, outlined in figure 7-3, is the result of a long history of intervention, involving rent control and tenants' protection legislation, extensive federal acts and programs of housing subsidies, as well as specific housing programs of the Länder and local authorities (especially the council housing program in Vienna). Housing assistance has taken six principal forms:

- low interest rate state loans for housing construction and more recently for housing rehabilitation;
- annuity subsidies for market rate loans for new housing construction, and for housing improvement;
- tax relief and benefits;
- state bonuses associated with the Bausparkassen contract system;
- rent allowances to low-income tenants in public housing and in the private rental housing sector to prevent excessive rent increases due to the housing rehabilitation activities; and
- housing allowances, primarily limited to low-income households occupying a newly built dwelling.

This section reviews the evolution of the policies in broad outline. A more complete analysis of more recent policy follows a cursory discussion of prewar housing policies. The periods chosen for discussion purposes have some of the arbitrariness of all historical periods; nevertheless, they capture some of the major shifts in the role of the state in the metropolitan housing market of Vienna. Table 7-13 outlines a summary of the major housing policies.

FIGURE 7-3
Public Intervention in the Austrian Housing Market.

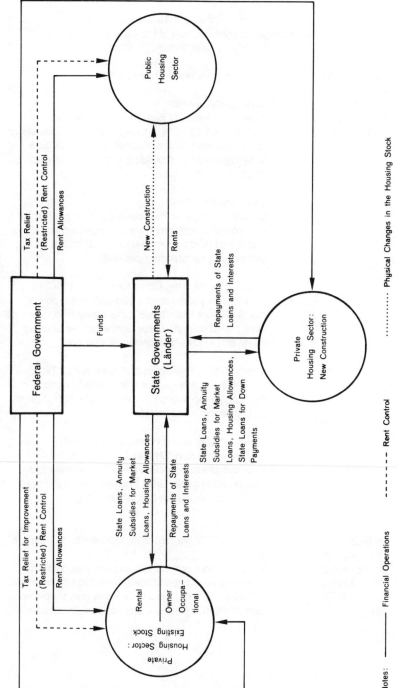

Notes: ——— Financial Operations - - - - - - Rent Control .... Physical Changes in the Housing Stock

TABLE 7-13
Different Stages in the Evolution of Housing and Housing
Related Policy.

Major stages	Housing policies and programs
Stage 1: The Early Stage (1859-1918)	*Building Code 1859* Specifies a series of regulations to establish minimum safeguards in the construction of buildings and to protect health and safety of the tenants; a planning permit and building line certificate was required for new construction. *Land-Use Plan 1893* Directed to regulate the spatial development of the city: zones of residential, industrial, commercial, and mixed land use are demarcated; height zoning and setback regulations are specified. *Housing for Working-Class Families Act 1902* Provides 24 years release from different types of housing taxes if landlords make newly built dwellings available to working-class families at low housing costs and restrict their profits to 5 percent. *Franz Josef I - Government Jubilee Funds 1908* Provides low interest rate state loans to nonprofit housing associations for new construction of physi- cally adequate and low rent housing. *Small-Sized Housing Promotion Act 1910* (amended version 1919 and suspended 1921) Provides direct financial sources for small-sized new housing to nonprofit housing associations as well as to local authorities (public housing).
Stage 2: The Period of Council Housing and Rent Regu- lations (1919- 1945)	*Rent Act 1922* (various amended versions, suspended 1981) Provides strict rent control and security of tenure. The rents are frozen to the level in 1914 (suspended in 1968); the rents have to be used only for covering construction, operation, and maintenance costs.

TABLE 7-13 (continued)
Different Stages in the Evolution of Housing and Housing
Related Policy.

Major stages	Housing policies and programs
	Public Housing Program in Vienna (1923-1934) Makes housing in good quality available to working-class families at low costs.
	Federal Housing and Settlement Funds 1921 (suspended 1968) Provides state loans and interest rate and annuity subsidies for small-sized new housing and settlements. Available to nonprofit associations and public corporations.
	Vienna Housing Rehabilitation Funds 1934 Provides state loans covering 50 percent of reconstruction and rehabilitation costs.
	Vienna Housing Repair Funds 1934 Provides a 20 percent grant to improvement and repair costs for private landlords.
Stage 3: The Period of Reconstruction and Rapid Growth (1946-1967)	*Housing Reconstruction Act 1948* (amended 1967, suspended 1968) Provides state loans covering all reconstruction costs with 100 years currency term (1967: 50 years currency term) for reconstructing the damaged housing stock.
	Housing Promotion Act 1954 (suspended 1968) Promotes the construction of small- and middle-sized dwellings, provides low interest state loans with 70 years currency term and annuity subsidies, or constructions grants, for rental as well as owner-occupied housing, to nonprofit housing associations, local authorities, and individuals.
	Specific Housing Construction Programs of the Länder (Vienna: loans of the municipality for new construction, 1951-1968, social housing programs, etc.)

TABLE 7-13 (continued)
Different Stages in the Evolution of Housing and Housing
Related Policy.

Major stages	Housing policies and programs
Stage 4: The Period of Consolidation and Reorientation (1968-1984)	*Housing Promotion Act 1968* (amended version 1972, 1975, 1980, suspended 1984) Introduced to reorganize and unify the whole subsidy system; provides supply-side subsidies (state loans with a shorter currency term and higher interest rates than in the past and annuity subsidies for market loans) for owner-occupied, cooperative, and rental new housing projects, but also demand-side subsidies (housing allowances and non-interest bearing loans for the applicant), down payments to income limited and young families as well as subsidies to the landlords for substantial housing improvement activities in the older housing stock with small-sized dwellings; the responsibility of the Länder is extended. *Specific Housing Programs of the Länder* (Vienna: social housing programs in 1968, 1969, 1970, 1974) *Rent Act*, amended version 1968 (suspended 1981) suspends the freezing of rents at the 1914 level. Allows free market rents for new lease charters. Fifty percent of these free market rents are at the free disposal of the landlords; the rest must be kept for seven years in a "rent fund" designated to finance housing repairs. Another amendment in 1974 introduces rent control again for substandard dwellings (i.e., without WC and bath). *Dwelling Improvement Act 1969* (suspended 1984) Subsidizes improvement activities in amendable houses and in small- and middle-sized dwellings in the form of annuity subsidies and housing allowances. Landlords as well as tenants are entitled. *Income Tax Act*, amended version 1974 Provides rent allowances available to income limited households in the case of excessive rent increases due to housing rehabilitation activities.

TABLE 7-13 (continued)
Different Stages in the Evolution of Housing and Housing
Related Policy.

Major stages   **Housing policies and programs**

Urban Renewal Act 1974
Facilitates the reconstruction of existing urban
structures and renewal of dilapidated residential
areas with poor housing conditions.

Land Acquisition Act 1974
Makes qualified undeveloped land available to the
communities for the construction of residential
buildings.

New Rent Act 1981
Provides restricted rent control for certain types of
dwellings (upper rent limits according to size and
quality), a forum for tenant complaints, a certain
form of security of tenure, and the right to the
moving tenant to get costs of specific dwelling
improvements refunded from the landlord.
Additionally, rent funds are extended to 100 percent
of the net rent revenue of the previous 10 years, and
landlords are entitled to an "investment bonus" of 20
percent in the case of investing the rent funds in
repairs.

Stage 5:   *Housing Promotion Act 1984*
New Era   Introduced to reorganize the subsidy system for new
(1985-present)   construction. Provides subsidies primarily in the
                                form of state loans (25 to 50 years currency term,
                                interest rates up to 6 percent, and fixed annuity
                                allowances for market loans). Länder receive extended
                                responsibility in implementing the act.

                                Housing Rehabilitation Act 1984
                                Introduced with the purpose to unify the subsidy
                                system of the different existing rehabilitation-
                                related acts and to extend the responsibility of the
                                Länder. Rehabilitation is to take priority over new
                                construction. Provides state loans with a 10 to 50
                                years currency term, annuity subsidies, and housing
                                allowances.

The Early Stage: The Rise of Housing Policy (to 1918)

The rapid and largely uncontrolled housing growth at the end of the last century provoked a series of governmental actions to improve housing conditions and standards. Building and zoning regulations were introduced to tackle the problems, but these instruments were not very successful. Thus, at the beginning of the twentieth century, more active public policies increasingly addressed housing problems.

Indirect subsidies began in 1902 when tax relief was granted for newly built small-sized housing offered at reasonable rents. Access to subsidized housing was restricted to low-income households, an element of housing policy that has persisted ever since. Direct subsidies for new construction of low rent housing were provided to nonprofit housing associations in 1908, and state loans were provided in 1910 to nonprofit housing associations and local governments for the construction of standard low rent dwellings (for details see Langer, 1982).

The Period of Council Housing and Strict Rent Regulation (1919-1945)

Although population growth stagnated in this period, the housing shortage and inadequate housing conditions remained urgent problems. The pauperization of the population caused even more severe housing problems than before World War I and resulted in sharp policy changes and serious government involvement in housing. Rent control became a central tool in regulating the private housing market.

During World War I, rents were restricted for the first time to the rent level of 1914. By the Rent Act of 1922, this temporary wartime measure was made permanent in order to protect tenants from excessive rent increases. Moreover, this act also brought almost total security of tenure and restricted the profits of the landlords. A fixed proportion of rental income was tied to maintenance of the structure. This legislation evidently made it very unattractive for private developers to invest in new construction or maintenance. To stimulate new construction by housing associations and other nonprofit organizations, the Federal Housing and Settlement Fund was re-established in 1921 to provide low interest state loans as well as annuity subsidies to market loans.

These federal acts and related programs were by no means sufficient to solve the acute housing problems of the municipality. In order to overcome the apparent inability of the private sector to build housing for the poor in sufficient quantity and adequate quality, the socialist government in Vienna started its socially ambitious and architecturally famous council housing program intended to provide adequate housing to low-income households at costs similar to those in the rent-controlled private sector. Between 1922 and 1934, the public housing program encompassed about 80 percent of all construction activity in Vienna. About 63,000 dwelling units, mainly located in large-scale tenement blocks with big inner courtyards and equipped with social and service facilities, were built by the municipality. Sixty percent of the production costs were covered by the communal budget and the residual by a property tax progressively differentiated by dwelling size. Rents were kept at a very low level; a working-class family had to spend 3 to 5 percent of its monthly income for housing whereas rents comprised up to one-third of the average income before World War I (for details see Kainrath, 1985).

With the end of the socialist government in 1934, the council housing programs almost came to an end, and housing production declined rapidly (see figure 7-2). From the establishment of the fascist regime in 1934 until the integration into the "German Third Reich" from 1938 to 1945, Vienna's urban development stagnated. The extensive wartime housing damage in 1944 -- about 90,000 dwelling units were destroyed in Vienna -- caused severe housing problems for the following period.

The Reconstruction Period (1946-1967)

The major emphasis of policies after World War II was to stimulate the reconstruction of the extensive war damage, but the provision of new housing was also an important objective. Although the main instruments of housing policy were adopted from the prewar times (rent control, state loans, annuity subsidies, council housing programs), the effective range and reliance on these policies changed.

The prewar Housing and Settlement Fund was reinstated, and the Housing Reconstruction Act of 1948 introduced new funds by providing interest-free state loans amortized over a century. For the first time, subsidies were offered to private individuals building for their own residential purposes. In the mid-fifties, reconstruction of war damage was largely complete, but nevertheless, the housing shortage was still an urgent problem. Thus, in 1954, the Housing Promotion Act was passed to provide low interest rate state loans and annuity subsidies to all types of developers.

Immediately after the war, the municipality of Vienna started its council housing program again. But facing a changed political situation, the strong social and redistributive emphasis characteristic of Viennese housing policy during the time between the wars diminished. The rents, however, were still kept at relatively low levels, and the excess demand implied long waiting lists for council housing.

The Period of Consolidation and Reorientation (1968-1984)

Until 1968, housing policy in Austria was mainly concerned with encouraging the construction of small- and medium-sized rental housing, but several major changes in the subsidization system have taken place since then. In the Housing Promotion Act of 1968, similar regulations and forms of subsidies were made available for new rental, cooperative, and owner-occupied housing, as well as for rehabilitation activities within the existing stock.

The major instruments used to stimulate new construction remained low interest state loans and annuity subsidies for market loans. The proportion of state and market loans for dwellings of different tenure categories was legally fixed. Local authorities, housing associations, cooperatives, legal entities, and private individuals had access to these supply-side subsidies. To qualify for the subsidy, each had to meet certain rules and regulations concerning size of dwellings, construction and land costs, and profit limitations (in the case of housing associations) or income restrictions (for individuals).

The system of financing council housing has changed over time. Until 1968, the budget of the local government financed public housing. Because of shifts in the communal budget towards cost intensive infrastructure projects, housing investments are covered by federal funds and market loans since the late 1960s (see Fischer, Purschke, and Schubert, 1985). Although the municipality provided land free of charge, housing costs in the public sector increased and reached the cost level of the rental sector managed by housing associations and cooperatives.

The provisions of the Housing Promotion Act of 1968 concerning subsidies for housing rehabilitation by landlords have been unsuccessful for two reasons. First, only costs directly related to repair works were subsidized, whereas losses of rent income and costs of displacing tenants were financed by the landlord. Second, profits were restricted since the rents of the improved dwellings were subject to rent control (for more details see Swoboda, 1981).

The Dwelling Improvement Act of 1969 enabled annuity subsidies for housing rehabilitation to be provided directly to the tenants. As the tenants were granted a quasi-owner status by the Rent Act, they became rather active in modernizing their dwellings. As a consequence, dwellings in Vienna are often in much better condition than the buildings in which they are located.

In contrast to other metropolitan housing markets, urban renewal in Vienna is largely concerned with increased maintenance and rehabilitation of the old housing stock rather than with demolition and rebuilding (for further details, see ÖROK, 1978).

The Housing Promotion Act of 1968 also introduced demand-side subsidies to specific households. Households living in a subsidized dwelling can qualify for housing allowances depending upon income, family size, and dwelling size rather than upon the tenure of their dwellings. Moreover, lower-income and young households applying for a newly built dwelling in the owner-occupied, cooperative, or rental housing sector may obtain noninterest-bearing state loans covering the down payment. The Income Tax Act of 1974 provides housing allowances for lower-income households whose housing costs increase because of the rehabilitation activities of landlords. The objective of these demand-side subsidies is to bridge the gap between housing costs and the amount of money households are supposed to be able to afford to pay for housing.

Although rent control has been a continuing feature of federal housing policy, the nature of the controls has changed. The Conservative Party, in power from 1966 to 1970, suspended price control for existing leases and abolished rent control for new rent contracts. The objective of these policy changes was to encourage investment in maintenance and rehabilitation of the overaged housing stock. The socialist government, however, reintroduced rent control for substandard dwellings in 1974.

The New Rent Act of 1981 brought major changes, including the introduction of upper rent limits linked to the consumer price index and varying with the dwelling category. In 1985, rent limits were fixed at:

- 6 AS per meter (0.30 $U.S.) for dwellings without running water and toilet;
- 12 AS per meter (0.60 $U.S.) for dwellings lacking either bath or WC; and
- 18 AS per meter (0.90 $U.S.) for dwellings with bath and WC but lacking central heating.

In 1986, the upper rent limits for modern dwellings (i.e. with bath, WC, and central heating) were suspended. Variations in neighborhood quality are not taken into account. There are several exceptions to these rent regulations--certain large-sized dwellings without central heating, dwellings built after 1953 without the support of public subsidies, dwellings in single- or two-family houses and others. Under existing leases, the landlord may raise the rent up to two-thirds of the corresponding upper limits if the landlord is investing in maintenance. This act also provides security of tenure and guarantees the moving tenant to a refund of the costs of his major dwelling improvements. It is interesting to note that the New Rent Act has been severely criticized by both landlords and the Conservative Party on the one hand because of its rent regulations, and by tenants' associations and many socialists on the other hand because of its large list of exemptions from rent control.

The New Era: From Construction to Improvement (1985-Present)

The problems of maintaining, repairing, and improving the physical quality of the older housing stock in Vienna became more and more urgent in the early eighties. The Housing Rehabilitation Act of 1984 reflects the growing dissatisfaction with this housing problem and provides the basic outline for a new and more comprehensive redevelopment policy. In particular, this act reforms and unifies the subsidy system applied to improvement activities and shifts attention from dwelling improvement to substantial rehabilitation (for further details, see Hofmeister and Rechberger, 1985).

Housing rehabilitation policy before 1984 was unsuccessful for two reasons. First, "repairs" to the housing stock were not subsidized: repairs had to be financed from the funds generated by rents or by market rate loans. Rent increases to cover amortization were limited to a period of ten years and had to be approved by a court (Schlichtungstelle). In contrast, in the case of "substantial improvement," a landlord could qualify for a state loan or annuity subsidies for a market rate loan but only if he or she was also willing to invest in housing repair. For both types of investment, repair and substantial improvement, the majority of the tenants had to agree to the expenditure program. The Rehabilitation Act of 1984 enables landlords to undertake housing rehabilitation without paying attention to the strong distinction between housing repairs and improvement. This change in the subsidy system is expected to encourage investment in maintaining, repairing, and improving the quality of the existing older housing stock.

Second, there had been no subsidies covering losses of rent revenues during the period of rehabilitation or displacement of current residents. The introduction of such subsidies may increase the clearance of blighted structures in the future and may encourage nonprofit housing associations to engage in urban redevelopment. The Rehabilitation Act of 1984 also strengthened the role of the Länder by increasing their flexibility in funding maintenance and improvement activities. The Länder may provide state loans (also covering the displacement costs of tenants), and interest rate and annuity subsidies, as well as housing allowances. The loans may cover up to 100 percent of the rehabilitation costs over a term of 10 to 30 years. Moreover, local authorities are given extended power to deal with housing rehabilitation problems in a broader and more integrated manner.

The New Housing Promotion Act of 1984 has adjusted the subsidy system of the new construction sector to accommodate a tighter financial situation: state loans providing steady repayment of housing funds have been extended, whereas annuity subsidies have been reduced. The expenses for annuity subsidies increased from 0.1 percent in 1974 to 12.2 percent of the funds available in 1982, because of rapidly rising interest rates. State loans as a fraction of construction costs decreased from 98.7 percent in 1974 to 80.5 percent in 1982, evidently causing a decline in subsidized new housing construction. Under the new act, the Länder are entitled to determine a shorter repayment term (25 to 50 years) for state loans and higher interest rates (up to 6 percent). Annuity subsidies for market rate loans were also fixed by the act and no longer support fluctuating interest rates.

Federal and local officials are just learning how to implement these two acts flexibly. The acts will only begin to operate extensively during the next years. Thus, it is far too early to evaluate the precise effects these acts will have on the Vienna housing market.

CONCLUSION: MAJOR IMPACTS OF HOUSING POLICIES

The assistance and control policies of the federal government and the municipality of Vienna have induced major changes in supply and demand for housing. The different forms of public intervention, however, interact in such a complex way that it is rather difficult-- if not impossible-- to understand their combined effects upon the housing market.

The Effects of Rent Control and Tenant Protection Legislation

The effects of rent control in a housing market largely depend upon the nature of the regulations. As noted previously, from World War I until 1981, rents were essentially frozen in nominal terms. This strong form of rent control considerably restricted the functioning of the housing market. Note that 68 percent of the total housing stock belongs to the rental sector in Vienna, and 94 percent of these dwellings are rent controlled. The only free market segment in the rental sector has been new nonsubsidized housing which constitutes only 4.5 percent of the total stock.

The combined operation of frozen rents and nearly total security of tenure has resulted in a series of (positive and negative) effects upon the housing market of Vienna.

First, rent control and tenant protection legislation, as well as low returns imposed by law, discouraged landlords from maintaining, repairing, and modernizing their properties (for further details, see Abele and Winckler, 1976). This is the principal cause for the existence of a relatively large, old, and substandard housing stock in the densely settled downtown area, where the rapid growth during the Founders' Period had taken place. The very low levels of urban development since World War I and the relatively efficient legal restrictions on demolishing older housing also contributed to this widespread phenomenon of housing obsolescence. According to Weber and Knoth (1980), about one-third of the total housing stock is obsolete and requires substantial reinvestment in maintenance and repairs. This housing problem has become a major policy issue in the last few years and resulted in the Housing Rehabilitation Act of 1984, which emphasized housing improvement and revitalization.

Second, security of tenure granted tenants practically freehold rights, encouraging tenants to invest capital to improve their dwellings. A consequence of the moderate housing maintenance and rehabilitation activities of the landlords and the rather active modernization of dwellings by tenants is the curious situation in which the dwellings are often in a much better condition than the buildings in which they are located.

Third, tenant protection over the last 70 years has had a pronounced long-term impact on residential mobility. Security of tenure, dwelling improvement investments, and a quantitative housing shortage reinforced the postponement of decisions to seek a new home. The resulting rather low degree of residential mobility is, however, a major reason why there is no clear evidence of social segregation in Vienna as compared with many other metropolitan housing markets. Furthermore, even if households decide to move to another perhaps larger and more comfortable dwelling, they often do not terminate their leases, but use them as second homes (see Körzendorfer and Kaufmann, 1981). This is because rents are extremely low, and children have the right to take over the rental contracts of their parents. As a result, the proportion of vacant or not permanently occupied dwellings has significantly increased during the seventies. Such dwellings now comprise about one-eighth of the total dwelling stock in Vienna.

Fourth, rent control and excessively increasing production costs of new housing have provoked large disparities in housing costs. Thus, housing costs in the new construction sector exceed those of the old stock by at least 50 percent (see Kaufmann, Knoth and Hartmann, 1979). Disparities also exist in housing costs between dwellings of the same quality even within the same building as a consequence of the vintage of the rent contracts. However, rent levels in the controlled sector do not vary at all with differences in neighborhood quality.

Fifth, as a result of excessive demand for rent controlled housing, the phenomenon of black market transactions has become an important element in the housing market of Vienna. Landlords often charge illegal key money in exchange for a valuable lease.

Sixth, the minor role of private (nonsubsidized) rental housing construction is an important side effect of the rent control and tenant protection legislation (for further details on this issue see Kainrath, 1985).

With the introduction of the New Rent Act of 1981, rent control was liberalized in two ways. First, certain types of dwellings were decontrolled. Second, rent increases for new leases were permitted and linked to the consumer price index. Rents were allowed to increase up to two-thirds of these limits in the case of pre-existing leaseholds. As a consequence, this liberalization pushed the housing costs up for tenants in the old rent controlled sector and the rent burdens of lower-income families increased substantially.

Finally, there is a very recent yet not very strong tendency to circumvent the rent regulations by transferring the dwellings from the rental to the owner-occupied sector (condominium conversion) when a lease is terminated.

The Effects of Subsidies

Any discussion of the success or failure of the subsidy system has to address the question of who benefits from the assistance policies. This is a complex and critical issue. Nevertheless, it is possible to identify some tendencies.

Although housing policy has been designed to prevent developers from making large profits, the actors involved in new construction-- (nonprofit) housing associations, mortgage lending institutions, and the private building industry-- benefited most. The (nonprofit) housing associations responsible for pricing have little incentive to keep construction costs down for two reasons. First, the associations are tightly linked with the larger building contractors and housing association profits are limited to 5 percent of the total construction costs, not to a fixed amount of money. Thus, housing associations increase their profits with increased costs and speculative land dealings. Comparing construction costs of different types of developers, it is evident that developers building with public subsidies incur the highest costs. Whereas the costs incurred by private builders are only 92 percent of posted construction costs, local authorities and housing cooperatives exceed these benchmark costs by 15 and 24 percent, respectively. Financial institutions have benefited from the fact that housing market loans are profitable and riskless. Building contractors and materials suppliers are able to raise prices above average because they are not subject to public control.

On the consumption side, middle- and upper-income households have profited most. Rising construction costs and interest rates for mortgage loans have led to a situation in which housing allowances have increased substantially in the last ten years. But even with the help of housing allowances and state loans for down payments, newly constructed dwellings in the owner-occupied, cooperative, and public housing sectors have become unobtainable to low-income households. Mainly the middle and upper classes have gained access to new construction through public subsidies. Those who have benefited least are all types of low-income people, especially young families, immigrants from the rest of Austria, and guest workers. The latter are still excluded from any form of housing assistance in Austria.

REFERENCES

Abele, H., and G. Winckler. 1976. Wohnungsmarkt. Ansätze zuener Mikroanalyse der Wohnungswirtschaft. Institute for Urban Research, Vienna.

Bobek, M., and E. Lichtenberger. 1978. *Wien. Bauliche Gestalt und Entwicklung seit der Mitte des 19. Jahrhunderts.* Vienna and Cologne: Böhlau.

Boleat, M. 1985. *National housing finance systems.* London: Croom Helm.

Bourne, L. S. 1981. *The geography of housing.* London: Arnold.

Bruckmann, G., C. Festa, R. Gisser, O. Lackinger, and J. Lamel. 1975. *Prognose des Wohnungsbedarfes bis 1985*. Linz: Trauner.

Czasny, K., and A. Kaufmann. 1985. *Erfassung des Wohnungsangebotes*. Institute for Urban Research, Vienna.

Fischer, M., H. Purschke, and U. Schubert. 1985. Urban development in Vienna - Summary. *Scandinavian Housing and Planning Research*, 2: 195-199.

Hofmeister, H., and W. Rechberger. 1985. *Wohnbauförderungsgesetz 1984 und Wohnbausanierungsgesetz*. Vienna: Verlag der Österreichischen Staatsdruckerei Wien.

Honies, H. 1984. *Bauen und Wohnen*. Vienna: Orac.

Kainrath, W. 1985. *Wohnungspolitik zwischen Staat und Markt*. Vienna. Mimeo.

Kaitna, W., and Reichel, R. 1976. *Mieten in Altwohnungen*. Institute for Urban Research, Vienna.

Kaufmann, A., E. Knoth, and B. Hartmann. 1979. *Wohnungskosten und ökonomische Situation der Haushalte*. Institute for Urban Research, Vienna.

Kleps, K. 1975. *Wohnbauförderung und Wohnungsverbesserung in Österreich*. Vienna, New York: Springer Verlag.

Koppel, F. 1979. Wohnbauförderung und Wohnungskosten, Vorschläge für eine Neugestaltung. In *Wirtschaft und Gesellschaft*, no. 12. Vienna: Arbeiterkammer.

Korzendörfer, H., and A. Kaufmann. 1981. Wiens Wohnungsmarkt im Spiegel von Zeitungsannoncen. *Wien Aktuell 6*.

Langer, E. 1982. Wohnbauförderung und Finanzierung in Österreich. *Schriftenreihe der Bundeswirtschaftskammer*, vol. 44, Vienna.

ÖROK. 1978. Regional planning in Austria. Austrian Conference on Regional Planning Publication, Series 15, Vienna.

Stahl, K. 1985. Microeconomic analysis of housing market: Towards a conceptual framework. In *Microeconomic models of housing markets*, edited by K. Stahl. Berlin, et al.: Springer.

Swoboda, H. 1981. Aktuelle Probleme des Wohnbaus und besonders der Stadterneuerung. In *Wirtschaft und Gesellschaft*, no. 20. Vienna: Arbeiterkammer.

Swoboda, H. 1982. Wohnbauleistung und Wohnbauförderung 1971-1980 unter besonderer Berücksichtigung Wiens. In *Wirtschaft und Gesellschaft,* no. 24. Vienna: Arbeiterkammer.

Weber, P., and E. Knoth. 1980. Sanierungsbedarf in den Städten. Institute for Urban Research, Vienna.

8

GLASGOW: FROM MEAN CITY TO MILES BETTER

Andrew Gibb
Duncan Maclennan

THE MESSAGE AND THE MEDIUM

This analysis of British housing policy takes the City of Glasgow as its medium of exposition. Glasgow has had a longstanding notoriety for its housing conditions. More recently the city has gained a reputation for innovative rehabilitation programs. With a current population of just under three-quarters of a million people, Glasgow forms the core of a relatively large metropolitan area. The functional metropolitan area, which is roughly coterminous with the administrative unit called Strathclyde Region, contains a population of approximately 2 million people. The city-region forms the fourth largest conurbation area in the United Kingdom, and is also its most northerly conurbation, with a latitude of 50°51' North.

This essay focuses upon housing in the city and the metropolitan area rather than the nation as a whole. The shift to an urban scale of description and analysis has a number of important advantages. More aggregate descriptions, by their nature, tend to focus upon the broad instruments of policy and their initial incidence. As a result, they provide little insight about the processes by which policy inputs transform themselves into system outputs. The urban scale of analysis facilitates a description of system processes, policy outputs, and an analysis of the links between housing and other sectors of the local economy, society, and polity. A clearer understanding of how national policies are shaped by local structures may emerge.

An additional consideration is that in some countries housing policy is not solely, or even primarily, subject to the sovereignty of central government.[1] City governments can influence housing outcomes in a range of ways. The municipality may be the strategic planner and enabler that permits centrally sponsored policies to be pursued. Municipalities may differ in their "grantsmanship" skills, which can be essential to capturing a large or disproportionate share of nationally funded programs. In Britain, for example, there are few more striking contrasts than the relative performances of "grantsmen" in Glasgow and Liverpool in the last decade. Finally, where the city has a local tax base, its capital investment and subsidy policy can complement or can run counter to national policies. In Britain, housing policy is irrevocably bound up with local politics and ideology; this has had a major effect upon the nature of the housing system, particularly the provision of government housing. During the last decade, the British central government has striven to regain considerable control over local housing policies, particularly the provision of council housing.

Case studies within national systems may provide useful overall insights about policy effectiveness. Within Britain, however, specific problems and policies differ markedly between the declining cities of the North and the rapidly expanding area of southeastern England. Housing and other policies designed to cope with growth may be quite different from those required to cope with the consequences of economic decline.

Thoughout the 1970s, Glasgow was regarded as the most problematic large city in Britain. A recent analysis of 1981 Census data for British cities (Eversley and Begg, 1987) indicates that Glasgow is still the most concentrated locus of social deprivation in Britain, even though parts of the city are improving steadily (see table 8-1). The city thus provides a useful site for analyzing the consequences of national trends such as the slow decline of the manufacturing sector, the growth of a large welfare state, with the growing concern toward urban deprivation, the cutback of fiscal commitments by government, and the privatization of social services. Glasgow reflects these changes in economic prosperity and in the priorities of housing policy on a dramatic scale. The next section describes the broad historical sweep of events which saw the city move,

---

[1] A further complicating factor, which is often pertinent in relation to housing policies, is the existence of sub-national but supra-municipal levels of government. In this essay concerned with Glasgow, this consideration is important. Housing policy in Scotland, leaving aside national tax and social security programs, is controlled from Edinburgh by the Secretary of State for Scotland. While Scottish housing policy is similar to that of England, as noted below there are several differences.

within half a century, from being the most rapidly growing to the most rapidly declining city in Britain. The development of the city's extensive social housing sector from 1920 to 1975 is charted. The subsequent sections concentrate upon the period from 1975 to 1985 in which a new pluralistic approach to housing policy has come to challenge the decaying dominance of council housing. This pluralism is, of course, relative: even today, only one household in three in Glasgow is housed by the private sector.[2]

Of international relevance in Glasgow are the ways in which multisectoral and multiagency strategies have been used to renovate older neighborhoods on a large scale and how the city now faces the challenge of remaking the social housing sector.

TABLE 8-1
Social Deprivation in Urban Areas in Britain, 1981.

Area	Social deprivation		Housing deprivation	
	Score	Rank*	Score	Rank*
Glasgow	-2.87	1	-4.38	1
Glasgow Peripheral	-2.50	2	-2.80	3
Inner Birmingham	-2.37	3	-0.83	-
Inner Hull	-2.26	4	-3.51	2
Inner Manchester & Salford	-1.77	5	-1.63	12
Inner Liverpool	-1.73	6	-1.26	16
Inner Nottingham	-1.70	7	-1.33	15
Areas comprising Inner London				
Docklands Special Area	-1.31	-	-2.22	5
Islington and Hackney	-0.82	-	-2.27	4
Lambeth Special Area	-0.66	-	-1.77	8
Other Inner London	+0.62	-	-1.98	6

*   Relative standing among U.K. cities and selected urban areas (1 =worst).
-    Not included.

Source: Estimates by Eversley and Begg based upon 1981 Census, as cited in "Inquiry into Housing Canditions in Glasgow," Glasgow District Council, 1987.

---

[2] In contrast, for the rest of Britain only one household in three is housed by the public sector.

TIME'S ARROW

An explanation of the current housing system in Glasgow requires some historical context. Political attitudes towards local housing problems and the institutions developed to implement local policies have been much influenced by the experience of the last 50 years. In the British context, and this is particularly marked in the case of Glasgow, there has been strong political emphasis on the means of housing policy, often more than on the results. In the last decade, however, there has been a welcome shift of focus toward ends rather than means. The city has become a leader in the crucial British policy area of rehabilitating older neighborhoods and in remaking social housing. However, the priorities of the present can only be clearly understood if the social and economic influences acting on the city during the last century are clear.[3]

Pre-1914

In the late eighteenth century, the novelist Jonathan Swift described Glasgow as one of Britain's more attractive towns. However, this small market town and university center was soon to be more fundamentally transformed by the industrial revolution than any other British city. In each decade from 1841 to 1911, the population of Glasgow increased by 10 to 20 percent; it surpassed three-quarters of a million people by 1900. The development of trade with North America was facilitated by the city's location at the northwestern edge of Europe, and this stimulated the growth of the tobacco and cotton processing industries. The beginning of large-scale exploitation of coal and iron ore in the 1840s also gave rise to a vast expansion in the local economic base. Mineral extraction, metals processing, shipbuilding, marine engineering, and the production of railway locomotives and rolling stock were all developed in successive waves of expansion between 1860 and 1910. This export base was extensively aimed at the developing sectors of the then vast British Empire and North America.

The labor supply for the expanding industries was largely drawn from the rush of landless peasants from the depopulating rural areas of Scotland and Ireland. These displaced rural laborers had few resources of their own, and as a result they were housed in rental units provided by private tenement landlords. The vast influx of low-income labor also had to be housed close to workplaces during the era of the "walking" city. By the 1890s, electric tramways allowed low-income housing to spread out along lengthy tentacles of tramway routes. (Map 8-1 depicts this development.) The land economics of the period

---

[3] For a more detailed discussion see Gibb (1983).

MAP 8-1

Outward Growth and Internal Replacement, Glasgow.

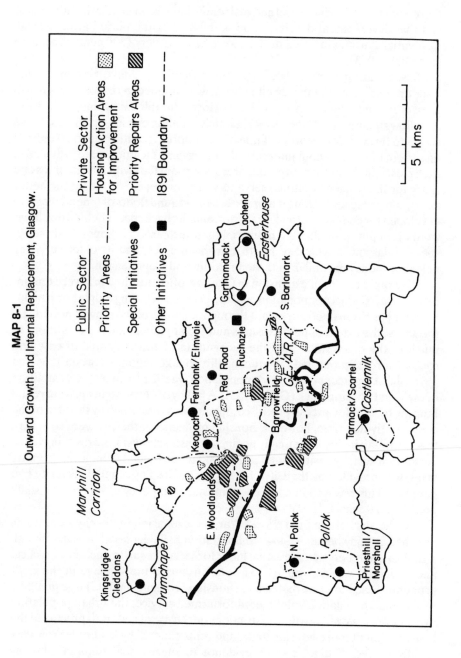

thereby dictated that industrial and residential land uses would exist side by side and that development density would be high. For the period around 1860, residential densities in the central city were on the order of 330 persons per acre (see Gibb, 1983).

The traditional urban dwelling form in Scotland, unlike England, is the walk-up tenement, and this dwelling form was supplied in response to growth pressures. These tenements were built of local, durable sandstone, in the form of hollow squares or rectangles within which common entries, or "closes," gave access to three or four storeys of houses. In poorer localities, up to 20 units of one-room houses, without internal toilet or washing facilities, were provided in each close. In the more prosperous areas, six-room flats with all amenities and space for the (then ubiquitous) servants were developed. In all but the better areas, and particularly along major routes, the ground floors of tenements were developed for commercial and retail uses, and the back spaces behind dwellings were often put to small-scale industrial uses such as workshops. In these respects, Glasgow is typical of North European cities, and its older surviving neighborhoods are similar to those in Berlin and Copenhagen.

The rapid nature of expansion in Glasgow often resulted in severe temporary shortages of accommodation, and the practice of selling lodging on a night-by-night basis remained important throughout much of the growth period. By the 1870s, the extent of homelessness and the appalling sanitary conditions of much of the older stock (and the recognition of consequential disease and social disorder) prompted the municipality to take action. Between 1866 and 1876, about 6 percent of the city's population was displaced by the demolition of the worst housing stock (Gibb, 1983). A policy of encouraging private rental housing by "not for-excess-profit" companies was developed by the turn of the century. By that time, however, housing problems in the city were so severe that the municipality had already begun to construct subsidized dwelling units. Subsidized social housing numbering 2,000 units, funded from local property taxes, was provided by the City of Glasgow before any other British city had done so. This was well in advance of any national policy of subsized "social" housing (see Smart, 1902).

By the start of the First World War, the expansion in the city's economic base had already begun to slow. Immigration had decreased in scale, though significant numbers of the existing labor force had begun to encounter cyclical and structural unemployment. The war disguised the slippage in the city's economic base but exacerbated local housing problems. While large numbers of the male population volunteered for armed service, the urban population expanded. However, wartime restrictions on the use of materials precluded the construction of more housing units, and rents charged by landlords grew very rapidly indeed. There is some evidence to suggest that rents in Glasgow increased by almost one-fourth in real terms between 1914 and 1915. This led to a series of major demonstrations and eventually to rent strikes. Glasgow was one of the first cities to manifest this anti-landlord shift of opinion. In consequence, rent controls were introduced which, although altered in detail over time, have remained essentially in place since 1915. Approximately 20 percent of the city's current housing stock dates from before that period, and this old housing still forms about half of the privately owned stock within the city. Thus, some 70 years of continuous rent controls and essentially anti-private landlord policies have dominated the economics of older housing.

1919 - 1945

After World War I, the British government faced major difficulties in attempting to persuade returning servicemen to accept the squalor of the homes they had left. The eminent anthropologist Ralph Glasser recalls living in Glasgow at that time. The area described below, Gorbals, was located adjacent to the central business district of Glasgow:

> *We lived in a mid-Victorian tenement of blackened sandstone...in the heart of the Gorbals, a bustling district of small workshops and factories, a great many pawnshops and pubs and little shops, grocers, bakers, fish-sellers and butchers and drysalters, tiny granny shops...public baths and a wash-house, many churches and several synagogues. The streets were slippery with refuse and often with drunken vomit. It was a place of grime and poverty.*
> (Glasser, 1987, p. 16)

His description of the dwelling unit is equally informative:

> *The Victorian building, in red sandstone blackened by smoke...was in decay. Splintered and broken floor boards sometimes gave way under your feet. The minimal plumbing hovered on the verge of collapse. Interior walls carried patches of stain from a long succession of burst pipes or ill-mended leaks. Rats and mice moved about freely.... On the common staircase six or eight flats shared two lavatories.... Going to the lavatory we had to remember to carry a supply of newspaper, not only for use as toilet paper but also to clean the soles of our boots of excrement and urine before going back to the flat.*
> (Glasser, 1987, p. 7)

It is pertinent to note that the dwelling unit Glasser describes survived for a further four decades, under strict rent control, until the post-1960 slum clearance campaigns.

The Royal Commission on the Housing of the Industrial Population of

Scotland reported in 1917 that as many as a third of the population could not afford "decent" minimum standards of housing without substantial economic help. In broad terms, the report of the commission implied that this group required subsidies of up to 40 percent of rent if the payment burden was not to be unreasonable. In 1919, the fear of a Bolshevist-type revolution in Glasgow and several other disadvantaged British cities was one of the factors that induced the national government to introduce public housing subsidies. At that time, it would not have been feasible to provide income-related allowances even if there had been a belief that the market could respond to demand subsidies. Instead, supply-side subsidies were introduced, tied to a minimum standard of housing consumption. Local government was deemed sufficiently well developed that the responsibility for constructing, owning, maintaining, and letting subsidized social housing units was given to municipal government. Indeed, it is not until the 1980s that this fundamental presumption of housing policy in Britain as a whole has been challenged and reversed by central government. There is a view that this subsidy strategy reflected central government's belief that most local governments would not be prepared to supply social housing. Central government finance also meant, however, that there was an additional source of revenue for social housing provision through local tax revenues. This role as key provider alongside its already key role as housing planner and facilitator put the British municipality in a position of great power in shaping local housing development. Glasgow stands out as the most highly developed and conspicuous attempt in Western Europe to implement local municipal socialism in housing provision.

The period between the two world wars also marked the development of a large-scale finance and subsidy system for housing in Britain. The broad structure of rental-sector finance which prevailed in Britain into the late 1960s was already in place by the 1930s. The private rental sector, aside from certain classes of new investment, was strictly controlled. Real rents declined until the late 1950s, when there was a short and abortive attempt at deregulation. In 1965 the introduction of a "Fair Rent" was intended to allow landlords a reasonable rate of return on capital via an administered rent system. Rapid rates of inflation and downward political pressure on rents meant, however, that in the regulated and controlled rental sector there were few incentives for private landlords to invest. This process, except in the uncontrolled sector (consisting of short-term, furnished lets), continues into the 1980s.

Council housing in Britain has been financed and subsidized by the same general processes from the 1930s to the 1980s, although subsidy details and spending controls have changed over time. Local authorities raise capital for housing (and other investment) from the general capital and bonds markets in the United Kingdom. The largest share of this money is raised via the intermediary of the Public Works Loans Board, since the large scale of its activities reduces interest costs, risks, and administration costs. The loans are amortized over 60 years for new housing investment and over 30 years for modernization projects. The interest costs are not directly subsidized by central government, as they often are in other European countries. Each municipality pools all of its loans and continually refinances the debt over time. Further, since 1935, separate accounts have not been maintained for each project or estate; rather costs and revenues are "pooled" across all the existing stock of the authority. Each year the housing authority has to generate revenues to cover the costs of loan amortization, interest, management, and maintenance.

The revenues arise from three main sources. First, rental income is levied on the basis of relatively simple pricing schemes which vary from authority to authority and may change over time. Second, municipal government may choose to subsidize council housing from local property taxes (known as "rates"). This is called the Rate Fund Contribution. Finally, subsidies from central government are included. From 1920 to 1975, these subsidies were generally tied to dwelling type. At a given date and for a given class of dwelling, authorities would be guaranteed a fixed nominal sum to be paid annually over a 40- or 60-year repayment period (see table 8-2). Until the late 1970s, and the reform of this system, income-related subsidies were of minimal significance. A further general requirement for assistance was that local authorities could not earn a surplus or profit on their Housing Revenue Accounts, and these accounts were balanced in relation to the historic costs of construction. This system may have kept rents low and, via pooling, assisted new project development. It did nothing, however, to ensure economical, efficient, and effective use of social resources.

Prior to the 1960s, aside from occasional subsidies to developers, the owner-occupied sector was largely unassisted. Social security spending for distressed owners was virtually nonexistent, and tax relief on mortgage interest was partially offset by taxes on imputed rental income. The improvement program for owner occupants was of little significance until the 1970s. The ways in which the system evolved, particularly after 1975, will be discussed later in more detail.

Between the First and Second World Wars, Glasgow's economic base remained problematic. The city never experienced the growth of owner occupation so characteristic of English cities in that period. Undoubtedly the sluggishness of the economic base contributed to this trend, but the local council's commitment to providing council housing pre-empted both land and resources for public sector development. Between the two wars the city developed more than 65,000 units for municipal rental to low-income households. These houses were initially built as semidetached units and other units with large gardens in almost "garden city" layouts (see maps 8-1 and 8-2). However, with a reduction in the real value of central government subsidies and a growing commitment to slum clearance in the 1930s, the principal form of new construction in the social sector became densely developed tenements.

TABLE 8-2
Central Government Housing Subsidies, 1938-1962.

Year of enactment	Type of property/occupant	Annual subsidy	Other
1938	three apartment flats	£10-10/-	Paid for 40 years
	four apartment flats	£11-15/-	Paid for 40 years
	five apartment flats	£13/-	Paid for 40 years
1946	three apartment flats	£21-10/-	Paid for 60 years
	four apartment flats	£23-	Paid for 60 years
	five apartment flats	£25-10/-	Paid for 60 years
1952	three apartment flats	£39-15/-	Paid for 60 years
	four apartment flats	£42-5/-	Paid for 60 years
	five apartment flats	£46-15/-	Paid for 60 years
	housing for new agricultural workers	£12-	Additional
1957	all approved houses	£24-	
	housing for incoming industrial workers	£30-	
	housing for agricultural population	£36-	
	housing for overspill development	£42-	
	development corporation	£42-	
	high-rise (six or more stories)	varies	
1962	all approved houses	varies	
	housing for incoming industrial workers	£32-	
	high-rise (six or more stories)	£40	

Source: Maclennan and Gibb (1986).

The oldest public sector units still form the most highly regarded areas of public sector housing within the city. By 1939 council housing provided about 17 percent of housing units in the city, about double the national average. Of British cities of similar size (between a million and half a million people), Glasgow built roughly double the amount of public housing of other cities, with the single exception of Birmingham.

Post-1945

The period immediately following the cessation of hostilities in 1945 merely exacerbated prevailing economic trends. The local economic base, which had been temporarily buoyed up by the demands for heavy armaments and shipbuilding in the wartime period, quickly succumbed to the footloose- ness of lighter and consumer-oriented industries. The traditional locational advantages of the city and the region were sharply eroded in the 1950s, and indeed the process of deindustrialization has continued unabated until the present. The presence of a strong regional component in national economic policy, the adoption of extensive social redistribution policies, and the trend towards national wage bargaining throughout the 1950s and 1960s all resulted in an upward drift of Glasgow incomes toward the national average. However, unemployment in the city and the region typically ran at double the national average. In addition, the city experienced a rapid decentralization of manufac- turing and service employment to the metropolitan periphery, but in turn, the region as a whole struggled as a structurally inappropriate entity in a competi- tively difficult location (see Cameron, 1971). As a consequence of these eco- nomic difficulties, net migration from the region rose steadily. With a reduc- tion in the net natural increase of the population, the city's population began to decline steadily from its peak of 1.25 million people in 1951. Population fell to less than 1 million by 1964 and to 750,000 twenty years later.

It may be that local housing policies had little impact upon the process of economic decline, though by the 1970s certain housing and environmental features of the city did act as a deterrent to growth. There is, in retrospect, little doubt that the housing policies adopted in the early postwar period exacerbated the decline of the city. It is important to stress that in Glasgow (and indeed in the wider British and European contexts) urban decline may be as much "policy led" as "market led." Policy decisions produced a housing stock which, in terms of its physical and tenure structures, became increasingly inappropriate in the postwar decades. After postwar restrictions on housing construction were lifted, the city began to implement strategic regional plans which had been for- mulated in the late wartime period. The underlying thesis was that the city of Glasgow needed to be "unpacked," with up to a third of its residents decentral- ized to less densely developed and more salubrious peripheral locations. It was estimated that some 40 percent of the city's housing stock needed to be demol- ished, partly due to wartime damage but mainly due to lack of reinvestment in maintenance and upgrading of the facilities of older housing. In older central wards, such as the Gorbals area described above, the target for demolition often constituted 80 percent of the existing housing stock. At this time, the local socialist commitment was quite consistent with the conservative central government's view that new record levels of council housing ought to be developed to meet crudely defined housing "needs" targets.

The city pursued two broad strategies. First, more than 80,000 people were relocated to "New Towns" built within 20 miles of the city or were sent to "Overspill" reception towns much further distant. At the same time, the city started to develop large-scale council housing schemes on the peripheral edges or corners of the city (see maps 8-1 and 8-2). The continued large-scale devel-

TABLE 8-3
Peripheral Housing Schemes in Glasgow.

	Year	Castlemilk	Drumchapel	Easterhouse	Priesthill/ Pollok
House completions	1958	7,926	7,926	3,659	5,278
	1968	9,578	9,845	12,997	11,395
	1978	9,747	10,345	14,959	11,566
Population	1976	36,521	34,002	30,868	24,459
Public ownership	1976	98%	98.8%	98.8%	98%
Overcrowded	1971	18%	21%	21%	20%

Sources: Strathclyde Regional Council (1976); Gibb (1983), Table 7v.

TABLE 8-4
Housing Tenure in Glasgow, 1961-1984.

	Percent of total housing stock				
Sector	1961	1971	1976	1980	1984
Public	38.0%	53.7%	61.0%	65.8%	62.6%
Owner-occupied	17.1	23.4	25.0	25.6	28.2
Private rental	41.2	22.5	14.0	8.6	9.0

Source: Census Enumeration, Abstracts, 1961 and 1971: Strathclyde Regional Council 1981. *1980 base projection to 1987*; *Population, Households, Housing*; Glasgow District Council Planning Dept. *1985 City Profile*.

MAP 8-2

Housing and Redevelopment Areas, Glasgow, 1918-1975.

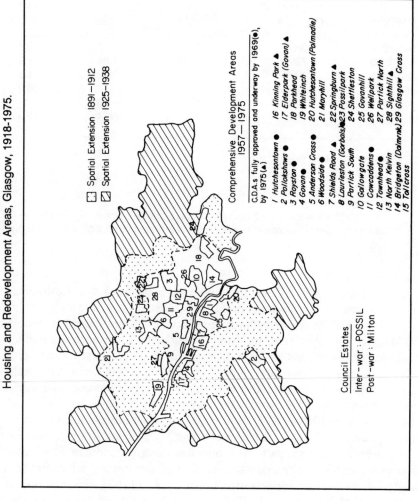

☐ Spatial Extension 1891–1912

▨ Spatial Extension 1925–1938

Comprehensive Development Areas
1957 – 1975

C.D.A.s fully approved and underway by 1969(●),
by 1975(▲)

1 Hutchesontown ●	16 Kinning Park ▲
2 Pollokshaws ●	17 Elderpark (Govan) ▲
3 Royston ●	18 Parkhead
4 Govan ●	19 Whiteinch
5 Anderson Cross ●	20 Hutchesontown (Polmadie)
6 Woodside ●	21 Maryhill
7 Shields Road ▲	22 Springburn ▲
8 Laurieston (Gorbals) ●	23 Possilpark
9 Partick South	24 Shettleston
10 Gallowgate	25 Govanhill
11 Cowcaddens ●	26 Wellpark
12 Townhead ●	27 Partick North
13 North Kelvin	28 Sighthill ▲
14 Bridgeton (Dalmrnk)	29 Glasgow Cross
15 Tollcross	

Council Estates

Inter–war : POSSIL

Post–war : Milton

TABLE 8-5

Municipal Housing Capital Investment, 1946-1947 to 1986-1987
(£m, in June 1986 prices).

| | | Capital expenditures | | |
Fiscal year	Housing revenue accounts	Other **	Total	Capital receipt
1946-1947	38.7	0	38.7	0.8
1949-1950	73.4	0	73.4	1.6
1956-1957	79.2	0	79.2	1.6
1966-1967	138.4	0	138.4	8.2
1976-1977	142.0	22.0	164.0	9.1
1986-1987*	65.0	41.4	106.4	12.3

Source: GDC Finance Dept.

Notes:
* Estimated.
** Prior to 1969, HRA and Non-HRA spending are not distinguished. Prior to the 1969 Housing Act, Non-HRA spending was a very minor component of total capital expenditure.

opment of the peripheral schemes is indicated in table 8-3, as is the dominance of public ownership of housing in these large areas (see table 8-4).

After the 1950s, new emphasis was placed on slum clearance rather than building to meet shortages, and from the early 1960s onwards, the municipal bulldozer removed 5,000 to 7,000 older central tenement units per annum. The city was, for renewal purposes, subdivided into more than twenty Comprehensive Development Areas (see map 8-2). As sites were cleared, high-rise and system-built housing appeared in these and other publicly owned locations. In the decade from 1965 to 1975, about 35,000 nontraditional housing units were developed by the city council, with more than 25,000 in multistory tower blocks.

The broad temporal pattern of council housing development is indicated in figures 8-1 and 8-2. The sharp acceleration of construction after 1945 generated peaks of social housing construction in 1954 and 1966, with the demolition process peaking in the early 1970s. The efforts of the municipality were augmented until the 1970s by those of the Scottish Special Housing Association (SSHA). The SSHA was formed in 1936 as a national agency to provide social housing units in disadvantaged areas. It was controlled directly and deficit-financed by the central government. The figures also highlight the minimal private sector investment in Glasgow's housing stock from 1960 to 1980.

FIGURE 8-1
Changing Roles in Housing Provision.

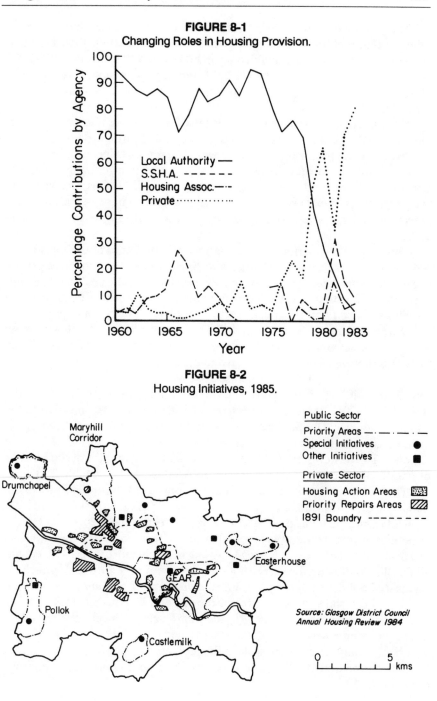

FIGURE 8-2
Housing Initiatives, 1985.

The volume of capital expenditures involved was considerable. Table 8-5 indicates that real housing spending nearly doubled between 1946-1947 and 1949-1950, and then nearly doubled again between 1949-1950 and 1966-1967. Over the period 1946-1947 to 1976-1977, this represented an investment of £3,000 million (including SSHA spending) in the social housing stock in Glasgow.

The Housing Revenue Account trends for Glasgow and a number of similar-sized English cities are indicated in table 8-6. Two main points are noteworthy. First, the proportion of costs covered by rents has increased markedly since the 1960s as transfers from the Rate Fund and from central government have declined. Second, comparing across cities, Glasgow has received relatively high rates of ex post subsidy from central government and, at the same time, required ratepayers to finance a high proportion of local social housing costs.

Throughout this period, the population and number of households in the city continued to decline. At the same time, development of new private housing for home ownership was virtually precluded by the city's land promotion policies, and there were seldom more than 200 new private houses built in the city each year (while the public sector completion rate commonly ran close to 5,000 per annum). Also the demolition process was largely clearing away the private rental sector of the small inner-city tenements that had been built from the 1840s onwards. Estimates suggest that, at the start of the Second World War, the city had a tenure structure that was roughly three-fifths private rentals, one-fifth council rentals, and one-fifth home ownership. But by the start of the 1970s, the city's tenure structure had diverged even more from the national average. The public sector had now come to provide around three-fifths of all units in the city, a degree of dominance rare outside of Eastern Europe. The owner-occupied sector included about a quarter of the housing provision, and the private rented sector took up the rest (see table 8-4).

The effects on local political economy from such a controlled process of municipal expansion are of interest. In the case of Glasgow, in the early 1980s, even following the modest retreat of the public sector, some 70 percent of the 66 political wards in the city had more than half of their units in council housing, and in about half of the wards social housing made up more than 70 percent of all dwellings. It is hardly surprising that the issues of tenure and rents have dominated politics of the city for almost a quarter of a century. But notwithstanding the socialist party control of the city and its housing stock, the last decade has seen a new pluralism in the approaches to local housing policy. There has been a new pragmatic approach made by politicians, who seem to have been so impressed by the scale of the problems created in the city that they have been prepared to relax centralized municipal control in order to improve conditions.

TABLE 8-6

Distribution of Housing Revenue Account Income and Expenditures: Glasgow,
Birmingham, Liverpool, and Manchester;
Various Years (in percent).

	1960-1961	1970-1971	1975-1976	1982-1983	1984-1985
Glasgow					
Income (percent of total)					
Rents	31.6%	47.6%	50.7%	49.2%	58.4%
Subsidies	29.6	23.2	34.4	26.8	17.6
Rate fund Contirbution	38.6	29.2	14.1	24.0	24.0
Expenditure (percent of total)					
Loan Charges	84.6	77.0	65.8	56.7	62.8
Repairs	11.6	14.1	25.6	32.2	23.7
Others*	3.8	8.9	8.6	11.1	13.5
Public Housing Stock	121,241	156,395	184,811	176,500	172,084
Birmingham					
Income (percent of total)					
Rents	68.2	66.0	42.7	69.7	78.6
Subsidies	18.3	22.1	38.2	21.5	17.3
Rate fund Contirbution	10.8	5.6	13.4	8.8	4.1
Expenditure (percent of total)					
Loan Charges	63.2	75.7	65.8	60.9	63.9
Repairs	21.1	12.7	19.8	23.4	22.1
Others*	15.7	11.6	14.4	15.7	13.9
Public Housing Stock	115,036	127,300	143,969	132,237	128,000
Liverpool					
Income (percent of total)					
Rents	47.1	72.9	43.6	84.6	--
Subsidies	16.7	23.4	41.5	12.0	--
Rate fund Contirbution	8.0	--	12.6	3.4	--
Expenditure (percent of total)					
Loan Charges	52.6	68.8	64.3	65.5	--
Repairs	11.6	17.9	19.2	19.7	--
Others*	35.8	13.2	16.5	14.7	--
Public Housing Stock	59,328	70,100	77,059	74,414	--

TABLE 8-6 (continued)
Distribution of Housing Revenue Account Income and Expenditures: Glasgow,
Birmingham, Liverpool, and Manchester;
Various Years (in percent).

	1960-1961	1970-1971	1975-1976	1982-1983	1984-1985
Manchester					
Income (percent of total)					
Rents	54.8%	70.3%	37.3%	60.7%	64.3%
Subsidies	23.9	24.0	37.9	10.2	5.6
Rate fund Contirbution	9.3	4.8	21.9	29.1	30.1
Expenditure (percent of total)					
Loan Charges	66.8	77.1	63.9	63.6	59.3
Repairs	20.8	13.7	23.1	15.7	19.9
Others*	12.4	9.2	13.0	20.8	20.8
Public Housing Stock	52,941	65,508	100,121	104,760	90,423

Notes: -- Not Available
         * Primarily supervision and management expenses

Sources: Chartered Institute of Public Finance and Accountancy: Glasgow Annual
          Abstract of Accounts

With this broad sweep of historical background material in place, we now move on to consider the dramatic shifts in the operation of the local housing system in the last decade.

NEW PLURALISM

While much has been made of the effects of the Thatcher government in reducing local housing subsidies and in promoting housing privatization, these policies did not cause the difficulties of social housing in Britain. Nor did they lead to the regeneration of Glasgow's private housing market. It would probably be fair to suggest (and this is dealt with in more detail in the final substantive section of the chapter) that government (at least into 1987) has precluded real attempts to solve these problems. In Glasgow, major housing problems have their origins in the period of massive postwar construction of social housing. Current problems arise from the technical, spatial, financial, and organizational structures developed in that period. In essence, there has been a failure to find a feasible, long-term form of social housing in Britain which is equitable, efficient, and effective.

Towards the end of the 1960s, the conventional postwar policy of providing peripheral or high-rise public units to house low-income families from emptied and then demolished private rental units came under increasing scrutiny for a range of reasons. First, with an already growing concern about the exchequer costs of demolition-rehousing, a number of government reports began to suggest that housing rehabilitation might be more cost-effective. In a relatively rare step in the essentially nonevaluative history of British housing policy, cost and benefit measures were developed (if rarely used) to establish the relative merits of demolition versus new construction. Second, officials began to recognize the real merit of earlier warnings, particularly by sociologists, of the harmful effects of demolishing communities. The alienation of the youth of the city in remote estates became palpable by the early 1970s. These estates had even then become, like Glasgow's Gorbals of half a century earlier, places of "grime and poverty" but without the public and private amenity provision of the older, central neighborhoods. Third, as early demolition schemes had largely followed a "worst first" path through the city, later schemes for demolition began to contain a larger proportion of units suitable for rehabilitation.

At this time, faith in the social housing sector as a mass and long-term solution to the problems of the city began to deteriorate rapidly. This process began earlier in Glasgow than in most British cities, but it has taken at least 15 years for the defenders and critics of social housing to suggest new forms and approaches. These new developments in social housing will be considered in the penultimate section. Here it is enough to note that these doubts manifested themselves in the shift towards the regeneration of the older central city.

The Shift to Rehabilitation of Older Neighborhoods

The pros and cons of a rehabilitation strategy were being seriously considered by the end of the 1960s, and by 1968 the government had introduced legislation to encourage area-based rehabilitation. However, two other pressures prompted a dramatically sudden shift. First, a growing number of communities in the older city had begun to voice dissent with programs of clearance designed to facilitate urban motorway development; this aroused local political interest. Further, in January 1968 a historic storm doubled, literally overnight, the number of older tenement units that were thought to be in need of major repairs or modernization. With about 90,000 units then in serious disrepair, it was quickly realized that there would be little of older Glasgow left if the policy of clearance were to be continued. At first the municipality tried to undertake rehabilitation of older, previously private housing by buying out the residents and creating "Housing Treatment Areas";

about 1,000 units were thoroughly rehabilitated in this way. However, the municipality recognized that its cumbersome and remote bureaucratic procedures were not effective. It was taking so long to improve streets that about half of the residents were displaced or deceased before the schemes were completed.

In 1974 the municipality welcomed new Scottish-wide legislation which provided the legislative and financial framework to facilitate one of the most extensive and successful housing rehabilitation programs in Western Europe (see Maclennan, 1984). The 1974 Housing Act (Scotland) gave the municipalities the powers to identify Below Tolerable Standard (BTS) housing units, with the standard being defined in relation to some ten items describing the housing amenities and conditions. Where more than 40 percent of the units in a small area, which in practice ranged from 40 to 400 units, were identified as being BTS, then a Housing Action Area (HAA) could be declared. At this point the area was designated for demolition or for improvement. The declarations were critical insofar as favorable levels of grant aid could be offered to improvers within these localities.

This legislation gave the municipality considerable strategic powers to shape the pattern and volume of rehabilitation in the city. It also left open to the municipality the identification of the agents of change within these areas. The municipality recognized its own inadequacies as the provider of improved housing. Either it could rely upon market-led responses of private property owners using grant aid, or it could use local housing associations, funded by national government, as agents to implement change. Grant aid for private sector home improvement had been available in Britain since 1948. However, in Glasgow the use of such aid had always run at minimum levels, particularly in the bottom third of the property value range, precisely where the BTS stock lay. The system of pricing utilized in rent controls, the "Fair Rent" system, actually offered landlords no more than a 5 percent nominal rate of return on investments from 1964 to 1984, when inflation was more than double that rate. (For a more detailed explanation of "Fair Rents" see Maclennan, 1982.) Only since 1982, with an upward shift in real rents, has it been permitted for landlords to resell improved property immediately (and with no grant payback). Even so, with higher levels of grant aid, small numbers of landlords are undertaking improvement activity. In 1984 it was estimated that less than 3 percent of major property improvement in the BTS stock was being undertaken by private landlords (Maclennan et al., 1985).

A detailed study of the Glasgow owner-occupied housing market in the mid-1970s (Dawson et al., 1982) indicated why improvement led by owner occupiers was not a suitable strategy. The study shows that the housing market, in which average dwelling prices are high for a British city, could be subdivided into at least seven submarkets. Four high-quality submarkets became the locus of choice for primarily professional/managerial workers. Dwelling units in these submarkets were almost entirely financed by building societies. These sectors formed chains through which households moved upwards and outwards as their incomes and family circumstances developed. The substantial price pressures prevailing in that sector also reflected the small stock of owner-occupied units available in the city. This pattern undoubtedly contributed to the sustained movement of middle- and upper-income households to the detached suburban municipalities. The sustained reduction in the population of the city throughout the 1970s is indicated in table 8-7.

In the other submarkets, encompassing the bottom three deciles of the housing stock, purchase was dominated either by lower-income, first-time buyers, or by older children of council house families who rejected social housing offers. The study noted the high propensity of the children of council house tenants to reject social housing offers for themselves. Analysis of neighborhood choices in the city indicates that while there was some income overlap between those households locating in the better and the poorer areas, the presence of younger children in the household was the key factor in explaining location away from central city areas. The study also revealed that in the bottom three deciles there was a high proportion of cash purchases or purchases involving unusual loans, with building societies providing less than 20 percent of the funds. At that time, the proportion of society funding in these locations appeared to be deteriorating as national societies progressively bought out smaller, locally oriented societies. This process of credit rationing is described in Maclennan and Jones (1987).

It is obvious that the key processes set in motion by national housing policy had negative impacts on central city areas. Inner-city decline had been further exacerbated by rent controls, which discouraged reinvestment. Tax expenditures to assist low-income owners had minimal impacts in the bottom three price deciles, especially where there were cash purchases. The social rehousing-demolition process had left behind a scarred landscape of blighted properties awaiting demolition and ugly vacant sites after demolition had taken place. It has taken Glasgow almost 15 years to recover from the negative externalities produced by the clearance process of the 1960s.

These negative effects of major housing policies dominated the improvement grant system (see table 8-8). During the 1970s there were only about a thousand grants to homeowners in the city. A survey of houses in the rehabilitation program in 1980 indicated, from a sample of 500 units, that none had been improved by landlords and fewer than 0.5 percent by owners. Owners did not even upgrade their units when a 90 percent rate of subsidy was offered, either because of prisoners' dilemma effects or because the 10 percent burden of payment was too much for this poor and generally elderly population. As is shown below, this scenario has now changed dramatically.

TABLE 8-7
Estimated Home Population and Movement, Glasgow District,
1973-1983.

Base year population	Natural increase/ decrease	Net migration	Other changes and adjustments	Total change	Population in succeeding year
923,995 (1973)	-775	-18,625	+437	-18,963	905,032 (1974)
905,032 (1974)	-957	-23,863	+405	-24,415	880,617 (1975)
880,617 (1975)	-8,815	-22,775	-15	-24,605	856,012 (1976)
856,012 (1976)	-2,386	-21,857	+328	-23,915	832,097 (1977)
832,097 (1977)	-2,795	-19,805	+182	-22,418	809,679 (1978)
809,679 (1978)	-2,603	-12,973	+213	-15,363	794,316 (1979)
794,316 (1979)	-1,471	-11,036	-115	-12,622	781,694 (1980)
781,694 (1980)	-1,100	-6,326	-200	-7,626	774,068 (1981)
774,068 (1981)	-1,886	-10,011	0	-11,897	762,171 (1982)
762,171 (1982)	-1,409	-9,748	0	-11,157	751,014 (1983)
751,014 (1983)	-1,445	-5,553	0	-6,998	744,016 (1984)
744,016 (1984)	--	--	--	--	737,018 (1985)

Note: -- Not available.
Source: Registrar General's Mid-year Estimate, obtained by GDC Planning Dept.

The municipality therefore preferred to use housing associations as agents of change within HAAs. The operation and impacts of these associations are discussed in detail in Maclennan (1985). Here only the broad outlines of this key process are recorded, while figure 8-2 indicates the spatial scale of their development.

The Role of the Housing Associations

After the municipality had identified potential HAAs, the Housing Corporation then set about developing associations within these territories. At first seven associations were developed, generally around the community nucleus of a residents' action group. Each association was then given a territory and a potential action programme of up to 2,000 units. In due course, more community pressures prompted a wider spread of associations, and by the 1980s the Housing Corporation had promoted or established ten more associations in areas with high concentrations of BTS stock. At present there are 26 territorially based associations operating in well-defined older neighborhoods. To date some 16,000 units have been improved, with a target to complete a similar number of units over the next seven years. The spatial pattern of spending by associations is indicated in map 8-3. Map 8-4 indicates the spatial patern in improvement grants.

TABLE 8-8

Approved Applications for Home Improvement and Repair Grants,
by Tenure, 1975-1985.

| | Discretionary | | Housing action areas | |
| | Owner | | Owner | |
Year	occupiers	Others	occupiers	Others
1975/76	741	139	9	3
1976/77	461	238	37	22
1977/78	368	272	18	35
1978/79	909	265	99	11
1979/80	2,111	455	133	10
1980/81	3,798	590	90	19
1981/82	4,412	625	138	56
1982/83	23,246	2,910	157	192
1983/84	22,554	3,006	319	30
1984/85	7,825	1,455	173	37
Total	66,425	9,955	1,173	415

Source: Scottish Housing Statistics, Form IMPI.

MAP 8-3

Expenditures in Housing Association Areas for Improvement, per 500 Meter
Grid Squares, Glasgow, 1975-1984.

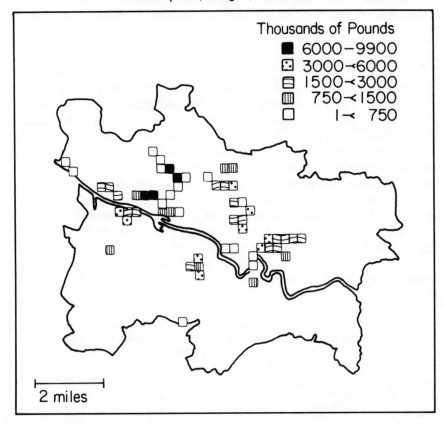

The associations are managed by elected committees of up to 16 local residents. There is clear evidence that these committees have formed an important channel for the considerable talents of the high proportion of redundant middle-aged workers who live in these locations. The committee then appoints development staff who put together rehabilitation contracts and consult with local residents before overseeing construction projects.

The nature of the historic tenement stock and the mixed land-use pattern present difficulties for comprehensive rehabilitation. Many of the major repair and improvement items required are related to the roofs of buildings, the internal service stacks, the exteriors of the buildings, and the attached backcourt spaces. Thus, comprehensive rehabilitation of the tenement requires agreement by all of the building owners and users. The provision of buyout finance to the associations has meant that there has been little resistance to improve-

MAP 8-4

Improvement Grants per 500 meter grid squares, Glasgow 1974-84
(total expenditure at 1983 price levels).

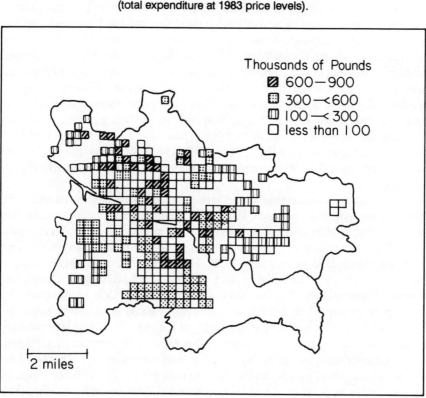

ment from low-income residents and private landlords. Both owner-occupiers and private landlords have usually been willing to sell their units to the associations. Residents are guaranteed a place in the rehabilitated units at "Fair Rents," and there is minimal involuntary displacement. Within association areas, the pre-improvement tenure structure is broadly split between 55 percent private lets and 45 percent low-income homeowners. After improvement, the private tenure share typically falls to about 10 percent. This pattern is changing, however, as some landlords now prefer to improve rather than sell. The proportion of homeowners retaining ownership has also doubled. The problem of uncooperative commercial users of properties, which had resulted in associations essentially avoiding closes with commercial units, has been eased. Since 1982, compulsory repair (but not improvement) legislation has been supplemented with means-tested repair grants for commercial users.

The packaging of houses and closes, which is not pursued within areas on a "worst first" basis, may take two years of development activity and planning, and construction activity may take another 18 months. The costs of this process are essentially financed by central government through the Housing Corporation. The cost of acquisition and works for comprehensive unit improvement in Glasgow is now on the order of £25,000 per unit. The rent of the improved property is then set at a "Fair Rent" level, and the discounted value of expected maintenance and management costs over a 30-year period is deducted from the discounted value of the rental income. The net surplus is then used to repay the mortgage taken out for the acquisition and renovation process. The gap between this mortgage amount and the actual outstanding loan is met by a Housing Association Grant (HAG) (see Hills, 1986). In reality, the HAG grant has covered more than 90 percent of the costs of most improvement projects in Glasgow.

The housing association program in the city, which has continued under the conservative government since 1979 with relatively minor disruptions, has represented a massive commitment of heavily subsidized government expenditure. The annual totals of spending run close to £50 million per annum and have done so, in 1985 prices, since 1978. The benefits have also been substantial. The condition of the housing stock and the associated neighborhoods has improved dramatically. Further, survey evidence shows that the beneficiaries of the policy have chiefly been low-income and elderly households, often the very individuals who had been disadvantaged for more than a quarter century by postwar housing policies. There is also growing awareness that, as rent levels rise over time, an increasing proportion of the initial capital costs will be captured in accounting surpluses. These costs are likely to be recouped by central government. If so, the HAG becomes an index-linked loan rather than a grant. It should also be noted that much of the HAG grant aid has been directed to the inner city of Glasgow which, according to the 1971 census, contained a disproportionately high share of the most disadvantaged households in the whole of the United Kingdom. Undoubtedly this factor, combined with political reaction to the extraction of Scottish oil, contributed to the initial support for the programme.

The benefits of the program have not been restricted to narrowly defined areas or income groups. Research suggests that, if the residents had received cash grants equal to the value of HAG, they would have spent less than half on housing; the grant would have been used to move rather than improve. It took policy makers five years, from 1974 to 1979, to realize that the program was bringing about neighborhood regeneration rather than merely fixing up inadequate units. It has taken the subsequent period to realize that the spatial and sectoral effects have had a wide and positive impact on the city as a whole.

The New Wave and Altered Images

Housing association zones have produced a sufficient cumulative impact that they could be labelled the growth poles in local urban redevelopment. First of all, in the period 1978 to 1982, the less deteriorated zones next to association territories experienced a 9 percent increase in real capital values over what could have been expected for otherwise similar properties. These spillover benefits occurred where external cleaning (of the stone walls, for instance) and environmental upgrading accompanied internal house renovation. Subsequently, the rate of usage of home improvement and repair grants grew dramatically in these locations. The pattern for the city as a whole is indicated in table 8-8. In the early 1980s, central government expanded the volume of grant aid available for private repair and improvement and, albeit temporarily, boosted the rate of grant aid to 90 percent. In this period, the city was now controlling private sector grant aid of more than £60 million annually. There was, in marked contrast to the 1960s, excess demand for these grants. The municipality channelled these grants towards relatively rundown areas and to low- and middle-income households; in consequence, gentrification via the use of grant aid by high-income groups has been minimal in the city. Through this process, more than 25,000 units have been improved in the city.

In the last decade, the combined action of associations and private improvement has reduced the stock of BTS houses by more than 40,000 units. This has occurred in the most densely populated neighborhoods. The overall geographic pattern of improvement grant spending in the city over the last decade is indicated in map 8-4. Recent research has also indicated that the proportion of building society lending in such areas is now in fact higher than the average for the city. This is in contrast to the credit disadvantage they previously faced. Further, a recent paper by Maclennan and Munro (1987) has made clear that even after allowing for increased capital values due to grant aid, the last decade has seen the shift of the bottom third of the market towards the city mean house price. It is only the worst 5 percent of the dwelling stock which has not been appreciating rapidly. The changing spatial pattern of prices in the city is displayed in map 8-5.

The upward trend in city house prices, although the urban economy is still declining, reflects the fact that the number of households has been growing rapidly during the last decade. Further, there is clear evidence that tenure choice is shifting intergenerationally. In the last five years, about 70 percent of the growth in home ownership in the United Kingdom has been from the purchase of local authority units under the sales discount scheme introduced by the conservatives under "right to buy" legislation in 1980. But this process has had minimal relevance in Glasgow, despite the city's large stock of social housing. The extent of its disrepair and the long acculturation of older households to renting have both acted to reduce house sales. Indeed, the city

MAP 8-5

Relative House Price Change by Census Area, Glasgow, 1972-84.

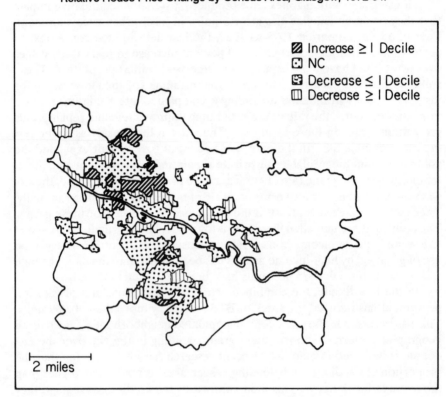

Legend:
- ▨ Increase ≥ I Decile
- ▣ NC
- ▨ Decrease ≤ I Decile
- ▥ Decrease ≥ I Decile

2 miles

has sold less than 3 percent of its stock since 1980. However, research undertaken (see Maclennan and Munro, 1985) indicates that tenure attitudes of the young are becoming polarized in favor of homeownership, with almost all young employed households preferring housing within the private sector. It is also clear from recent research that the city has become increasingly effective in attracting the children of households who had gone to the new towns and outer metropolitan suburbs in the 1960s back to central city areas.

The strong back-to-the-city movement currently experienced in Glasgow is not a high-income shift of already established households, but is dominated rather by single and two-person households setting up for the first time. We

TABLE 8-9
Glasgow Private Sector Completions by Type of Site,
1980-1984.

Year	New ('Greenfield')		Redeveloped ('Brownfield')		Total
1980	787	87.7%	110	12.3%	897
1981	568	52.6	511	47.4	1,079
1982	656	54.6	545	45.4	1,201
1983	586	45.1	713	54.9	1,299
1984	305	22.3	1,064	77.7	1,369

Source: NB2 and H LAND1 returns to Scottish Development Department; Planning
Department.

have already noted the successive waves of policy which introduced the housing associations and reinforced their impact through private improvement grants. Since 1980 there has been an important wave of unsubsidized investment (that is, unsubsidized apart from the tax treatment of homeowners). In the late 1970s, private developers, who had built no more than 250 units in any single year in the period 1955 to 1975, began to take an increasing interest in brownfield sites lying vacant in the central city. Many of these sites were in public ownership, but conservative cutbacks on spending for public housing encouraged their transfer to the private sector. Thus, even during a period of considerable economic uncertainty and high real interest rates, private developers have provided more than 1,000 new units per annum in the city every year since 1979. The share of these units going to brownfield sites is now more than 80 percent, and the city's share of residential construction for the metropolitan area as a whole has increased from about 10 percent to more than 25 percent (see tables 8-9 and 8-10). These early sites were almost invariably clustered on vacant land adjacent to housing association zones. Initially, development focused on "starter" homes for single people and childless couples. Now there is growing evidence of a demand for higher-value units, and more than 300 of these units have been marketed successfully in the last year.

Research on the Glasgow market over the last decade indicates that the rehabilitation program has not only fulfilled important distributional objectives but has also created a context for the restructuring and growth of the private housing market in the city. Old submarket boundaries have begun to

TABLE 8-10
Housing Building in Glasgow as a Proportion of Strathclyde,
1976-1984.

Year	Sector	Number of completions		Glasgow as percent of Strathclyde	
		Strathclyde	Glasgow	Public	Private
1976	Public	6,361	2,307	36.3%	
	Private	4,344	426		9.8%
1977	Public	3,958	1,754	44.3	
	Private	4,372	530		12.1
1978	Public	3,958	1,719	43.4	
	Private	5,149	347		6.7
1979	Public	2,659	711	26.7	
	Private	5,007	817		16.3
1980	Public	2,242	484	21.6	
	Private	4,250	897		21.1
1981	Public	3,450	2,000	58.0	
	Private	3,803	1,079		28.4
1982	Public	1,403	484	34.5	
	Private	4,230	1,201		28.4
1983	Public	1,011	312	30.9	
	Private	4,372	1,299		29.7
1984	Public	1,264	267	21.1	
	Private	5,316	1,369		25.8

Source: Centre for Housing Research, Glasgow University.

disappear, and housing search patterns now range over a much wider set of neighborhoods. Locations that upper- and middle-income households avoided as recently as the 1970s now attract buyers from a wide range of socioeconomic groups. The overall social mix in the central city has diversified, there has been a flourishing of central city entertainment and service outlets, and Glasgow has been pronounced by all and sundry as "miles better." And, of course, the reconstruction effort (which, including all forms of rehabilitation and private investment, is estimated at around £125 million per annum since 1980) has had major construction employment effects-- of the order of 5,000 jobs. The long-term test for jobs is to establish whether the improved image of the city will affect the flow of mobile service and high-tech industries to the city. This remains to be seen.

This section has indicated how carefully planned public sector investment can significantly improve badly deteriorated neighborhoods. The rehabilitation experience of central Glasgow in the last decade should be encouraging for other city governments. It demonstrates clearly how an entrepreneurial bureaucracy, giving urban marketing equal priority with urban planning, can effect dramatic transformations when combined with the confidence and participation of citizens. Glasgow needs now to apply the same imagination to the problems encountered with social housing stock on its outer edges. In these fringe areas, Glasgow is still a mean, indeed meaner, city. We now examine these issues in the last section of the chapter.

REMAKING COUNCIL HOUSING

The provision of large-scale council housing was warmly welcomed by the citizens of Glasgow and their elected representatives throughout the three decades from 1945 to 1975. The Second World War contributed to socialist attitudes and behavior in postwar Britain. Late wartime news film compared the plight of the poor in Britain's northern cities, including Glasgow, with the fate of the still unliberated cities of Eastern Europe. The population had become used to bureaucratic methods of allocation, and, to paraphrase Sir Alec Cairncross, there was every confidence that the political centralization which had won the war could just as easily ruin the peace. Housing in Glasgow reflects on a mass scale both the virtuous objectives of the British "welfare state" and the ineptitude of its design and implementation.

The motives of the providers and the initial satisfaction of the tenants upon moving into uncramped, sanitary dwellings of their own, often on the suburban edge of the city, cannot be doubted. The neighborhoods, like the dwellings, were fresh and new, and tenants waited with impatience to be housed under the protection of council and away from the vagaries of private landlords and the polluted, smog-ridden atmosphere of the older tenements. In addition to their attractive housing and environmental attributes, the schemes were viable in spite of their remoteness, because rents were significantly subsidized (by about 40 percent of costs). The excess demand for these units was reflected in long waiting lists, and this combined with the dwelling allocation priorities adopted by the municipality to minimize problems with antisocial tenants.

It was not considered a stigma to be a council tenant in Glasgow, and in broad terms it still is not. The problems of these estates were, however, built in from the start. Within a short time, families recognized the costs of disruption of the extended family networks that had characterized life in the central city. There was now no nearby grandmother to look after children if mothers wished to enter the labor force. Employees quickly learned, especially when plants where they were employed relocated to another sector of the city, that travel to work was expensive and time consuming (Glasgow still has the lowest rate of auto ownership, 42 percent of households, of any British city). At the same time, overtime work hours were being reduced. Families stayed in the schemes because the housing subsidies, which were tied to specific units, were extensive, and they offset labor market disadvantages. Of course, the subsidies were not portable from place to place even within the local authority. From data collected in 1985, we know that the average council tenant changes dwellings once every 14 years. This is roughly half the crude mobility rate of homeowners in the same context. Even in 1985, almost one-quarter of all council tenants were the first tenants of the houses in which they lived. Even those who do move tend to move within the council sector and within the same broad estate. Council housing allocation produces a great deal of locational inertia resulting largely from the nature of tied dwelling subsidies.

Another obvious feature of the estates from the outset was that "good housing" was defined in extremely narrow terms. Housing problems were defined in terms of the shortages of sanitary shelter units, and the neighborhood and locational aspects of housing amenities were largely ignored. The lack of transport, shopping, recreational, leisure, and cultural facilities stood in marked contrast (and still does) with the rich heritage of nineteenth century public amenities which tenants had left behind in the inner city. The almost complete absence of private land and property in the large estates precluded markets for these services; they were provided, and only in some areas, by the mid-1970s.

By the mid-1960s the deterioration of these estates had become quite marked. The city had never implemented a planned housing maintenance system, and the political preferences for low rents resulted in undermaintenance of units from the start of the settlement of these areas. Recent comprehensive modernisation of social housing units built as recently as 1953 requires expenditure of around £18,000 to put a house in good order, largely because the units have been under maintained for a quarter of a century.

In 1985, for the first time, the local authority undertook a citywide survey of the condition of housing units in the city. This survey confirmed that much still needs to be done to improve housing quality in the private sector. However, the study also confirmed that 13 percent of the city's municipal stock now also fell below the Tolerable Standard, and even more worrisome, almost half of the housing stock required repairs exceeding £3,000 per unit. This figure represents an amount 15 times greater than what the municipality spent on repairing the average house in 1985-1986. Moreover, the average outstanding repair requirement per unit in the council sector, at £3,533, was almost three times greater than the estimate obtained from similar surveys in London and Northern Ireland.

This massive repair problem represents one of the fundamental problems of bureaucratically managed social housing. Politicians will often be tempted to take a short-term perspective and restrain rents, both to secure electoral support and to avoid offending the party ideology of low rents. Until decay is well advanced, and previously hidden deficiencies become evident, tenants will also prefer low rents. Indeed, tenants had no direct involvement in rent setting in the first place. Such a system, which in broad terms represented British council housing into the 1980s, is not feasible in the long run. Moreover, the external environment, which may have seemed neat and logical on paper, becomes degraded if there are no defensible spaces, particularly where large families are housed at high densities with few amenities.

The environmental quality of Glasgow's outer estates is simply appalling. In the 1985 survey, environment was the "trigger factor" most often cited by tenants who wished to leave their present neighborhood. About 40 percent of tenants want to leave their existing units and about half of these cite the quality of the neighborhood as the key motivating factor. Over 20 percent of tenants in social housing in the city report that they do not like their neighborhoods. This contrasts with a figure of 4 percent for a similar income group of households in the private sector. Proximity to the greenfield serves only as a painful reminder of how things were in the past.

The council sector, albeit with large injections of new units every year until 1976, matured in the aggregate as well as at the individual estate level. By 1980 it had become apparent that there were sharp social subdivisions within the council sector. The lowest income groups were increasingly segregated into poorer housing areas, at the same time as areas of obviously better quality were emerging. A number of hypotheses have been advanced to explain this phenomenon (see Clapham and Kintrea, 1986). It has been argued that housing offices, even after explicit point schemes were introduced to rank the assessed needs of particular households, would tend to allocate more respectable households to better, more stable areas. It was also argued that status conscious tenants would seek to transfer out of more problematic areas, leaving behind less advantaged groups. Economically successful households could always walk away from poor social housing options and enter the private or owner-occupied sector. More recent research has indicated that in the housing allocation process, less disadvantaged households will turn down poor areas offered to them either because there is less temporal urgency in their need for housing or because the lower end of the private market is still an option for them. Unless the minimum standard of social housing is moderately high, further income segregation will occur within the public sector. This process has accelerated because post-1965 buildings have often technically deteriorated within a decade.

The consequences of adverse income separation have been exacerbated because the authority does not implement a unit pricing system related to the absolute or relative quality of units. The pricing system adopted is based on dwelling type, size, and amenities, with little importance accorded to age of property. One consequence of this system is that the worst housing may be relatively low in amenities but still command a higher rent than older and more attractive units. In this way, there may be an important cross-subsidization of richer by poorer tenants. Indeed, this may be an implicit mechanism by which the city encourages higher-income tenants to remain within the social sector. Social diversity at the tenure level may actually be rather costly, with few benefits at the estate level. The same rental system, with a rather flat pattern of rents, may also then encourage tenants of larger family units in older but attractive areas to remain in these units long after their families have left home. This results in a high proportion of older, childless couples living in larger houses with gardens while younger families live in overcrowded high-rise dwellings. This kind of size mismatch now appears to affect about fifteen percent of the social housing stock.

A second process, which became more important after the start of the 1970s, was the gradual immiserization, at least in relative terms, of a significant proportion of council tenants. Council housing, by the very nature of its social objectives, is disproportionately comprised of households with a lower and less secure labor market status than is the ownership sector. A review of the various sample studies undertaken in the city in the last decade suggests that the average unemployment rate for council tenants is roughly three times that of the owner-occupied sector. This is partly explained by the propensity of homeowners who experience financial difficulty to move to council housing. (It should be noted that in 1985 more than 5 percent of new tenants in Glasgow were households moving from the owner-occupied sector.) And, of course, there is the longstanding assumption, seldom statistically tested, that home-owners are more mobile in the face of job loss.

In 1987 the average unemployment rate for the city was 22 percent. In the owner-occupied wards, this rate varied from 6 percent to 12 percent. In those wards in which council housing predominates, the unemployment rate in the more favored areas was on the order of 11 percent, but the rate was seldom less than 33 percent in the postwar peripheral housing schemes. The high unemployment rates in these schemes reflected the preponderance of unskilled workers in the resident population, who have been particularly susceptible to the impacts of economic decline in the city since the 1960s. Whereas studies of 1971 census data emphasized older tenement areas as the key loci of deprivation, the 1981 census clearly revealed that the largest pockets of socioeconomic deprivation now lie in council housing on the edge of the city (see map 8-6).

MAP 8-6
Social Deprivation in Glasgow, 1981.

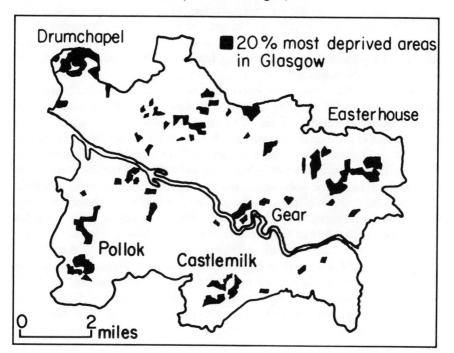

A recent detailed study of a poor area of council housing (which contained 2,200 households) indicated that, although the official unemployment rate was 31 percent, only one household in three had even one employed household member because of the high concentrations of the sick, disabled, and prematurely retired population in the area. Housing and neighborhood decay have thus coincided with deteriorating labor markets. It is important to emphasize that for many of these residents, both jobs and homes were less problematic a decade ago.

The exact extent of immiserisation is difficult to assess from published records because a second process has contributed to the declining socioeconomic status of the residents of the peripheral housing schemes. From 1955 to 1975, the majority of those allocated housing units were employed families. Now an increasing proportion of the waiting list for social housing includes the unemployed, young, single persons, and single-parent families. Through the processes referred to above, these groups tend to be allocated disproportionately into the worst areas. The worst areas have a turnover rate of up to a quarter of their units in a single year period, in contrast to the 5 percent turnover rate in the best council housing areas. Hence it is to these low-quality areas that those in most urgent need of housing are allocated. In the distressed area referred to above, some 75 percent of lets in the last year were made to unemployed persons and single-parent families. This process has become known as "residualization."

In our view, the maturation process emerged from the inherent structures developed for council housing and could now be susceptible to change from new directions in housing policy. The immiserisation process is primarily a consequence of local economic decline. It reflects the increasingly impossible task that social housing is being asked to confront. Residualisation stems in part from the processes of economic decline, but it also reflects shifts in government policy which have polarized attitudes towards council housing. Residualization has also been affected by the adverse maturation of council housing. For instance, with sustained real income growth for the majority of households in the city, the inability of the social sector to meet new qualitative housing demands almost inevitably implied a shift to home ownership. It is commonplace in the British literature to equate residualization with the consequences of the large-scale sale of council units. Actually council sales are neither a necessary nor a sufficient condition to create residualization; in Glasgow the process has been extensive, but not primarily driven by sales of council units.

New Directions

There is a growing tendency in Glasgow, just as in the rest of the United Kingdom, to lay the blame for the emerging crisis of housing quality on the housing finance policies of central government. This is much too simplistic. As noted earlier, however, the lack of a clear central policy for the social rental sector may be the barrier to the solution of the problems rather than the cause of the difficulties per se. At present, central government seems loathe, and not just because of spending restraints, to see reinvestment resources channelled through the local authority. The pro-privatization policy that dominated British housing policy in the early 1980s appears to have passed. Now unwillingness to spend partly indicates a vacuum of new ideas for social housing in Britain. Central government remains unconvinced that large-scale bureaucratic, monopolistic provision of council units will produce efficient pricing systems, a fair utilization of subsidy, resident involvement, and value for money in service provision.

It is to the city's credit that it is now, after almost half a century of minimal change in organizational style, attempting new approaches to social housing provision and contemplating partial privatization of the housing stock. However, all of these changes are predicated upon an increased injection of housing capital expenditure into the social housing sector. An independent inquiry into housing in the city (in 1986) has called for a £2 billion injection, to be largely financed and subsidized by the public sector. It should be noted, however, that this sum is close to the total of public capital spending for the whole of England and Wales. At present rates of investment, such a program would take 20 years, even supposing that housing conditions in the city would not deteriorate further. In this sense, Glasgow's housing crisis is a reflection of the broader economic and social difficulties that confront the nation. Glasgow's problem cannot be solved by special pleading, nor can it be solved by a short, massive burst of government money. The resources of citizens, renters, and local communities must be effectively organized into new styles of social housing to prevent the inefficiencies and inequities of the present system from reappearing. As a precondition, the approach to municipal housing finance must be overhauled.

Financing Council Housing

Since the mid-1970s there have been a number of changes that have reduced current subsidies and led to increased central government control over spending on council housing. In 1978 the departing national Labor government introduced a new Housing Support Grant system for council housing. Under this system, the Secretary of State would estimate a national rental revenue for the city and compare this with allowable expenditures depending upon housing types, management, and interest repayments. If allowable costs exceeded national rental income, then the deficit would be met by a Housing Support Grant. This related the distribution of council subsidies more closely to the needs of authorities than the older method of distribution.

At the same time, central government relaxed its detailed evaluation-specific grants for capital spending and distributed "block grants" for housing purposes to local authorities. At present in Scotland, unlike England and Wales, central government splits the block into HRA (council housing) expenditure limits and a non-HRA program (improvement of private stock, etc.).

Towards the end of the 1970s, the Scottish Office attempted to relate capital allocations and current subsidies more precisely to local needs; thus block grants were introduced. The new freedom for municipalities to select their own priorities, in the belief that broad shortages had been resolved and that local quality problems were now paramount, was however quickly circumscribed by a sharp reduction in both capital spending allowances and current subsidies. The pattern of change for Glasgow, including the changing composition of the Housing Revenue Account, is indicated in tables 8-11 and 8-12. The figures from 1980 to 1986 represent a sustained period of anti-housing sector action on the part of central government.

TABLE 8-11
Housing Revenue Account, 1980-1981 to1985-1986
(£m, 1985-1986 prices).

	1980-1981	1981-1982	1982-1983	1983-1984	1984-1985	1985-1986
HRA expenditure						
Loan charges	120.9	118.7	112.8	103.6	101.7	96.7
R & M	63.2	61.3	61.0	45.6	40.1	32.3
S & M	21.5	20.4	20.3	21.7	20.2	19.9
Other	3.5	3.8	4.7	8.1	4.3	3.8
Total	209.1	204.2	198.8	179.0	166.3	152.7
HRA income						
Rent & other	90.3	103.1	102.9	103.1	94.7	101.3
HSG	73.1	55.4	48.3	35.9	31.1	24.8
RFC	45.7	45.7	47.6	40.0	40.5	26.6
Total	209.1	204.2	198.8	179.0	166.3	152.7

Note: "HSG" is the Housing Support Group; "RFC" is the Rate Fund Contribution.
Source: GDC Finance Dept.

Public sector investment in Glasgow housing has decreased sharply since 1978. This reduction commenced under the Labor government but has been less drastic than for the rest of Scotland and the United Kingdom as a whole. A number of pertinent points are conveyed by table 12. Between 1980-1981 and 1986-1987 there was a real overall reduction in investment of 11 percent. However, government allowances to spend on council housing (now mainly for modernization) were 30 percent lower, and low levels of sales receipts in Scotland have meant that the overall scale of the capital program has been reduced by some 26 percent. Spending on non-HRA programs (largely improvement grants to owner occupiers) in 1986-1987 is 330 percent of the level of seven years earlier, even following program contraction from 1984 onwards. Further reflecting the biases of government policy, SSHA spending (largely on social housing) has been reduced by 62 percent, whereas Housing Corporation spending (largely on rehabilitating older tenements) has been maintained at its 1980-1981 level. The sectoral and spatial consequences of these unbalanced investment programs have already been noted above. Clearly, if social housing areas are to be improved, investment levels have to be increased.

Currently, rents are rising much more rapidly than inflation as subsidies are being reduced. Support from the Housing Support Grant program in 1986-

TABLE 8-12

Public Sector Capital Investment in Glasgow, 1980-1981 to 1986-1987 (£m, 1985-1986 Prices)[1].

	1980-1981	1981-1982	1982-1983	1983-1984	1984-1985	1985-1986	1986-1987[2]
Housing Revenue Account							
Net Capital	83.3	72.2	47.0	63.6	40.6	50.8	58.0
Capital Receipts	7.6	5.5	20.2	17.0	9.0	10.2	8.9
Capital Gross	90.9	77.7	67.2	80.6	49.6	61.0	67.0
SSHA	26.1	17.2	16.8	14.9	15.1	8.5	9.9
Capital Expenditures on Public Sector Housing	117.0	94.9	84.0	95.5	64.7	69.5	76.9
Capital Bids[3]	128.0	128.0	116.0	165.0	150.0	193.0	250.0
Non-HRA							
Net Capital	11.8	14.0	29.7	73.9	73.1	35.2	39.2
Capital Receipts	8.3	7.9	8.4	8.1	12.4	8.8	0.8
Capital Gross	20.1	21.9	38.1	82.0	85.5	44.0	40.0
Housing Corporation	43.2	50.0	57.1	59.2	47.4	44.1	44.0
Non-HRA Capital Expenditures	63.3	71.9	95.2	141.2	142.9	88.1	84.0
Capital Bids[4]	--	--	--	--	--	--	65.5
Total Gross Public Capital Investment	180.3	166.8	179.2	236.7	197.6	157.6	160.0

Notes: 1. September 1985 prices.
2. Estimates at out-turn prices.
3. GDC bid or estimated requirements per annum over five-year period.
4. Full requirements not calculated prior to 1986.

1987 was one-third of its 1980-1981 level (see table 8-11). At the same time, the municipality was restricted, by new central government legislation and penalties, from increasing the flow of local tax revenues used to subsidize social housing. Indeed, the Rate Fund Contribution has fallen sharply since 1982-1983. As these measures began to bite, the city actually halved its maintenance spending from an already patently inadequate level. The revenue situation was exacerbated in 1984-1985 when the city government, in an election year for council seats, permitted no annual rent increase, even though Glasgow rent increases have lagged behind the Scottish average for most of the 1980s.

Glasgow's approach to rental increases is open to question on two counts. First, the average rent-to-income ratio for tenants not receiving Housing Benefit (the income-related subsidy) is just under 7 percent. Second, the impact of rising rents upon tenants throughout this period was greatly alleviated for the lowest income groups by the widespread uptake of Housing Benefit. This subsidy defrays housing costs on the basis of household income. By 1985 more than three-quarters of tenants in the city received some Benefit, more than half received full recompense of their housing costs, and it has been estimated that this centrally funded subsidy covered around three-quarters of the increase in rental income in any year after 1982. In this context, a low rental-low quality of service policy does not seem to make a great deal of sense for the municipality.

The pooling of rents also ensures that there is no necessary relationship between the quality of a unit and the rent charged. Tenants can be exploited, as can central government, through the system of Benefit payments. In our view, an end to pooling and the development of pricing schemes which reflect the quality of units are preconditions for the reforms set out below. There is nothing in the present finance system to ensure efficient provision of management services. Until recently, the city had a monopoly in the provision of repair services; these services were expensive, slow, and unsatisfactory in relation to other Scottish local authorities. Management services have also been subject to criticism, with, for instance, 75 percent of tenants regarding the authority as a bad manager of maintenance services (Maclennan et al., 1987). Annual maintenance spending on dwelling units has, in consequence, rarely exceeded 1 percent of the value of dwelling units. The current quality crisis in the council housing stock cannot disregard this history of neglect. Politicians in the city must now convince central government that it must relax spending controls, and also persuade tenants and citizens that they must make a greater financial contribution to restoring the stock.

Housing politicians in the city may not like the tenor of the financial comments made above, and reform may be slow to emerge. However, there has been a range of innovative proposals by the same key individuals aimed at creating more attractive forms of social housing. The main thrusts of change are set out below.

Privatization

The previous section has indicated how the private housing market has grown rapidly in the city in the 1980s. In most of the United Kingdom, growth in home ownership in the 1980s is attributable to the sale of council houses, at much discounted prices, to their existing owners. Glasgow, in common with a number of other socialist-inclined local authorities, has sold with little enthusiasm since national legislation gave tenants the right to buy their houses in 1980. Most sales have been in areas of larger semidetached units set in higher-quality neighborhoods. At the margin, and in the very long run, sales to existing tenants may help to sustain or enhance the socioeconomic status of a neighborhood. But this effect is likely to be minimal in Glasgow. Sales have been in council housing areas with an already favorable socioeconomic status. The purchasers, who are mostly middle-aged adult with offspring making their own job and housing decisions, would probably not have moved out into the ownership sector. This kind of privatization strategy has few positive effects on the stabilization of the more problematic council housing areas. There, the low quality of the housing units and the extent of disrepair, the low incomes of the residents, and the rental sector advantages of Housing Benefit all act against any extensive use of the right to buy.

In Glasgow, the privatization of social housing units in such areas has only occurred when the process of public neighborhood decline results in substantial vacancy generation or pervasive abandonment. In some areas, the quality decline has become so extreme that not even the most needy housing groups will accept these homes at an effectively zero rent. The coexistence of large blocks of vacant housing, with the pervasive negative externalities of vacancy quickly spreading to adjacent sites, along with minimal capital spending allowances for the municipality, has effectively forced the city to attempt to market more than 3,000 units into the private sector.

Two broad strategies of selling contigious housing subdivisions have been adopted. Between 1980 and 1984, some 2,000 units were sold in an unimproved condition, at minimal prices, to potential "homesteaders." The purchasers could then apply for generous private sector grant aid (which, unlike resources for council housing, was then readily available). The properties were not rationed by price, and some 11 persons applied for each house, all of which were eventually sold. The houses were mostly sold to young two-person employed households who generally had some skill or trade that would facilitate the provision of sweat equity. More than half of the purchasers indicated they had some previous connection with the area in which they purchased, and some 40 percent stressed that their second choice would have been to wait for a council house. Since 1984 the council have de-emphasised their homesteading program, and home improvement grants for new owners have been less widely available. More recently, the council have instead marketed, again at minimal transfer prices, around 1,000 dwellings in three areas to developers who will upgrade and then resell them. Once again, demand forecasts indicate that these units will sell to moderate income households with a previous background in council housing who had lived in the areas undergoing change.

Both of these sales strategies, which have been most extensive in the peripheral estates, have been directed towards selling empty houses. Since fiscal cutbacks had prevented the refurbishment of these dwellings within the public sector, it could be argued that upgrading had been associated with a reduction in vacancies rather than displacement of less-advantaged groups. But in reality, the less-advantaged new council tenants or waiting-list applicants have been displaced. The policy, however, has created more socially mixed and economically viable neighborhoods, and it has certainly provided an option whereby council tenants whose real incomes were growing did not have to relocate in order to satisfy their tenure preferences. The real success of these policies can only be assessed a decade or so from now. Privatization policies have therefore had a limited, if locally important, effect upon rundown social housing areas, affecting only about 3 percent of the stock in these locations. The scale of the existing problem is such that solutions will have to be found within the social sector.

Initiatives in the Social Sector

The city has taken a number of important steps to stimulate resident involvement in the planning and management of social housing. New approaches to management have been suggested, and the repair system is being scrutinized. There has been a growing realization that social housing is for the consumers rather than the local politicians or bureaucrats. The city is currently attempting to decentralize service provision to about 30 area offices. But there is already an awareness that the proposals still leave rather large administrative units which have relatively limited control over key policies such as repairs, housing allocations, etc. Indeed, the pace of new ideas is so great, as increasing political commitment swings behind the realization that social housing can be remade, that policies are undergoing constant revision.

During 1985 the city began to put in place a radical plan, by British standards, for its social housing stock. After studying models of provision and revitalization in Scandinavia, France, and the United States, the municipality decided that both management efficiency and tenant involvement could be enhanced by transferring ownership of the municipal housing stock to cooperatives formed from existing tenants of social housing. At present, some six cooperatives, initially financed as housing associations for convenience, have been formed from more than 2,000 units. Twelve more areas of similar size have been identified and development work initiated. A recent report of the council has proposed transferring some 25 percent of the stock to cooperatives by 1990. It should be stressed that these initiatives preceded the provision of tenants' rights to opt out of council management, which was included in the conservative election manifesto of 1987. Glasgow has finally begun to adopt a potentially feasible form of social housing, almost a century after rejecting cooperative models of housing provision.

These coops, or housing associations formed in social housing areas, can break the monopoly of council housing provision. They will have rents assessed in relation to the quality of the units, and tenants will be directly involved in management and in deciding the key trade-offs between rent and expenditure or quality of services. However, a number of cautionary notes are needed. First, the Glasgow shift has to be regarded as a bold experiment. We do not have a priori knowledge that the costs and benefits of management arrangements will be preferable in the long run. Second, the incentive for participation in these coops is modernization of the units and areas. Although rents may rise to help finance these improvements, central government will have to relax capital spending limits in order for the schemes to proceed, even if they are to be self-financing. There may also be a cost to government in terms of increased Housing Benefit spending levels. Third, reinvestment in the peripheral public housing estates will not necessarily have the same widespread regenerating effect as the revitalization of older tenement areas. The monolithic land uses of these estates and the absence of private nonresidential property will have to be considered as barriers to neighborhood regeneration. A fifth consideration is that the city is set upon having par-value coops, and this may not be the best option for reducing public sector costs and maintaining long-term resident involvement. Some form of progressive equity sharing would probably be more appropriate. Finally, the unemployment rate in these locations is likely to remain high even if there is a remarkable recovery in the British economy, so to some extent these schemes must retain an element of "ghetto gilding."

Although higher rent levels may resolve some of the issues and improved efficiency of resource use could create positive benefits, it is clear that Glasgow's outer estates will continue to deteriorate as the rest of the city is restored. The city has already decided that this is not acceptable, and indeed civic commitment by certain more affluent citizens is directed against further deterioration of these areas. Glaswegians care about their city. In rescuing it from bureaucratic indifference, they will strive to improve it; the egalitarian strain in Scottish culture remains strong. However, for improvements to become realities, central government must also devise a purposive and informed strategy for social housing. There are, after a decade of despair, some signs of such a strategy emerging. This is not a plea for more subsidies, but rather a call for central government to abandon its anti-housing stance in public spending policies and to examine more carefully its restrictions on capital spending.

CONCLUSION

This chapter has indicated how major thrusts of national housing policy may be reinforced or offset by local circumstances. In Glasgow, national housing policy has had major and long-lasting impacts on citizen well-being, and programs have been dramatic in their scale. The essay has also indicated how successive policy initiatives, with objectives increasingly running counter to preceding policies, have to operate within accepted political, economic, and geographic structures.

We have also illustrated how large-scale housing programs in Britain, while funded in a spirit of generous commitment, have focused upon short-term quantitative outputs rather than long-term qualitative impacts. In particular, postwar social housing transformed Glasgow without putting in place organizational or incentive systems that would generate a feasible, long-term social housing system. Housing policy in Glasgow from 1950 to 1975 is a globally important example of lack of foresight in the use of policy resources.

The last decade of experience in Glasgow, however, offers a more optimistic prospect for effective state action in housing provision. The large-scale, nonmunicipal, rehabilitation program is a clear example of how state investment can generate citizen involvement and private investor confidence. The older neighborhoods of one of Europe's most disadvantaged cities have been successfully revitalized with positive impacts on local image and employment.

The key task now facing Glasgow, as so many other European cities, is to diversify and regenerate rundown social housing areas.

REFERENCES

Cameron, G.C. 1971. Economic analysis for a declining urban economy. *Scottish Journal of Political Economy*, 18: 315-345.

Clapham, D., and K. Kintrea. 1986. Rationing, choice and constraint: The allocation of public housing in Glasgow. *Journal of Social Policy*, 15: 57-67.

Gibb, A. 1983. *Glasgow - The making of a city*. London: Croom Helm.

Glasser, R. 1987. Growing up in the Gorbals.

Hills, J. 1986. When is a grant not a grant? Welfare state programme, Discussion Paper no. 12. London School of Economics.

Maclennan, D. 1982. *Housing economics*. Harlow, Essex: Longmans.

Maclennan, D. 1985. Urban housing rehabilitiation: An encouraging British example, *Policy and Politics*. 13: 413-429.

Maclennan, D., D. Donnison, C. Jones, and G. Wood. 1982. The cheaper end of the owner occupied housing market. The Scottish Office, Edinburgh.

Maclennan, D., and A. Gibb. 1986. Policy and process in Scottish housing, 1950-1980. In *The economic development of modern Scotland*, edited by R. Saville. Edinburgh: John Donald.

Maclennan, D., and C. Jones. 1987. Building societies and credit rationing: An emperical examination of redlining. Urban Studies, 24: 205-216.

Maclennan, D., and M. Munro. 1987. Intra-urban changes in housing prices: Glasgow 1972-1983. *Housing Studies*, 2: 65-81.

Maclennan, D., and M. Munro. 1985. The growth of owner occupation in Britain. In *Low cost home ownership*, edited by P. Booth and A. Crook. Gower: Aldershot.

Maclennan, D., A. O'Sullivan, M. Munro, and K. Kintrea. 1987. Housing and environmental change in the G.E.A.R. area. In *The GEAR review*. Glasgow: Scottish Development Agency.

Maclennan, D., D. Robertson, D. Carruthers, and M. Munro. 1985. Improvement grants and their impact in Glasgow. Glasgow District Council.

Royal Commission on the Housing of the Industrial Population, Scotland, Cmnd. 8731, HMSO, London 1917.

Smart, W. A. 1902. *Housing and the municipality*. Glasgow: Adeshead Press.

Strathclyde Regional Council. 1976. *Urban deprivation*. Glasgow: Strathclyde Regional Council.

INDEX